John Masters, who was born in C[...]
fifth generation of his family to ha[...]
at Wellington and Sandhurst, he [...]
join the 4th Prince of Wales's O[...]
active service in Waxiristan in 19[...]
war, in Iraq, Syria and Persia. [...]
brigade of General Wingate's Chindits in Burma, and later
fought with the 19th Indian Division at the capture of
Mandalay and on the Mawchi Road.

Masters retired from the army in 1948 as a lieutenant colonel
with the DSO and OBE. He went to America and turned
to writing. He is best known for his novels, published by
Sphere Books Ltd, most famously BHOWANI
JUNCTION.

John Masters died in New Mexico in May 1983, at the age of
sixty-eight.

CASANOVA

John Masters

Cardinal

For Tony and Chris Charnock

SPHERE BOOKS LTD

Published by the Penguin Group
27 Wrights Lane, London w8 5tz, England
Viking Penguin Inc., 40 West 23rd Street, New York, New York 10010, USA
Penguin Books Australia Ltd, Ringwood, Victoria, Australia
Penguin Books Canada Ltd, 2801 John Street, Markham, Ontario, Canada 13R 1b4
Penguin Books (NZ) Ltd, 182–190 Wairau Road, Auckland 10, New Zealand

Penguin Books Ltd, Registered Offices: Harmondsworth, Middlesex, England

First Published in Great Britain by Michael Joseph Ltd 1969
Published by Sphere Books Ltd 1989
1 3 5 7 9 10 8 6 4 2

Printed and bound in Great Britain by
Richard Clay Ltd, Bungay, Suffolk

Author's Note

The first acknowledgment I must make is to Casanova's own wonderful autobiography, *Histoire de ma Vie*. The full and accurate text of this work was first published in 1960 by the owners of the manuscript, F. A. Brockhaus of Wiesbaden, and by Librairie Plon of Paris. By kind permission of these firms I have been able to quote liberally from Casanova's own words.

At the time of going to press four volumes of Casanova's manuscript (out of twelve) have also been published, as two double volumes, in a meticulous English translation by Willard R. Trask. I thank the American and British publishers (Harcourt, Brace & World, Inc.; Longmans, Green & Co. Ltd), for permission to quote passages from this translation. I also thank F. A. Brockhaus and Librairie Plon for allowing me to translate, myself, from Casanova's original French, passages which have not yet appeared in Mr Trask's translation.

My second acknowledgment is to that dean of Casanova students, Mr J. Rives Childs, who has devoted many years of skilled and patient research to Casanova's life and writings. I am particularly grateful to him for reading and commenting on my book in typescript, and for the help he has given me. He is, of course, in no way to be held responsible for my judgments or manner of presentation.

Thirdly, among many who have helped me with particular points, I thank Dr R. R. Willcox and Mr Richard Cavendish of London; Professor Polišenský and Mrs John of Prague; and Mr Zada of Duchcov.

Finally I am happy to acknowledge the arduous labours of those who have been responsible for editorial advice: John Hadfield, Joy Law, James Laver, Chantal Coural, Tony Raven and Margaret Crawford.

J. M.

Contents

Prologue

In the last years of his life Casanova wrote his memoirs. Here are the first words of the preface:

I begin by declaring to my reader that, by everything good or bad that I have done throughout my life, I am sure that I have earned merit or incurred guilt, and that hence I must consider myself a free agent. The doctrine of the Stoics, and of any other sect, on the power of Destiny is a figment of the imagination which smacks of atheism. I am not only a monotheist but a Christian whose faith is strengthened by philosophy, which has never injured anything.

This is the man he wished the world to remember – an urbane and sophisticated Christian gentleman. The truth, as so often with him, is less glossy but much more interesting.

His name has passed into our language as a synonym for 'great lover'; and so he was, but he was also a devout Catholic and a superstitious astrologer; a low-life scoundrel and a fearful snob; a sceptical Freemason and a servant of the Establishment; an ingenious adventurer and an excellent writer. In a life that alternated between extravagant ostentation and abject penury he met and conversed with Voltaire, Rousseau, Franklin, Catherine the Great, George III, Frederick the Great, and two popes. He was generous, mean, vindictive, proud, fawning, honest, lying, brilliant, stupid, unstable; and for part of his life his profession can most simply – though not quite accurately – be described as Confidence Trickster Extraordinary. And in all this he was the embodiment of Europe at its splendid, decadent peak, and of his age, the Age of Reason and of maniacally spendthrift gambling; the age of satin in the parlour, and excrement in the passages; the age when every day science grew stronger and faith weaker; the age when the aristocracy was nearing the limit of its power and the peasantry the limit of its patience.

For himself, then, and for the century and the continent for whom he stands as so vital a symbol, I give you Giacomo Casanova . . . with a word of warning: like Casanova, I generally cloak farmyard activities in drawing-room language, but that cannot disguise the activities themselves, which are incessant, shameless, and often contrary to all laws of God and man. *Caveat parentus.*

I

Springtime in Venice

In *The Story of My Life* Casanova lists a genealogy by which he traces his descent from a Spanish hidalgo of Zaragoza. Its tale of grandees and colonels, of runaway heiresses and papal dispensations, is highly suspect. It was not important because it was true, but because it made a sanctuary for Casanova's self-esteem. As a child he had to have some secure place to retreat into from society's barely veiled slanders, which he must soon have learned were only the plain truth.

That truth is as follows. A certain Gaetano Giuseppe Casanova, born at Parma in 1697 with no money and of no family, and growing up with no talents except a handsome face and nimble legs, went on the stage as a dancer. At that time, 'stage' was almost synonymous with 'brothel'. All the women were available at a price; most of the men pimped for them, or for themselves. The social position of actors and actresses was, as usual, equivocal – worshipped in theatre and boudoir, scorned in street and court. Casanova's genealogy claims that while performing in Venice this Gaetano (supposed scion of the Spanish line) met Zanetta Farussi, the beautiful sixteen-year-old daughter of a shoemaker, and eloped with her. The Patriarch of Venice, Pietro Barbarigo, married the pair on 27 February 1724; but three weeks before that Zanetta's father died of chagrin at his daughter's misalliance. Of this marriage our Giacomo, born on 2 April 1725, was the first child. Having married a social pariah Zanetta now had no recourse but to go on the stage too, which she at once did.

Two unpleasant rumours cloud this romantic picture. The first is that Giacomo's father-by-the-flesh was not Gaetano Casanova but Michele Grimani, of the patrician family which owned the S. Samuele theatre, where Gaetano and later Zanetta played. It is likely that the theatre owner had his will of all the actresses and hangers-on at his theatre; quite probable that he met no resistance in the process; and when he got a girl into trouble he would arrange for a peasant or underling to marry her, for a consideration. Such things are not unheard of even nowadays. All her life Zanetta was a woman who knew how to look after herself. Her pregnancy cannot have been the cause of the marriage, for Giacomo was not born until thirteen months after it; but she may have used an earlier false alarm to put pressure on Grimani, or she may have simply asked for the marriage as reward for a long relationship with him. Whatever the motivations, or the means, Zanetta in the end got herself respectably married and at the same time established an obligation by the Grimanis. In the patrician oligarchy of old Venice this would be useful to herself and invaluable to her children. Casanova certainly believed himself to be Grimani's son. He said so in a later pamphlet; and, in writing this chapter of his early life he sets down the following sentence: 'My mother came back to Venice with her husband'; not, notice – 'with my father'.

According to the other rumour Gaetano was not the father of Zanetta's next child, either. Francesco, born in London in 1727, is said to have been conceived while she was the mistress of the Prince of Wales, later King George II. Of the rest of the family, only three reached maturity: Giacomo's brothers Giovanni Battista, born in 1730, and Gaetano Alvisio, born posthumously in 1734; and his sister Maria Maddalena Antonia Stella, born in 1732.

Zanetta Casanova left Giacomo and the rest of her brood in Venice, in the care of their maternal grandmother, while she pursued her profession, or professions, all over Europe. Giacomo was sickly and upset and suffered from nosebleeding. He claims that his first memory is of something that happened when he was eight, but it does not take a psychologist to guess that there were painful earlier memories subconsciously suppressed. Those first years, so full for most of us of mother love, of sibling play, of widening discovery in nursery and school, laid the foundations of Casanova's character. He says that he was slow and dull-witted, but we know that in fact he was of marked intelligence and quick wit. If he suppressed those qualities it was because he knew he would not like what they would force him to understand: that his mother did not love him, and was barely distinguishable from a whore; and that the family's social position was one step above the gutter – with the other foot still in it.

The stuff of that first memory, as of the second which he places six weeks later, is of great interest. The first was of a particularly heavy nosebleed and of how his grandmother cured it, of a witch and being shut in a box, of incantations and shrieks, of a beautiful golden-haired woman coming down the chimney with presents, of oaths of secrecy.

3

The second memory was simpler; he stole a crystal and when his father started to look for it he dropped it into his brother Francesco's pocket. Francesco got a beating and Casanova chalked up the first score in another of his remarkable skills, the art of making enemies. Consistently unwise, he could not resist telling Francesco what he had done, a few years later. 'He never forgave me and never missed an opportunity of getting his own back', he wrote plaintively; but in fact he saw a lot of Francesco during his life and the relationship between them was not hostile.

Casanova himself did not seem to realize how closely those two memories fit the pattern he imposed on his life: beautiful women, representing his missing mother, coming down from nowhere with gifts and cures for whatever ailed him; and a lifelong attempt to avenge himself on the world, by trickery, for its original unjust punishment of him.

An eminent doctor was consulted, by mail, about the nosebleeding. His diagnosis, also sent by mail, was that it was caused by the density of the lad's blood, which in turn must be caused by the density of the air where he lived. To cure him, the air must be changed. In other words, he must be taken away from Venice. By now his 'father' was dead and Zanetta turned to the Grimanis for help. So it was that his mother, his grandmother, and the Abbé Grimani, brother of Michele, took him by boat down the canal from Venice to Padua, and lodged him in a boarding house there. The boarding house keeper was a Slav woman from Venice's territories in Dalmatia, and they gave her six sequins to feed and lodge Giacomo, keep him neatly dressed, and have him educated . . . for six months. Six sequins was worth about 13 dollars or £5 10s.

Everyone went away, heaving sighs of relief, the Abbé back to Venice, Zanetta somewhat farther – to St Petersburg in Russia. Writing more than fifty years later the moment is as stark to Casanova as it was on that day at the beginning of his tenth year. 'So they got rid of me.' This, not the urbane philosopher of the Preface, is the true Casanova, an acutely sensitive man who in that single sentence accuses all the world, more particularly his family, and, most bitterly, his mother, of bequeathing him a hundred causes for shame and leaving him to shoulder them alone.

The Slav woman, a grenadier with a pendulous bosom and an imposing moustache, ran a hell-hole where Casanova shared his miseries with three other little boys. The beds jumped with fleas and the bedding crawled with lice. To eat, she gave them a small portion of dried cod, thin soup, and an apple; to drink, water in which grape-stems had been boiled. Rats scampered about the attic and ran down the walls to gambol on the boys' pillows. Casanova could not sleep at night, so he slept in class. His teacher saw the state he was in, saw the bites covering his small body, and went to inspect the boarding house. Some improvements were made, but not enough. In truth, as Casanova said, the money being paid did not allow of anything better.

But the change did mend his health, and his body began to grow apace, his appetite with it. Hungry as only a growing boy can be, he began to steal food, but he could never find enough. Fearing, at last, that he would starve to death if he was not rescued soon, he wrote secretly to the Abbé Grimani and to his grandmother. Grimani told him to shut up. Old Signora Farussi, who was both mother and grandmother to him, came hotfoot to Padua and worked out an arrangement whereby he was to board with his teacher, Dr Gozzi.

Gozzi was a priest, then twenty-six. From Casanova's description he may have been a suppressed homosexual. He was certainly terrified of women. His parents were simple peasant folk, and he lived with them. His mother worshipped him and every time she said 'My son the priest' she was struck dumb with the miracle that it could be true. His father was a shoemaker, who worked hard, and got drunk on feast days; everyone loved him. The fourth member of this warm household was Bettina, the priest's younger sister (there had been ten other children, but none survived infancy). Bettina was seven years older than Casanova, though he politely narrows the gap.

Here Casanova passed his later boyhood and embarked on the confused and confusing years of adolescence. He attacked learning with the same sharklike appetite he had already shown for food. Bettina looked after him and his clothes, washed him, and did his hair. She – the new mystery of the female, with her secret differences and strangeness – began to obsess him. She encouraged him, but he was too shy, too young, and too much aware of Sin to respond. She decided to make her wishes clearer. One day she told him that his thighs were dirty, and set about washing them. While in the neighbourhood she paid a call on the boy's private parts. They, and his voluptuous sensations, grew until they could grow no more. She relieved him of his torment.

Casanova was overwhelmed at what had happened, and at the emotions aroused in himself. She had given him to eat of the Tree of Life; but also of the Knowledge of Good and Evil. Had he somehow defiled her? Surely she, an angel in human shape, was incapable of really *meaning* to do what she had done? Surely she could know

5

nothing of, let alone share, the extraordinary lusts that she had aroused in him?

After much wrestling with these metaphysical problems, Casanova decided in the end that she did in fact share those satanic desires. The reason she gave in to them was that she was a weaker vessel, a woman. It was up to a man (aged eleven now) to save her from herself.

Alas, he was prevented by the appearance of a rival, a great hairy brute of fifteen. Casanova soon found him in bed with Bettina. Horror! Worse – insult! He had given his love and it had been spurned. He meditated murdering both of them; but Bettina fell sick, and then she got smallpox, and he caught it, and when that was over, all passion was gone. Bettina married two years later. As souvenirs of his first, unconsummated love Casanova carried with him to the grave a warm memory of her, and three pockmarks on his face.

Meantime, he kept growing. At the age of twelve he began attending the University of Padua. He still lived with Dr Gozzi, who also taught him to play the violin, but now he was allowed a key and could come and go as he pleased. His mother and the Grimanis were determined that he should be an ecclesiastical lawyer, but Giacomo wanted to be a doctor, 'a profession in which charlatanism takes you even further than it does in the legal profession'.

The freedom of university life went to Casanova's head and he quickly gambled and squandered himself so deep into debt that he had to beg his grandmother to send him money. The wise old lady sent him nothing, but went to Padua and brought him back to Venice. Dr Gozzi shed tears and gave him a holy relic which he would certainly have kept all his life – if it had not had a gold setting.

In Venice he seems to have worked in the legal office of one Giovanni Manzoni, shuttled back and forth to Padua to register 'assiduous attendance' at the university, and continued his studies in a desultory fashion. On 22 January 1741 the Patriarch of Venice admitted him to the four minor orders of the Catholic clergy. These entitled him to call himself *abate*, and enjoined him to wear a gown, carry no sword, and refrain from duelling; and that was about all.

He soon registered his first (and last) ecclesiastical triumph. He preached a sermon of such limpid eloquence that the collection netted him over a hundred dollars and several *billets doux*. This shower of gold and proffered caresses turned his thoughts to the future he might enjoy in that then rather specialized branch of the Church; and certainly nothing could have suited his temperament better. But next time he preached over-confidence betrayed him. He did not properly memorize his sermon, and he ate and drank too much before going to church. Once facing the expectant congregation, he forgot his masterpiece and had to stumble down from the pulpit half fainting from shame and chagrin.

The general pattern of his life was shared by many another young man; but the details were peculiarly his own. He fought relentlessly with his guardian Grimanis and his priestly tutor, Giovanni Tosello, and in his spare time succeeded in making more enemies. One was a Venetian senator, Malipiero, who might have become Casanova's patron if he had been more careful. Malipiero, at seventy-six, was obsessed with the charms of a young actress, Teresa Imer, then seventeen. (Teresa's father, Giuseppe Imer, was a famous theatrical impresario, friend of the playwright Goldoni, and for a time official lover to Casanova's mother.) As the gouty old man proclaimed himself impotent, his intentions towards the girl are not clear, but he was certainly very jealous, and when he came upon Giacomo and Teresa engaged in biological study – they were examining the difference between boys and girls – he set upon Casanova with a stick and drove him from his house.

The boy received his degree of Doctor of Law from Padua in 1742, being then seventeen years of age. During a summer visit to the village of Pasiano di Pordenone his finer nature held him back from sexual correspondence with a peasant girl called Lucia, although she spent whole nights in his bed with him. She was too young and innocent, he thought, forgetting that he had made *that* mistake with Bettina, and look what had happened to her! (Bettina's marriage was already unhappy; soon after this she left her husband and went back, with her children, to live with her brother the priest.) Sure enough, when Casanova returned to Pasiano next year Lucia had gone – seduced by some lecherous brute, made pregnant, turned out to a life of sin and misery. If he had not been so scrupulous, Giacomo reasoned, this dreadful thing would not have happened, because Lucia would not have been innocent. Nor was it possible that any other man could have bowled her over so readily if Casanova had loved her.

So he came to his first actual affair, his first complete sexual experience with a woman. The only unusual, and prophetic, aspect of it is that not one girl but two were involved, simultaneously. The girls were Nanetta and Marta Savorgnan, then about fourteen and sixteen, distant relatives of the Grimanis. The venue was their aunt's house in Venice, on a street now vanished.

He met the girls originally as friends of Angela Tosello, the niece of his hated priest-tutor. Angela was a tease, the sort of stop-go-stop girl who frequently reaches the end of her coquetry in such places as Epping Forest or Van Cortlandt Park, half-naked and strangled with one of her own stockings. The type was to hold a disastrous, almost hypnotic fascination for Casanova all his life. Nanetta and Marta felt sorry for him, and to punish Angela he returned their affection. Soon they arranged for him to spend the night in their garret room – unknown, naturally, to their aunt. (There was no one who cared in the least what Casanova did, or where he slept.) His description of the double seduction which followed is of such singular sweetness that I am sure he is telling the whole truth, not only of fact but of emotion, about himself and about the girls:

I woke only when they came and got into bed, but I at once turned away and resumed my sleep, nor did I begin to act until I had reason to suppose that they were sleeping. If they were not, they had only to pretend to be. They had turned their backs to me and we were in darkness. I began with the one toward whom I was turned, not knowing whether it was Nanetta or Marta. I found her curled up and covered by her shift, but by doing nothing to startle her and proceeding step by step as gradually as possible, I soon convinced her that her best course was to pretend to be asleep and let me go on. Little by little I straightened her out, little by little she uncurled, and little by little, with slow, successive, but wonderfully natural movements, she put herself in a position which was the most favourable she could offer me without betraying herself. I set to work, but to crown my labours it was necessary that she should join in them openly and undeniably, and nature finally forced her to do so . . .

. . . I turned the other way to do the same thing with her sister . . . I found her motionless, in the position often taken by a person who is lying on his back in deep, untroubled sleep. With the greatest precautions, and every appearance of fearing to waken her, I began by delighting her soul, at the same time assuring myself that she was as untouched as her sister; and I continued the same treatment until, affecting a most natural movement without which I could not have crowned my labours, she helped me to triumph; but at the moment of crisis she no longer had the strength to keep up her pretence. Throwing off the mask, she clasped me in her arms and pressed her mouth on mine . . .

In opening their bodies to his, the two girls also opened his eyes, and his mind, to a vista of permanent ecstasy. Concealed between their thighs he found his life's avocation. He pursued it with a will. At Pasiano again, he found opportunity to make love to a recent bride during a carriage drive. He took advantage of her fright at a tremendous thunderstorm to pull her onto his lap. Women then wore no knickers or underpants, and since the rather silly young wife clung paralysed to him at every flash and crash, the rest was easy. Certain of having behaved properly this time (without his bold action the unhappy woman might have gone the way of Bettina and Lucia), he tipped the leering coachman a ducat – about a week's wages.

His grandmother, the only person who had returned the love he was so eager to lavish upon all the world, now died. His mother entrusted the business of disposing of house and furniture to the Grimanis; but Casanova, finding himself short of money, sold the furniture on his own account, reasoning that it had been left to him, not to his mother. The Grimanis sent a bailiff, Razzetta, to frighten him into some sort of responsible behaviour. When Razzetta found how much furniture was missing he had the house sealed and guarded. Casanova instituted suit against him. He had to withdraw the suit after a severe talking-to from the Abbé Grimani, but he did not forget Razzetta. The Grimanis now sold the house over his head. The Casanova children, who had no family feeling and no desire to live together, scattered to different lodgings. The Grimanis arranged for Giacomo to live in a house they owned, where also lived an actress called La Tintoretta, more eminent for her prowess in bed than on the boards.

Up in the wilds of Poland his mother had become friendly with an Italian monk called Bernardo de Bernardis, then Master of Theology at the royal court. The monk wanted to be a bishop. The Queen of Poland's daughter was Queen of Naples. The King of Naples had the right of nomination to bishoprics in his domains. Would the actress, who was known to be on intimate terms with the queen, please speak on the monk's behalf? The actress would – but Zanetta Casanova never did anything for nothing. If de Bernardis became a bishop, he was to take Giacomo Casanova into his episcopal family and see to his advancement in the Church.

The thing was done as planned. Pope Benedict XIV appointed de Bernardis to be Bishop of Martorano, in southern Italy. Casanova was sent the news by his mother, and received it with wild joy. A bishop's palace, gold and embroidered silk, colour and riches, learned canons, witty monsignors, gracious countesses! And with it all, an assured path to further glory! The purple! The thrice-crowned white! . . . Infinitely better, in any case, than poring over dusty law-books. Also, it would take him away from the supervision of the Grimanis, with their sneering pretensions. (And yet, as a passionately loyal Venetian, he always respected the name: it had been written in the Golden Book, the roll of the patrician families of Venice, in 1297.)

Signora Manzoni, his lawyer-employer's shrewd wife, tried to calm his transports. He did not know his own nature, she said; he didn't know the bishop; and he didn't know Martorano. The association would not last long. But nothing could dampen Casanova's enthusiasm.

In far-off Poland his mother learned where he was lodged. She wrote urgently to the Abbé Grimani: her son the priest living in the same house as an *actress*? That wouldn't do at all, especially as the bishop-designate would soon arrive to pick up the boy. The Grimanis obediently put Casanova into the theological seminary of S. Cipriano at Murano, the little town — now famous for its glass — built on an island in the lagoon of Venice.

It is hard to decide whether the seminary or Casanova was the more unhappy with this arrangement. He was a Doctor of Law of Padua University, but in his sulking fury he pretended on admission to have no training at all; so they put him in a class with the youngest seminarians, who could hardly read. The youths all slept in long rows in dormitories and, since the directors of the seminary expected the worst, while making no allowance for the nature of the young male animal, the worst duly happened. Another youth, with whom Casanova had become very friendly, got into his bed. They were discovered. Casanova swore that nothing sexual had taken place, but the rector ordered him to be beaten, and the sentence was carried out forthwith.

He left the seminary, and at once sued the rector for battery. The Grimanis, furious, had their thug Razzetta lure him into a gondola and row him across the lagoon to the island fortress of S. Andrea. There he was made prisoner. Why? Because the Secretary of War said so. For how long? At the Secretary's pleasure. To be exact, Casanova thought, at the Grimanis' displeasure — which might last for ever.

It was not as bad as that. The period the Grimanis had in mind was, say, six months, when de Bernardis would pass through and Casanova could be handed over, *got rid of.*

Casanova's first concern was to avenge himself on Razzetta for the old and new indignities. Razzetta had at all times acted merely as an agent for the Grimanis, but Casanova knew better than to make direct assault on a patrician of Venice. His imprisonment was not very strait, so he arranged for a gondolier to row him secretly ashore one night. After checking on Razzetta's routine, he returned to the fortress, where he made his re-entry undetected. On the chosen night he feigned sickness and pretended to have sprained an ankle. He called his soldier-servant's attention to himself to establish the time. Then, dismissing the servant, he slipped over the wall into the waiting gondola, went fast ashore, masked himself, beat up Razzetta, threw him into a canal, was rowed fast back to the fort, jumped into bed, and, pretending to feel sick again, yelled for the servant and the doctor . . . who came running, establishing another exact moment at which he was known to be in bed at the fort. When the beating-up of Razzetta became public there didn't seem to be enough time between the servant's two visits for a crippled Casanova to have got ashore, committed the assault, and got back.

Of course, the truth soon became known, although Casanova was never formally accused. He didn't care. On the contrary, he hugged himself with pride at his growing reputation as a young fellow not to be lightly crossed. He was also painting a clear picture of himself in the minds of the Venetian Establishment as a man of infinite resource, but no sagacity. But he didn't care about that.

He passed the slow weeks playing cards with the officers of the Albanian garrison (Albania then belonged to Venice) and writing letters for that majority of them which could neither read nor write. An ensign's wife gave him his first dose of venereal disease, probably gonorrhoea. For the rest, he walked on the ramparts of the lonely fort, gazed at Venice shimmering in the heat across the bay, thought of Nanetta and Marta pining for him in their garret, and waited impatiently for the coming of de Bernardis.

The bishop arrived at last, and the Grimanis had Casanova released from S. Andrea. De Bernardis interviewed him, and was un-favourably impressed. The Grimanis had, besides, undoubtedly given him a lurid picture of the youth's character; so, instead of taking Casanova with him, he told him to follow later. At Ancona a certain priest would have money for him; from there he could find his own way to Rome, where he would join up with the bishop and go with him to Martorano.

Ancona is 180 miles from Venice. That is the last I shall see of him, de Bernardis was perhaps saying to himself: a joke's a joke, but did that good woman really think I was going to saddle myself with her delinquent byblow for the rest of my life? If they'd given me a decent bishopric, perhaps . . . but Martorano!

However, now that he was no longer a child, it was not so easy to 'get rid of' Casanova. The bishop could have gone to Zanzibar, leaving no word and no money, and Casanova would have turned up. The Grimani reins had begun to chafe intolerably and by now he must have well understood just what his relationship with them implied about himself, his mother, and his whole family. So, having got himself attached to the train of Andrea da Lezze, the new Venetian ambassador to the Holy See, and after a last night in the arms of Nanetta and Marta, he crossed the bay and reported to da Lezze's major-domo at Chioggia, nineteen miles from Venice on the outer line of sandbanks guarding the great lagoons. In his purse he had forty sequins (about 90 dollars or £35), which was to see him to Ancona and through the period of quarantine he must pass there.

This was on or about 10 October 1743. The true chronology for this period of Casanova's life is largely guesswork. He says for instance that he was in southern Italy, when his dated signature as witness to a legal transaction shows that he was in Venice. He was writing fifty years later and, although he had somehow managed to keep an amazing number of papers, there was obviously much that he could neither document nor accurately remember.

At Chioggia they had to wait three days. In those three days Casanova got involved in a faro 'school', lost all his forty sequins and a good deal more on credit, caught his second dose of gonorrhoea, composed and recited a sonnet in honour of macaroni, ate such a quantity of it that he was named Prince of Macaroni, and pawned his trunk, containing all his belongings, to pay his gambling debts. The young *abate* had displayed for the first time the demoniacal speed with which he could get himself into real trouble. He had not yet perfected his techniques for getting out of it.

One disaster followed another. The ship set sail, Casanova owning nothing but some underclothes and a pair of shirts. At Orsara, the next stop, he passed his disease on to a complaisant housekeeper. Then, penniless and ill, he turned for help to a young Franciscan monk also making the voyage.

It is hard, today, to imagine the state of the Roman Catholic Church in the eighteenth century. There were, of course, dedicated and religious priests at all levels; but for tens of thousands in the monastic orders and in the bureaucracy of the Curia in Rome, the Church was a giant freemasonry of quacks. Brother Steffano was a whole-hearted rogue and an accomplished cadger. Casanova had never met anyone like him, and was alternately repelled and fascinated by his extraordinary personality. The monk could not read, got drunk at every opportunity, and lived off the gifts of the devout. When Casanova told this man of his troubles, Steffano was delighted, for he saw that with a combination of Casanova's good looks, education, and quick wit, and his own monkish skill at begging, they should do well indeed. And so they did. Casanova was dumbfounded at the rivers of wine, the mountains of food, that were provided merely for the asking. Looking at the man who was obtaining all this, he certainly thought, 'If that coarse oaf can get that much, what could *I* not get?' He may not, as yet, have decided that 'there's one born every minute'; but he certainly saw that a man could live very well indeed without ever putting himself to the degrading boredom of work.

Recovered from gonorrhoea, and shut up in the Ancona lazaret where travellers had to pass the quarantine, Casanova looked about him for another woman. The selection was easy: a Greek slave-girl who had ogled him from the lower courtyard. Turning invitation into consummation was much more difficult, for he was up, she was down, and both were guarded. They tried everything. Floorboards were prised loose, bags of sugar piled to make steps, muscles cracked. After much sweating and straining the girl got her head as high as Casanova's loins, where her lips, at least, could reach the root of the matter; but Casanova, up above and mad as a rutting stallion, could by no means get down to the girl's strongbox. She, as frustrated as he, begged him to buy her from the Turk who owned her. As she was a Christian, he would be compelled to sell her; and she would steal some of his diamonds and give them to Casanova as her dowry. He was tempted, for he truly believed himself to be in love with the girl: this was always his charm and the biggest factor in his success with women . . . but, in the middle of the final attempt to achieve a more perfect union, when he had his hands under the girl's armpits and was lifting her bodily up to his balcony, his guard saw them. The girl dropped ten feet to the courtyard, Casanova got shaken like a rat, and all was over . . . the period of quarantine, too.

He set off to walk to Rome, 190 miles away across the mountainous spine of Italy. At Loreto he met Steffano, and they went on together. Steffano announced that he planned to walk no more than three miles a day. He refused to go any faster, or farther, unless Casanova carried his cloak. Casanova innocently agreed, to find that the cloak was full of huge pockets, and the pockets so loaded with food and wine that he could barely stagger along under it. Steffano's drunkenness, his thieving, and his boorish behaviour to devout and simple people, soon brought the two to blows. They separated, and Casanova went on alone at a fast pace. But his troubles, far from abating, increased. He left most of his money behind at Tolentino; sprained his ankle near Serravalle; and was directed to the house of the chief of police to lodge. That official tried to sodomize him, and he fled to the village inn. Calling in a doctor to treat his ankle, he had no money to pay doctor or innkeeper. With two minutes left before Casanova was to be taken to prison, Steffano arrived, cackling like a madman, and paid off his debts. They went on together, Casanova now superstitiously convinced that his destiny was linked to the villainous monk's. And so, for the moment, it was.

Soon after leaving Serravalle, while crossing the bleak upland of the Marches, Steffano selected a poor hut as their inn for the night, and descended upon it. Only Goya could match Casanova's description. In the hovel they found an old man dying on a pallet, two crones, three stark-naked children, one cow, one huge dog, and every sign of extreme poverty. Casanova was so horrified to hear the monk demand food and lodging that he tried to leave, but the women wailed, the dog grabbed his coat, and he had to stay.

The chicken was so tough it could not be eaten. The wine, which the old man swore he had been keeping for twenty years against just such a visitation, had turned to vinegar. Casanova took some food out of the monk's cloak, where there was enough to feed everyone for a week.

Night fell. They lay down on the straw, the crones crawled in beside them, the monk yelled 'Murder!' Casanova tried to break free, the great dog rushed snarling from his throat to Steffano's, the old man bleated and sighed. Casanova, stiff with terror, showed his mettle by becoming stiff in another department and allowed his crone to get her satisfaction from him. 'When the lamp is taken away all women are alike', he quoted philosophically; but, he added, 'without love this great business is a vile thing'. Steffano's virtue was of a stronger fibre, or he really had no taste for women; besides, he had a monk's heavy robe to protect him from the women's lascivious parts and the dog's teeth. Breaking free from his harpy he jumped up, grabbed his staff, and laid about him. Shrieks, thumps, and screams. The monk lay down again, saying he thought he'd killed one of the women. Casanova thought he'd killed the old man and the dog as well. They went to sleep.

Morning showed the old man lying like dead, a bruise on his forehead; and women, children, cow and dog vanished, together with the contents of Steffano's cloak. The monk was furious, but Casanova thought that if the women had stolen food and money they would not be reporting the murder of the old man. The two men met a carriage going their way, and went on towards Rome. No one ever heard another word of the theft, or the murder. That was how things were in the Papal States, in A.D. 1743.

A couple of days later Steffano proudly showed Casanova a sack of truffles he had stolen from their hostess of the night before. Casanova had been much taken by this woman. His temper, equally violent in the service of good or evil causes, overcame him. He grabbed the monk's stick, cudgelled him with it, threw him into the ditch, and went on alone. That night he sent the truffles back to their owner.

Two more days . . . and Rome! Casanova hurried to the address the bishop had given him. No bishop: he'd gone on to Naples. He had not left any money. Casanova took the earliest coach. (From his description I see him jump into a passing carriage, calling 'Follow that bishop!')

In Naples he hurried to the address given: no bishop. He hurried to the monastery of the bishop's order. No bishop: he *had* been there, yes, but had left ten days earlier for Martorano. No, he had not left any instructions about giving journey money to *abate* Giacomo Casanova. He had not left any instructions at all.

Casanova tried to find a coach onward. But unless he paid in advance none would take him, and he had no trunk. He possessed just eight carlini (about thirty cents), so he started walking. He reached Portici, took a room at an inn, ate well, slept, and went out for a walk, wondering how he was to pay for his food and lodging. While sightseeing at the royal palace, he met a prosperous-looking man who introduced himself as a Greek, native of an island then subject to Venice. He offered to show Casanova round the palace, but Casanova saw in the man's subservient manner toward him – a Venetian – a prospect of getting money. He embarked on the first of those many frauds which were to lose him, time and again, the rewards his talents and his generosity had earned.

This first was a simple, not to say simple-minded, piece of chicanery, and even at this distance of two centuries one is baffled by the Greek's gullibility. Casanova undertook to increase a quantity of mercury, at a trifling cost. He did it by adding bismuth and lead to pure mercury. The resulting amalgam was of great mass but, of course, of correspondingly less purity, though Casanova did not mention this latter point. The greedy merchant offered to buy Casanova's secret for the equivalent of one thousand pounds sterling. Casanova accepted the offer, gave the merchant the formula, and got his bill of exchange for the money. The merchant went off to perform the magic but soon came back complaining that the mercury was not now pure. Casanova suavely pointed out that it was of the same purity as the mercury with which he had demonstrated, and on which the contract had been made.

The merchant was in a quandary. Casanova held his signed bill for a thousand pounds, for a secret which was worthless. He could refuse to pay, of course, and take the matter to court ... and admit that he, a wily Greek, had been bamboozled by a beardless eighteen-year-old *abate*? Already the mocking laughter rang in his ears ... He proposed a settlement, and Casanova was wise enough not to open his mouth too wide. For fifty pounds he gave the merchant back his bill of exchange.

The merchant bore no grudge. The young Venetian's aplomb seems rather to have awed him, and, as though awarding the diploma of a business college, he presented Casanova with a case of silver-handled razors and a vat of muscat wine. They parted good friends and Casanova could at last buy some clothes to replace those he had pawned during the disastrous stay in Chioggia.

He was beginning to establish a pattern in his life; at nineteen miles from home he had lost everything he owned, and more beside: 400 miles farther on he had regained it all, and more besides. He had learned that city slickers are just as easily duped as country yokels; and that although you could get food and drink from people's devoutness, from their greed you could get money, and plenty of it.

He went on southward, now foppishly dressed, heavily perfumed, and thoroughly content with himself. At Martorano he finally ran Bishop Bernardo de Bernardis to earth, having shown that sheer determination was one of his qualities, or failings, depending on what he was determined about.

In Martorano he took one look at the harsh Calabrian landscape, the bishop's tumbledown palace and 'most canonical of maidservants', and decided that Martorano was not for him. He told de Bernardis he was leaving, and strongly advised the bishop to come with him. They would make their fortunes together. The bishop spent the day alternately laughing at Casanova's outrageous proposal and sighing at the dreary prospect that his refusal would leave him; but, of course, refuse he had to, and Casanova went off alone to win his fortune, armed with flattering letters of introduction to various of the bishop's friends.

The manner of his going illumines the event with a sharp significance. He took money the bishop pressed on him, but in return insisted that the bishop accept a gift worth more than the money – the set of razors he had just been awarded for his fraud in Portici. If he had merely taken the money and gone his way, he would have been just another young man on the make in a corrupt society; the bishop would not have remembered him and the world would never have heard of him. But he was Giacomo Girolamo Casanova – on the make, certainly; not for money – that was incidental – but for the thing his birth had denied him: respect. In different ways he had already earned the respect of three older and more experienced men – Razzetta, the Greek merchant, and now the monk-bishop of Martorano.

Casanova went to Naples. He had plenty of money and good introductions, and the Marquis of Arienzo soon offered him a post as tutor to his great-nephew, the ten-year-old Duke of Maddaloni. Casanova did not accept the offer but kept up an intimate relationship with the Duke for many years. It is not irrelevant to note that the Duke grew up to be impotent, but his wife had a son; who in turn married, only to have the marriage annulled by Pope Pius VI . . . for his impotence! This peculiarly decadent family was at the centre of all Casanova's adventures in Naples, now and later.

Our Giacomo flew higher. He met a nobleman also called Casanova, and happily recited his family tree. He was pressed to present himself at Court. But now he smelled danger, for the Queen of Naples was the daughter of the Queen of Poland, from whom his mother the actress had begged a bishopric for de Bernardis. At Court the whole story would come out and his pretentious genealogy would be made ridiculous in face of the actuality . . . *dancers!*

He left for Rome, sharing a carriage with a lawyer on his way to pursue a case in the Vatican's courts, the lawyer's wife Lucrezia, and her sister Angelica. Lucrezia encouraged his amorous advances, and on the second night, at Marino, an uproar caused by troops squabbling in the town gave him a chance to press his suit. It is, again, a scene from Goya's brush or Chaucer's pen, and we cannot today understand how it could have taken place without an understanding of the eighteenth century's codes of morals and behaviour. From lack of privacy and plumbing they accepted as normal much that we, at least in the western world, regard as shameful or indecent.

The inn, for example, offered the travellers two rooms, one of which had the dining-table and a bed; the other, hardly more than a closet, could only be reached through the first, and contained another bed. The two women took the closet: Casanova and the lawyer, who had only met the day before, shared the bed in the dining-room. When the fracas began outside, the frightened women called for a light. The husband went to look for one, but Casanova, whose forte was in keeping his wits and his erection when all about him were losing theirs, slipped into the closet. The spring of the door-lock broke, so he couldn't get out and the lawyer couldn't get in. He leaped on Lucrezia, the bed collapsed, shouts and shots boomed in the street, Lucrezia begged him to leave, mad with lust he tried again and in the black pandemonium lifted the nightie of the wrong lady . . . Note that Lucrezia, in originally encouraging Casanova, accepted that any sexual outcome would take place in the same bed with her sister. These were not abnormal people, but, as life and housing were then organized, the sex act was in general no more to be hidden than the act of eating.

They reached Rome, and Casanova presented the letters of introduction he had been garnering along the route, especially to Cardinal Acquaviva and Father Giorgi. Cardinal Acquaviva was the most powerful man in Rome after the Pope . . . and some said, before. He was not only the King of Spain's ambassador, but was governor of a large part of Rome which belonged to Spain, not to the Pope. His income, as titular bishop of Monreale in Sicily, came to £14,500 a year, equivalent to perhaps £50,000 (125,000 dollars) today, with no taxes. Father Giorgi was Procurator General of the Augustinian Order in Rome, and had a strong personal influence over the Pope.

Acquaviva gave Casanova a position, and Giorgi undertook to guide his career in the Church. Casanova slipped joyfully into the life of Rome like a duck into a succulent, slimy pond. Acquaviva held a brilliant court, where Casanova met the élite of Rome, with their mistresses, pimps, and hangers-on. He heard about Cardinal B., who did not pay his handsome young *abate* 'except for certain extra services which he demanded in his nightcap'. He met the Cardinal Sciarra Colonna and his mistress the Marchesa Catrina Gabrielli. He kissed the Pope's slipper, told him the story of his adventures, and begged a dispensation to read forbidden books; which the Pope gave him, but not in writing. He met the Pope a second time, at the Villa Medici, and heard the Pontiff, after listening to someone's petition, tell the man to commend himself to God. Casanova told the Pope that the man was not going away happy; for presumably he had prayed to God and received no satisfaction before coming to the Pope, God's prime minister; and now the minister had referred him back to the master. The Pope laughed; Casanova begged for a dispensation from eating fish, which he said inflamed his eyes. It is also possible that he did not like fish.

Behind the bravado and the bounce there hid still a boy who waited, terrified, for some aristocrat to point a finger and cry 'Dancers!' In the middle of the vivacious narrative some sentences linger like cries of pain: 'I knew that she must know that a haughty air is unnerving,' and 'In the most brilliant company, if but a single member of it stares me up and down, I am undone; I become ill-tempered and stupid'.

For work he had to make précis of documents for Cardinal Acquaviva. He lived free of cost, and with an ample stipend beside. The silken manoeuvrings for power and place wove and unravelled under his watchful eyes, and he missed little – except the pitfalls in his own path. He had plenty of time to make love to Lucrezia, notably on day-long picnics which turned into copulating marathons among the ornamental arbours of Frascati or Tivoli. He also succeeded, with Lucrezia's cheerful advice and on-the-spot encouragement, in taking the virginity of her sister Angelica, thus saving the girl's fiancé much trouble.

When writing his *Story*, Casanova always tried to hide the identity of his women, unless they were strumpets or actresses, by using false names. Nevertheless, devoted casanovists, with James Rivers Childs in the van, by searching legal and church records, tax rolls and the like, have established probabilities about some and certainties about others; but not, of course, as to whether they really had affairs with Casanova. This Lucrezia was probably Anna Maria d'Antoni. She married Alessio Vallati in 1734, ten years before she met Casanova. She is also another example of his excessive chivalry about women's ages – or, perhaps, of his attempt to conceal his need of older women as mother-substitutes. He describes her as 'young', although she was in fact ten years older than he.

The sun shone. Cardinal Acquaviva thought highly of him, Cardinal Colonna still more so, for he composed love poems to the latter's mistress which the Cardinal (barely thirty-six years of age) passed on as his own. The Marchesa knew better; she rewarded the *abate* with a wink and, at a suitable moment, a brief exploration under her skirt. Father Giorgi thought he was intelligent but flighty and warned him several times to be careful. Father Giorgi said that there was no such thing as bad luck. In Rome no one was interested in excuses, only in success or failure. These were the precepts that led to power, for those to whom power was all. But Casanova did not want power. He wanted respect, and for him the first necessity was self-respect, according to his own warped but deeply felt emotions. It was this praiseworthy quality which now undid him.

His French teacher, Dalacqua, had a daughter called Barbaruccia, and Barbaruccia had a secret lover, an earnest, amiable, but distinctly square young man. One day the lover came long-faced to Casanova, to say that Dalacqua had surprised him in bed with Barbaruccia, thrown him out of the house, and locked her up. She was pregnant and they were going to elope. All was ready, except that they had no money. Would Casanova lend them some? He did.

Rumours began to fly. Casanova was horrified to learn how much attention Romans of every rank paid to the most minor scandal. It was said that Barbaruccia's father had gone to the papal offices and asked for an order to imprison a young man who was about to elope with his daughter. But who was the young man? No one knew, except that he must be living in the Spanish Quarter, where the Pope had to ask permission of Cardinal Acquaviva before his Holy Order could be carried out, for it was known that such permission had been asked. Presumably it had been granted. The papal police would strike at any moment.

Worried by the gossip, Casanova returned to his room in the Cardinal's palace to find Barbaruccia there, disguised as an *abate*. The police had seized her lover in the act of elopement, she herself had just got away. She was in tears, desperate, didn't know where to turn ... so she'd come here. That made Casanova desperate, too. The doorkeeper had seen the girl come in and her disguise would not have deceived him for a moment. What should he do? What would Father Giorgi advise? Hand Barbaruccia over to the police, of course. When the Pope and Cardinal Acquaviva had agreed to seize her, who would be blamed for failing to help her?

To Casanova, *he* would be, by himself. He would be acting just as they would expect an actress's bastard to act. A gentleman, on the other hand, a gentleman by birth, the sort who didn't care *who* stared at his clothes, would do the gentlemanly thing and damn the consequences.

He sent the girl direct to Acquaviva, to throw herself on his mercy. The Cardinal took pity and let her escape the city with her lover. It only remained to sacrifice someone in her place, so that the Pope and his police would not later refuse some favour the Cardinal wanted. With perfect acumen and in the most kindly manner possible, he sacrificed Casanova. He told him with great personal regret that he must leave his service, and Rome itself. He, the Cardinal, was fortunate enough to know influential people in all parts of the country, indeed, of the world. Anywhere that Casanova wished to go, he would send him, well provided with money and as though on a secret mission (he had seen the importance to Casanova of a good appearance, above all). He would give him the best possible introductions. Now, where did he want to go?

Casanova, his eyes welling with tears, begged once to be forgiven; then, seeing that there was no hope of that, drew himself up and said, 'Send me to Constantinople'.

2

The Philosopher's Stone

With the ball at his feet, Casanova had kicked it away. The disaster in Rome marked the end of his first attempt to make for himself a respected position in the world. He did not actually abandon his orders until a little later, but clearly he now had made up his mind that the devious patience of the Church Political was not for him; he had no pastoral instinct, and was too independent a thinker to become a sound theologian. That left nothing.

He left Rome for Venice, on the first leg of his roundabout journey to Constantinople, in a footloose frame of mind. The Church was 'out'. What next?

On reaching Ancona he at once began a high-handed quarrel by demanding food which the innkeeper was forbidden to serve, it being then Lent and this a city of the Papal States. Casanova claimed that he had the Pope's permission to eat meat in Lent, but he could produce no document to prove it. Threats and insults flew, tempers became frayed. It was pointless, petty, and ridiculous – a good example of the lengths to which Casanova would go in his obsessive longing for a respect greater than his appearance or his performance merited.

When he had calmed down he turned his attention to some fellow guests – a theatrical family of the kind which Casanova despised, always fell in with, and was naturally perfectly at home with. This family consisted of mother, two daughters, aged twelve and eleven, and two brothers, Petronio and Bellino. The two girls were whores, Petronio a male prostitute, and Bellino a *castrato*. Casanova tackled them systematically. The two little girls prettily allowed themselves to be persuaded into his bed for a small sum (paid in cash and handed at once to Mother). Petronio's approach was politely refused. Mother was eliminated, and that left only Bellino, the *castrato*.

At this period several sovereigns, among them the Pope, forbade women to appear on the stage as inciting to licentious behaviour.

Women's parts were taken by *castrati* – boys or men who had been castrated as children. A castrato's voice would not break and his body was likely to assume the more typically female shape, including an enlargement of the breasts and hips. Very considerable numbers of boys from poor families were castrated to be sold to the theatre or the Church (for choirs). The material rewards could be considerable, especially when the alternative was starving in a hovel, along with a dozen brothers and sisters. As for public morality, the substitution of *castrati* for pretty women naturally and inevitably led to homosexual relationships as the deviates of each city paid court to the pretty boys, whose mutilation and its psychological consequences had forced them into homosexuality.

Bellino, who appeared to be about sixteen years old, now began to obsess Casanova. He says that he had already made up his mind that Bellino was not a *castrato*, but a girl: though after a few days Bellino pointed out that his passion had grown to a point where he no longer cared. Casanova was madly enamoured of the person he saw, whether it was male or female. His infatuation, however, did not prevent his having a lightning copulation with the Greek slave-girl of the lazaret, this time on a ship, and in front of Bellino. Bellino, knowing nothing of the previous history, stood frozen with horror and amazement at the sudden coupling, almost under the Turkish owner's nose. Casanova was not sorry that Bellino had witnessed this display of his mental determination and physical equipment.

Bellino tried to defend himself against Casanova's ardour, and by design gave him the chance to see that he had a penis. Casanova persuaded himself that it was not a penis but a gigantic clitoris, and continued his assault. At last, on the journey northward towards Pesaro, he got Bellino to himself. They spent the night in Sinigaglia. There was only one bed in the room. Casanova, keeping his voice neutral in spite of his passion, asked Bellino whether he would prefer that Casanova took another room for himself. Bellino smiled nicely and said 'No'. They went to bed together.

I had scarcely got into the bed before I was overcome to see him moving toward me. I clasp him to me, I see that he is fired by the same transport. The exordium of our dialogue was a deluge of mingling kisses. His arms were first to slip down from my back to my loins. I stretch mine still lower, it is revelation enough that I am happy, I sense it, I feel it, I am convinced of it. I am right, I am vindicated, I cannot doubt it, I do not want to know how, I fear that if I speak I shall no longer be happy, or be happy as I would not wish to be, and I give myself, body and soul, to the joy which flooded my entire being and which I saw was shared. The excess of my bliss seizes all my senses with such force that it reaches the degree at which nature, drowning in the highest of all pleasures, is exhausted. For the space of a minute I remain motionless in the act of mentally contemplating and worshipping my own apotheosis.

She was a girl. The thing he had seen was a little device worn by actresses who wished to play their usual parts in cities where they were not permitted to, and so posed as *castrati*. It was a false penis made of gut, attached to thin, transparent hide or skin tissue, the whole being stuck with gum over the woman's vulva, completely obliterating it. The examination of actors was usually conducted by aged clergymen, local agents or the Roman Inquisition, and the deception would serve, remembering that a *castrato* would not in any case possess testicles and would have a generally female appearance. As soon as the examination was over the actress took off the false apparatus and lived her normal life.

Casanova was in love. Her name was Teresa. (Actually it was Angela Calori, born in Milan in 1732.) He would marry her! She was divine, perfect, wonderful! In a rare and touching gesture he wrote her a long letter, in which he confessed the truth about himself and his background. She had thought him a rich young nobleman. He was not; he was no more than she – if possible, less.

She accepted his offer of marriage. They would go to Venice, she would take off her man's clothes and be a woman, a wife, a mother. But first she had to perform a contract at Rimini.

She got there. Casanova didn't. He had managed to lose his passport, so when he came to the outposts of the Spanish Army at Pesaro, they arrested him. He had lost his wallet on the way to Rome. Fifty years later one can hear the grating of his teeth as he writes, 'I suffered these misfortunes once and once only'. But for the moment he could only write to Acquaviva in Rome asking for a new passport, and suffer imprisonment until a reply came.

He whiled away the time by losing money to a military cardsharper who at this time called himself Don Bepe il Cadetto. There was nothing else to do. After about ten days, while taking an early stroll, he saw an officer ride up, leave his horse and walk away. Casanova wondered to see the beast stand so still, with no one aboard. He took the reins . . . tested the stirrups. Goodness, one climbed up like this, and here one was, astride the monster's back (for the first time in his life). He must have given the intelligent animal some secret equestrian signal, for it took off at full gallop. He was quite unable to direct it or stay its course. At full speed it tore past the Spanish picquet lines.

23

Ignoring the sentries' shouts, it galloped on, musket balls whistling around. At the Austrian outposts it came to its senses and stopped.

The sentries demanded to know where Casanova was going, at that speed. Quick-witted, he answered that that was a military secret which he could only divulge to the Commander-in-Chief. The Austrians sent him under escort, at full gallop, to General Prince Lobkowitz. Casanova was ushered at once into the presence — (one is struck, time and again, by the lack of barriers in the eighteenth century; wear the right clothes, tell a plausible, or sufficiently implausible, story, have the nerve, and you could get to see anyone, any time) — where he wisely told the simple truth. Lobkowitz laughed and had him escorted out of the city, free to go where he would: except that they took the horse, pointing out that it didn't belong to him.

He was free. But the city outside the wall of which he now stood was Rimini, and inside Rimini was Teresa/Bellino. A string of mules came in from the country. It was raining, cold, miserable. The muleteers trudged through the mud, heads bowed under old sacks. Such human animals were never stopped by the soldiers — war was nothing to do with them. Casanova put his hand on a mule's neck, began to walk, head bent, trudging in the rain . . . past the gates, past the unseeing guards, right back into Rimini.

He spent a day and a night with Teresa and then, considering it dangerous to stay in Rimini, smuggled himself out and took the stage-coach for Bologna.

Here he set himself to thinking. In the Church he had not been respected: no churchmen were, except cardinals, and perhaps true saints, if there were any. To tell the truth only the army was respected, because people were afraid of it. The army wasn't afraid of anyone. The army wasn't quite respectable, of course, but one didn't have to be respectable to be respected: in fact the two things seemed to be mutually exclusive. Be respectable and the world laughed at you for a ninny. An idea germinated, took root, and reached full flower in no time at all. He would become a soldier . . . an officer, of course.

Today the word 'army' conjures up a picture of millions of faceless young men in drab green or grey, under identical helmets: dully gleaming weapons of great complexity: the highly organized arm of a highly organized state. An eighteenth-century army contradicted this description in every particular, especially in Italy. States were not well organized for anything, and their armies less so. Administration, supply, training and discipline were of the sketchiest, or non-existent. Officers lived how they wished and soldiers how they could. There was always war going on somewhere in the ramshackle peninsula among the various dukedoms, republics, principalities, legateships and dependencies, all of which were just as likely to hire someone else's army, or mercenary freebooters, as to use their own troops (if they had any). What were these Spanish and Austrian armies doing at Rimini? What were German troops doing at Marino, the night Casanova first tried to seduce Lucrezia? One could explain, of course; and at the time a few high-ranking officers knew and cared. For the rest the army was a way of life, and it didn't matter a damn who provided the fighting, the looting, the billets, or the girls. It was also – and this is vitally important in understanding Casanova – one of those semi-closed societies (others were the Church and the Law) through which the landed aristocracy held the power without being put to the troublesome details of actually governing or administering. It was through these 'clubs' that Society gave employment, reward, and recognition to all classes lower than its own; but most particularly to that middle class which might otherwise have overthrown it and governed in its stead.

Having decided to be an officer, Casanova designed himself a uniform, and had a tailor make it up for him. It was white and blue, with gold aiguillettes and sword knots. In it he strutted about Bologna, revelling in the wonder he caused, careless how much of it was derision at his peacock posturing and how much admiration of his truly astounding nerve.

Now arrived a long letter from Teresa in Rimini. She would certainly join him, as they had planned, if he ordered her to, but there was a complication: the Duke of Castropignano had offered her a great deal of money to become *prima ballerina* in his new theatre in Naples. What was she to do?

Casanova wrestled with his emotions. He loved Teresa. She was divine, perfect, wonderful . . . on the other hand, he had enjoyed her charms, and down there where the fascinating false penis hung she was just the same as the dreadful hag who had raped him on the road to Rome. The mystery of exactly what was lurking between any particular woman's legs obsessed him until he had seen, touched, and entered it. He could see now that Teresa was really not much better than a whore. She would certainly have lovers, like this old duke (who was fifty-five); then he, Casanova, would appear to be living off his wife's immoral earnings, just like other theatre husbands.

He faced, for the first time, one of the recurring problem-themes of his life: how to rid himself, with honour, of a woman he had seduced and, in the excess of his good nature, offered to marry or care for eternally. It took him a little time, but he came up with the answer. Taking his pen he wrote to her with a heavy heart, advising her to accept the Duke's offer. He would join her in Naples when he came back from Constantinople. Meanwhile she was to engage a suitable (meaning ugly) chambermaid and act with discretion.

His heart almost visibly lightening, he set out for home. Dodging the quarantine by various subterfuges, changing his Austrian black cockade to one of Spanish red when he passed into Spanish-controlled territory, he reached Venice on 2 April 1744, his nineteenth birthday, having ridden post fifty-eight miles that day. In no time he was back in bed with Nanetta and Marta, his 'little wives'.

The Grimanis, led by the Abbé his guardian, had no trouble concealing their joy at his reappearance in Venice, in uniform. Perhaps by their influence, he obtained a posting to go with the uniform, and bought a commission as an ensign in the army of Venice. Commissions were bought and sold in most of Europe at that time: they were in England until 1871. His regiment was stationed at Corfu, and he stipulated that as soon as he had reported for duty he must have six months leave to complete his secret mission to Constantinople.

He set off for Corfu. The ship's first stop was again at Orsara, as on the journey to Ancona. He was certain, as he strutted the quayside, that no one would recognize in the gorgeous, warlike ensign of the Republic the meek cleric of last year. He was wrong. The town doctor recognized him, and hurried up to offer him anything he wanted. Casanova had given the complaisant housekeeper gonorrhoea; and she gave it to another friend; who gave it to his wife; who gave it to ... The doctor had made his fortune, treating half the town. When was Casanova coming back?

The ship sailed on. A storm blew up, and a priest on board urged the sailors to help him exorcise the devils in the clouds, while Casanova urged them to keep working the ship. Casanova was right, but one sailor tried to throw him into the steep Adriatic seas, the rest threatened his life, and only the soldiers on board saved him. The priest said that God sent the storm because Casanova had in his possession an impious parchment of black magical origin. Oddly enough, Casanova did have just such a parchment on him. He had bought it for ten shillings from a Greek at Malamocco, just before setting sail. Of course, *he* wasn't fool enough to believe such nonsense, but some simple people held the laughable superstition that the parchment made women fall in love with the possessor of it. The priest triumphantly confiscated it and set fire to it. Being parchment, it took a long time burning, and writhed like a tortured gnome in the process. The storm abated. The sailors believed the priest had saved them. Casanova had had another demonstration of the power of self-deception.

Arrived at Corfu he turned to gambling, the obsession that was to be his curse, just as women, in spite of all, were his benediction. The game he played – *the* game everywhere in Europe throughout his life – was faro. Here is Hoyle's description of it:

The Tailleur [banker, or dealer] and Croup sit opposite each other at a large oval Table covered with a green Cloth, on which is a Line marked by coloured Tape, or a wooden Rim about an Inch High and Eight from the Edge of the Table, for the purpose of separating those Cards punted on from the others. Money is placed either loose in a well, or done up in rouleaus. The Tailleur is to deal while the Croup pays and receives, guards against Errors, and shuffles another Pack of Cards . . . [The Banker then turns up two cards at a time, setting one down on his right, the other on his left.] He wins when the Card equal in Points to that on which the Stake is set turns up on his Right Hand, but loses when it is dealt to the Left. The Punter loses half the Stake when his card comes out twice in the same Coup [that is, when the Banker turns up two of the same value. This provision is the basis of the built-in odds enjoyed by the Bank, although the odds against the punter also increased with every Coup dealt].

The game allowed for all kinds of plays, starting with a *paroli* (double) which the punter intimated by bending one corner of his card upward. From here he could go via *Sept et le va* (gambling a successful *paroli* plus the original stake, for a sevenfold return), through intermediate steps to *Soixante et le va* for sixty times the stake. These and all other calls could be shown by bending and mutilating the cards, without speaking a word; which enabled strangers of different nationalities to play with no inconvenience, and, together with the masks worn in many cities (especially at Venice) at certain times, enabled gamblers to play without being known, either by face, voice, or costume – only by the manner of play; but there one was obviously in deep waters.

Casanova quickly lost all his money, but just as he was about to go under for the third time, his ship arrived, and he set out for Constantinople. En route they stopped briefly at the Venetian penal colony of Cerigo (Cythera) where he met a certain Antonio Pocchini, enduring exile for pimping. He should have noticed the face, and the crime, more carefully . . .

Casanova's account of his stay in Constantinople has been questioned. It has been said that he may have invented his whole visit, using names of people who were publicly known to have been there at the time. He was, remember, writing when almost everyone who could have asked questions was dead. But the probability is that he did go, not once but twice, and in his *Story* intermingles incidents from both visits.

Two Turks dominate the tale. There is a Bad Turk called Ismail, a libertine and worse – indeed, a sodomite. (Most Europeans of the period believed all Turks to be devotees of this rite. Most Europeans were correct.) The Good Turk is called Yussuf.

Yussuf is wise and good and has a nubile daughter by an earlier mariage. His current wife is also young, nubile, and unsatisfied. Yussuf becomes a father-figure, gives Casanova an extremely sensible talk on masturbation, and offers him the hand of his daughter in marriage, plus great wealth and a high position. To win all this he has only to become a Muslim. Casanova is torn . . . How can anyone *respect* him if he turns apostate? What sort of a reception can he expect where it matters – in Venice, Paris, London – if he changes his religion? He refuses the offer by allowing it to lapse. (His still extant offer of marriage to Teresa/Bellino does not cross his mind.) Instead he tries to kiss Yussuf's wife, and is rebuffed. What he should have done, he is advised later, was simply raise her skirt and get to work, as Turkish women were only modest about their faces.

The Bad Turk, Ismail, starts by making an improper advance, which Casanova virtuously declines. Later, wily as only a deviate Turk can be, he sets Casanova's volatile blood afire by letting him meet and dance with a Venetian girl from his harem (in sexual matters, Ismail was double-barrelled). The girl makes a secret rendez-vous, but when Casanova arrives, in a high state of anticipation, who should be waiting but Ismail. Ismail offers to show him something worthwhile. Hidden behind a window, they watch three girls disporting naked in a pool. One of them is the Venetian dancer. Since the girls are out of reach, Casanova has to slake his lust in the only human object at hand – Ismail. Ismail is kind enough to return the compliment several times. When it is over they part with mutual expressions of esteem.

Casanova's words at the end of his description are significant: 'This was the only pleasure of the sort which I enjoyed at Constantinople, and imagination had a greater share in it than reality.' Did they, or didn't they? Casanova isn't saying – here. He seems rather to be testing the temperature of the water: suppose he *did* have homosexual tendencies, just suppose . . . would it be possible to admit it, and not lose respect?

He left Constantinople loaded with presents by the tearful Yussuf, and returned to Corfu in the ship carrying the retiring Venetian ambassador home.

Corfu is a small island at the southern end of the Adriatic, close to the eastern shore at the point where modern Greece borders Albania. Today bikini'd girls imprint their breasts and buttocks in the warm sand; for Casanova it was a remote military frontier. The power which faced the Grand Turk all along this coast-line was Venice, for Greece had not yet been reborn. The eastern shore, which belonged to Venice, was barren and poverty-sticken, inhabited by half-savage peasants who grazed goats on the rocky slopes. Malaria riddled the whole area.

Casanova's orbit in Corfu was at first aimless, then gradually that of a satellite about a lady he calls Signora F. Her name was probably Foscari; she was wife to a commander of a galley and mistress to the Governor of the Galleasses, Giacomo da Riva. Casanova became adjutant to da Riva, and lost no time in making a few enemies. One was the other adjutant, or aide-de-camp as we would call the job today. He had 'rotten teeth, a blond wig, dirty complexion, and stinking breath' – a marvel of precise observation and concise writing here, because Casanova detested the fellow as a witness to Signora Foscari's total lack of awareness of him. It is only when he describes the women he loves and the men he admires that he becomes mawkish, wordy, and vague.

Another enemy was Casanova's batman, a jolly enough fellow, and full of pranks, until he fell ill and came to death's door, probably with malaria. Being confessed, he produced a grimy paper which proved he was the Prince de la Rochefoucauld, and said he wished to be buried in that station. The century dearly loved a prince, and a prince disguised as a private soldier was a special titillation. The paper was rushed to the Governor, who believed it. Casanova gave him the contradiction direct, saying that the man was a French deserter and a mountebank, nothing more; the famous lady whom the man claimed was his mother would now be about 140 years old. Casanova was right, but it is never wise for a second lieutenant to know more than a governor, and he was dismissed with a sharp snub. The paper was sent to Venice for checking.

The batman-prince was now ill-advised enough to recover. The deferential treatment he met went to his head and he attacked Casanova for doubting his story. Casanova waited for him in a dark alley and gave him a thrashing. Since the wretch was carrying a sword, and did not use it in the face of this physical violence, Casanova *knew* he was not a gentleman, or even a prince.

Well satisfied, he went to his favourite coffee-house, where an officer soon appeared and told him to put himself under arrest on board the flagship of the galleys, by order of the Governor. This sort of arrest meant being chained to the deck of the ship. Casanova left the coffee-house, walked to the end of the quay, got into the first boat he found and rowed out to sea. There he transferred to a passing caique and from that to a large fishing-boat. He ordered the skipper to put him ashore at the first opportunity, which was done, and Casanova went to sleep on the empty beach.

In the dawn he found he was on the Kassiopi peninsula, on the north shore of Corfu. There was a small village, a church with a miraculous fig tree, a few wild shepherds and a superstitious Greek Orthodox priest. Casanova, determined not to surrender to unjust and degrading imprisonment, organized twenty of the shepherds into a private army and twenty of their sisters into a corps of seamstresses to make shirts for himself. The girls would soon have manufactured more shirts than Casanova could use, had he not transformed them into a *corps de harem*. (Collecting and converting seamstresses must have filled some special need in him: he managed to get himself into this particular situation, master of a room full of girls busily sewing, at least twice more in his life.)

A few young men, who did not appreciate the education Casanova was giving their fiancées, complained to the priest, who put a dreadful curse called a *cataramonachia* on him. Casanova did not fear curses but he knew a good deal about poison. He went straight to the church and told the priest that at the first sign of illness he would come and blow his head off. The priest became assiduous in inquiring after his health.

Back on Corfu no one knew what had happened to him. It was presumed da Riva had hidden him until the trouble blew over, but da Riva knew nothing. Finally word of the strange doings at Kassiopi reached the capital and the Governor sent to get him. Casanova would have liked a large ship to come, with a company of soldiers. Then there could have been a stimulating scene, a little battle perhaps. But it was only one man, a lieutenant, his friend, who urged him to return and face the music. It wouldn't be so bad, because the bogus prince's paper had come back from Venice labelled a worthless forgery, and the man himself had been committed as a galley slave.

Casanova allowed himself to be persuaded, sent his girls back to their fiancés and his soldiers to their goats, and returned to Corfu.

For a brief while he basked in glory, and he had the sense not to rub in their folly to the Governor and the ladies who had taken the false prince's side. Then he was transferred, as adjutant, from da Riva to Foscari, and found himself in the same house as the Signora, who became his official mistress in one sense, and whom he wished above all to make his mistress in the other.

The Human Comedy evokes tears as well as laughter, and we weep and smile in the same moment as we look back, over two centuries, at the work and wiles of that great teaser, Signora Foscari. She gave Casanova enough encouragement to keep him always at her beck. It can have done her no harm socially, in that time and place, to have it seen throughout the garrison that the young hero of the Rochefoucauld affair was at her feet. Casanova, for his part, went out of orbit into the uncontrolled zoom of a man who is for the first time really in love. It is easy to see, and to say, that his passion was caused by the lady's skill in sitting on it, but that does not lessen the force of his brainstorm. He worshipped, he begged, he fell on his knees; he was insulted one moment and was prettily begged forgiveness the next (asking him to fasten her shoe, for which she put one foot up on a chair). He stole her hair, she reproached him, he burst into tears, she gave him some of the hair (and a glimpse of her breasts). He had the hair ground up into powder, mixed into a good recipe, and made into sweetmeats. The sweets became the talk of Corfu, and no one knew what was in them. But she wormed the secret out of him, swooned with pleasure, twisted her ankle (and had Casanova change her shift for her). The husband and da Riva being away, they passed hours in what Casanova would call dalliance. The next day, having underestimated either her own powers of resistance or Casanova's urgent accuracy, she dropped her guard for a moment, and, *presto*, the cat was in the bag. With a shriek she jumped up, giving the poor boy a fearful shock and nearly snapping off his instrument. It was too much. Casanova stormed out. A well-known whore called him into conversation . . . then into her room. Gratefully, and for a consideration, she finished what Signora Foscari had begun.

It is surely needless to add that she gave Casanova his third dose of venereal disease.

He was miserable, and now everything went wrong. He could not continue his pursuit of Signora Foscari. He had to undergo a cure, and everyone in Corfu knew why. His luck at faro changed for the worse, and he lost the resources which had been enabling him to live extravagantly. The military authorities, who had promised to promote him to lieutenant, gave the vacancy to another man. The volatile Casanova threw himself with gusto into the deepening gloom. He saw himself now not as a bright and brilliant young officer but as a tongue-tied, poverty-stricken bastard, sickly and pitiable, descended from a long line of dancing-masters and theatrical whores. By determined hard work he quickly became all the things he thought he was.

His regiment returned to Venice and he with it, only to resign from the army at once: then, surely, back into bed with Nanetta and Marta while he decided what to do next? But Nanetta had married and Marta entered a convent on Murano. There was only old Signora Manzoni, to laugh at the fulfilment of her predictions, laugh when he swore that he was going to be a lawyer, and laugh, though perhaps not so hard, when he thought of becoming a professional gambler.

In the end he tried, almost for the last time, to find another honourable profession. Dr Gozzi had taught him the violin, as well as Latin. He never pretended to play it well, but he did play, and here he was, back where he had come from, among the actors and musicians of Venice, his mother's people. In December 1745 he became second violinist in the orchestra of the S. Samuele theatre, at a salary of about seven shillings a day. It was a sad descent, for whereas the world might have respect for aged prelates and dashing ensigns, it had none for third-rate fiddlers.

Seven or eight wild young men, including Casanova and his brother Francesco, formed a gang which perpetrated all kinds of midnight pranks, to the annoyance of solid citizens. For instance, going late into an inn they saw a respectable weaver drinking with his wife and two friends. The gang leader, taking a fancy to the wife, led the band back outside and made a plan: they would return to the inn, masked, as representatives of the Council of Ten, and take the weaver and his friends away, while two would pretend to take the wife home, but in fact would rendezvous with the others as soon as the three men were out of the way. No sooner said than done, and now, as such methods always will, the ruthless secrecy in which the Council of Ten ruled Venice defeated its own purposes. At the mention of the dread title the three men turned pale and went. No one dared ask questions. The masked scoundrels took them to the island of S. Giorgio where no one would see them till daybreak, and rowed away.

Back at the rendezvous, the lady's terror turned to relief when the band gathered, took off their masks and revealed themselves as cheerful young men. They promised her that no harm would come to her on her husband; she had only to say nothing . . . and please lie down here. The leader, a young patrician of the Balbi family, served first.

The lady made a pretty show of resistance, but soon entered into the spirit of the game, especially after Casanova (who served second) made her realize that all eight were going to do her the honour of playing in her court. (He was wrong; his brother Francesco said he didn't feel well, and cried off.) After the orgy, and plenty of wine, they took the lady home and scattered, well pleased with their prank.

The husband complained to the Council, with details, except that the lady had the sense to say that no one had molested her; the young men had merely taken her home, treated her politely, and left her. All Venice, except the husband, knew better. A patrician soon retailed the full facts to Casanova, naming all the names. The Council of Ten did not act, in spite of the insult to their majesty, probably so that the exploit would be the sooner forgotten; but Casanova had again invited attention to himself, and the Venetian Government never forgot.

And now a brief chance, boldly seized, gave Casanova a new father and a new life. In the spring of 1746, being about twenty-one, he was playing at a wedding ball at the Palazzo Soranzo. Leaving late, he saw a red-robed man in front of him drop a letter. The red robe meant that the man was a senator of Venice, hence a patrician. Casanova picked up the letter and returned it to the senator, who insisted on giving him a ride in his gondola to wherever he wanted to go.

They had hardly set off when the senator said his left arm felt cold . . . then his head . . . his leg . . . Casanova acted fast. Recognizing at once that the senator was having a stroke, he made the gondoliers stop, leaped ashore (it was near where he had beaten up the wicked Razzetta) and found a surgeon. The surgeon bled the senator, and Casanova sacrificed his shirt to make a bandage. Then they took the sick man home, and Casanova learned that he was Matteo Giovanni Bragadin. The Bragadins were a family of extreme antiquity and great influence.

At the senator's palace the servants hurried off to tell his best friends, Marco Dandolo and Marco Barbaro, of his misfortune. The two patricians came at once. Casanova was not the man to bow out of such a situation, and he stayed close to the centre of affairs while, over the next few days, a surgeon attempted a radical cure. His method was to apply ointment of mercury to the patient's chest. Casanova saw that it was having a disastrous effect on the senator, who was getting burnt and suffering from an inflammation which his heart and arteries were in no state to combat. Casanova awakened the two old friends in the middle of the night, but he did not ask them what to do. He told them, and he did it. He removed the doctor's medicaments and washed the senator's chest. The senator went peacefully to sleep.

This action was of extraordinary courage, for if the patient had then died Casanova could have been accused of murder. Doctors today can be extremely unfriendly to unlicensed practitioners of their art, and they were no different in 1746. The doctor in this case coldly resigned his patient into Casanova's hands. The three aristocrats hailed Casanova as a genius, which he was, but not in quite the way they meant. He expanded under their praise, quoted all kinds of medical textbooks which, as he is scrupulous to point out, he had never read, and posed as an expert on everything under the sun. Since he was well educated, and exceptionally quick and intelligent, he impressed the three old men considerably.

Casanova, from the viewpoint of extreme youth, thinks of them as old. In fact at this time Bragadin was fifty-seven, Dandolo forty-two, and Barbaro fifty-eight. They were all three bachelors and had been gay blades in their youth. By birth they were influential and by inheritance rich; but in middle age they had turned their energies toward the forbidden sciences of cabalism and alchemy. Yet they were far from stupid. Why, then?

The year was 1746. Not only were such inventions as radio, television, electricity and the internal combustion engine in the womb of the future, but also the steam engine. An Ancient Roman, returning to earth, would have found that little of what he had known or used was out of date, and that much (good roads, plumbing, and central heating) had been forgotten. The Renaissance, the rediscovery of the classical world, had awakened men's minds without satisfying them. The vastness of the universe was known as it was not to the ancients, and telescopes were beginning to explore it. Microscopes probed new vistas in the other direction, the substructure of matter. Man was becoming aware, first, of the extent of his ignorance; second, that there *were* solutions to all mysteries: it only remained to find them.

Today when we say there are things we do not yet understand we mean extra-sensory perception, or ghosts, or telepathy, or the creation of life; in 1746 these were merely some among a million mysteries yet to be solved. An intelligent man of the age would certainly have predicted that telepathy would be solved before the art of sending coloured pictures ten thousand miles through space.

In this atmosphere, thickened by a general ground-fog of superstition, it needed a stern common-sense, a puritanical grasp of the true foundations of knowledge, *not* to believe in such things as the Philosopher's Stone (which would turn base metals into gold) and the cabalist ciphers by which the ancients had communicated with Being.

Giacomo's universal wisdom convinced Bragadin that he could not be as young as he seemed. He must have some supernatural gift, some cryptic communion with Hidden Ones . . . surely? To Casanova a nod was as good as a wink; and he had been with the three men for some time. He guessed that they were secret cabalists (secret because the Church forbade it on pain of the Inquisition, and death), and were asking if he were too. In response to the senator's veiled invitation, he at once leaped into the deep waters, and did not drown.

Why yes, he hinted, he *did* have a secret calculus. It had been given to him by an old monk on a mountain while he was with the Spanish army a year or two back. Frankly, he had not found it of much use. It was terribly obscure. He couldn't understand the answers it gave him to the simplest questions. Its only recent sensible communication was to tell him to leave the Soranzo wedding ball precisely at four in the morning, and that was how he had come to meet Signor Bragadin.

The old men were struck dumb with wonder. As Casanova was still diffident about his calculus, they put it to the test. Dandolo asked a question of which only he could know the meaning, let alone the answer. Casanova turned to his calculus, and since he had no idea what the question was about, put out the answer in verses composed of meaningless groups of figures. To win the game, Casanova had only to keep his mouth shut, because, as the history of human self-deception proves, the three old patricians were going to find what they wanted to find – however long it took.

I intend to go into cabalism in more detail later, when Casanova was using a more sophisticated system than at this time; but I must explain here that the cabala was basically a method, Jewish in origin, of writing down a symbol which in some magical way *was* God, and therefore omniscient and all-inclusive. Plenty of people believed that if you wrote down a certain thing in a certain way you were not invoking God, but actually creating His presence. In 1700 a book was published entitled *De la Cabella intellective, art majeur*. It explained how to construct a magic pyramid of letters and from that to abstract the answers, in hexameters, to any question put to it. The calculations were long and complex. As Casanova says he answered Dandolo's question in verse, this is probably the method he used. He may have found the book when he was a prisoner in Pesaro, more likely in Bologna, and studied it during his spare time in Corfu.

Now Dandolo set to work to translate Casanova's random figures. He found his answer. They were all astounded (none more than Casanova). The old monk on the mountain had given him a secret beyond price, they cried. Would he . . . could he, consider selling it to them? Why, certainly Casanova said; of course, he would drop dead within a week, as the monk had warned, but that was a mere nothing, a pleasure, for friends such as these gentlemen. They begged him to keep his secret. They would all work the cabala together, with Casanova as head occultist.

Senator Bragadin came to him with an offer. Those who had tried to make him in turn a priest, a soldier, a lawyer, a musician, were all wrong. What he was, and ought to be, was a rich young man about town, an expert in the occult arts, and the confidant of three lonely, elderly aristocrats. In brief, would he become Signor Bragadin's adopted son?

Casanova had deserved this staggering offer by his sheer nerve. He could rise now from the gutter, for the third time. They were offering him a place in the upper chamber, and clothes of silk. It occurred to him that, as a man of honour, he should tell the good senator he didn't believe in the occult, or the cabalists' calculus, or the sacred symbols, or the Philosopher's Stone. But, as with the girls he had refrained from seducing, what good would that have done? Dandolo had just proved to himself, and his two friends, that Casanova *did* have the cabalistic secret. They were determined to spend their money on a practitioner of the occult, and if it were not Casanova it would be some grasping charlatan.

He states his decision with simple dignity: 'I took the most creditable, the noblest, and the only natural course. I decided to put myself in a position where I need no longer go without the necessities of life; and what those necessities were for me no one could judge better than I.'

He accepted the senator's proposal and moved into the Bragadin palace at once.

3

Tu oublieras aussi Henriette

Quivering with anticipation, Casanova settled down to his life's work – living in extravagance off the gullibility of the rich. There were few better places in the world than Venice in which to do it. The ancient city, long past its power, glowed with the phosphorescent splendour of decay. The black fleets of gondolas, weaving and passing in the canals, carried a masked traffic of pleasure rather than of commerce. In the narrow alleys the crowds jostled toward the countless squares, each sheltered by the mass of an ancient church. There poets and lutanists improvised for a few pence. Fortune-tellers on high platforms whispered secrets down long tin trumpets into gullible ears. Mountebanks tumbled, harlequins pranced with dominoes, charlatans cajoled, herb doctors cried quackish cures: and everywhere there was the smell of fish, of water, of the over-ripeness of history, a city of the sea, settling under the weight of past riches, vivid, beautiful, *morbida*, a queen turned courtesan.

The life of the city, and the Republic of which it was the head, was governed by the whole body of the patricians, who delegated their power to the elected Doge and Council of Ten (in reality, seventeen). They in turn left much of the day-to-day administration to the three Inquisitors of State. It was the most efficient and ruthless oligarchy in the world; and secrecy – not freedom – was the motto emblazoned on its standard.

Casanova moved confidently now into the rhythmic tides of Venice. To add a touch of respectability to a life which the Inquisitors might regard as flighty he did a little legal work for Manzoni. Thus equipped with a home, a father, and a job, he set about losing all the money he could lay his hands on.

His gambling mania intensified, but he had not yet learned the gamester's elementary rules for self-preservation. He lost so much money at faro that Bragadin had to bail him out. He was fleeced by crooks who knew that a pretty face, and a promise of more to come, would deaden the watchful faculties. Bragadin taught him the facts of life with a marvellous urbanity. Having played on his word alone, and lost a large sum to a pair of sharpers, he had to beg from his 'father'. Bragadin said it would be attended to. Casanova, expecting to be given money to pay his debt, was astounded next day to receive instead a note saying that the play on his word had been just fun. Bragadin, of course, had privately advised the cheats that if they didn't write such a note, they might find life difficult for them in Venice. He gave Casanova two sound pieces of advice – only to play for cash; and never to punt, only bank. But the real lesson was: know the right people.

Another time that Casanova approached him for money Bragadin advised him to ask a certain Frenchman, Abadie, for it. Abadie had applied for the post of Inspector General of the Venetian Armies, an appointment that needed the ratification of the Senate. Casanova asked him for the money. Abadie turned him down with the cold charm of which only a Frenchman is capable. Casanova told Senator Bragadin, who smiled a warm Venetian smile. Abadie's appointment was all but delivered, but he did not get it, because Bragadin spoke out against him in the Senate. When they next met Abadie yelled at Casanova that if he had known he had to buy him off in order to get the appointment, of course he would have paid. Casanova retorted that a man with the brains for an Inspector would have guessed it. Abadie angrily told the story all round Venice, meaning to discredit Bragadin and Casanova; but he was only demonstrating still further the depths of his failure to understand the Venetian mind. The actual effect was that Casanova now had no trouble borrowing money.

Or women. Drinking at a remote tavern one night he saw a gondola arrive, and a hooded young woman get out, alone. She did not seem to know what to do or where to go. Casanova, who would have made a great cavalry leader, moved into a reconnaissance with care and dispatch. So began the second affair (Bellino/Teresa is the first) in a pattern which Casanova made his own, and used for the rest of his life. Thus: he sees a girl, A, in some sort of difficulty, often with her lover, B. He gets her out of the difficulty, and in the process falls madly in love. Her gratitude and his obviously genuine passion cause the girl to succumb. After a period of violent sexual athletics Casanova discovers that he is unworthy of her, and arranges for her to marry, or be taken over by, a more suitable man, C.

The girl in the gondola was Countess A.S. Probably from Bologna (Casanova conceals the city), she had allowed a lustful suitor to climb into her bedroom and spend a night with her, as a down-payment on the marriage he promised (in writing). The wretch absconded. The girl followed, hoping to find him and force him to marry her, or . . . she showed Casanova a stiletto. Casanova knew the man, Zanetto Steffani. He was a Grade One Secretary in the Chancellery, a useless lecher whose mother kept him short of money. Casanova had no difficulty in persuading the girl to give him up as a bad job; she would do better to get her father's forgiveness. She agreed, and Casanova fell in love, madly, crazily in love. She was adorable, sweet, accomplished, marvellous. She succumbed. Sexual athletics began. Casanova set about arranging the reconciliation with the father. He managed it rather cleverly by using his three old aristocrats as stalking-horses, and causing his cabala to give the mystic directions which brought father and daughter together. It was in these operations that Casanova's personal contact with the Infinite, the power that spoke to him through the cryptics of the cabala, revealed his name: Paralis. This was the first appearance of the word, which later became Casanova's own name in the mystical society of the Rosy Cross. He probably formed it on the pattern of Gabalis, used in the title of a well-known book on the occult sciences.

The intrigue reached a happy ending just in time, for the girl's father arrived, and the Inquisitors' police, after some inquiries, had already given him a list of ten men who might be holding the girl in their charge. The tenth name on the list was *Giacomo Casanova*.

Weeping bitterly for the loss of the Countess (who quickly married and wrote begging him to forget all that had passed between them), Casanova returned to the gaming tables, now at Padua, where he and the three old men had gone for a change of air. He was fleeced again, playing at the house of Ancilla, a famous dancer and courtesan, but this time he noticed the cheating and drew his pistol. The banker challenged him to a duel which they fought at once with swords, Casanova wounding the other. This man, 'Count' Tommaso Medini, was Casanova's lifelong enemy; he had Casanova's tastes and inclinations but was surly where Casanova was haughty, vicious where Casanova was witty. They met again, many times, twice more with swords.

Casanova returned to Venice and more gambling. Being short of money, he decided to pawn a diamond. (It wasn't his diamond, of course; Signora Manzoni persuaded a friend to lend it to him.) This could not be done in Venice, where there were no pawnshops, so he had to go to Treviso on the mainland. In the gondola were an old priest and his niece, returning from Venice where they had been trying to get the girl a husband. She was young, simple, and so lovely that Giacomo could overlook her terrible country accent and the goat's grease she used to thicken her hair; soon he forgot them altogether. The uncle was a parish priest of the old school, simple and poor..

Cristina was looking for a husband, was she? Well, what about the fine upstanding young fellow speaking to them? The girl looked Casanova up and down, and thought she would have no difficulty in learning to love him. The play continued its predestined course. The priest went to say mass. Casanova felt the familiar symptoms. The girl was adorable, sweet, wonderful . . . he was going to marry her, and she would make him happy for the rest of his life. Cristina gave herself the opportunity to discover that Casanova suffered from cold feet. He returned to Venice to arrange the marriage.

From Venice things looked different. The girl really couldn't pass *here* with that accent. She was much too gauche to be Signora Casanova. Her husband ought to be some simple straightforward fellow who needed her dowry to set him up in life.

Bragadin, Barbaro, and Dandolo were consulted. A suitable young man whom Casanova calls Carlo X.X. was found and inspected. Casanova took him out to the country, unaccountably feeling a bit of a cad, and, right at the end of the visit, let fall the information that *this* was the man Cristina was going to marry. He himself . . . unfortunate misunderstanding . . . quite unworthy of her . . . know how these things are . . .

Cristina did know. She took X.X. (his real name was Bernardi, and he was a clerk in the city administration), married him, and lived happily ever after, not omitting to beg Casanova to forget all that had passed between them. An affair could not really be considered to have ended until this last rite had taken place.

Casanova continued gambling and goating. His touchy pride, his absolute inability to accept humiliation, led him to two almost simultaneous disasters. First, he bought the temporary use of a girl from an old harridan in the belief that the girl was a virgin. The impeachment may or may not have been true; Casanova never found out, as the minx twisted herself about so adeptly that he wasn't able to get a fair run at her. As he had paid in advance, he was well and truly had, which is more than one can say of the little hussy. He took his stick and gave her a thrashing. She ran off.

Then, on a visit to the country, a fellow prankster half-sawed through a plank bridge Casanova was in the habit of using. The plank broke, causing him to drop into deep muck. He decided he could not take it in good part. He had been made an object of ridicule; furthermore, he smelled. To avenge himself he dug up a recently buried corpse, hacked off one arm, and concealed himself with it under the joker's bed. Then he tugged at the bedclothes. The joker, laughing heartily, said he didn't believe in ghosts, he wasn't to be fooled that way. Casanova tugged again, the man grabbed to catch the person responsible, Casanova gave him the dead hand to pull at, then let go. After a fearful scream there was silence and no movement. Casanova went back to his room. He had had the last laugh.

The man suffered a stroke, nearly died, and was paralysed for life. The religious authorities didn't care about him, but they did care about the blasphemy of digging up a grave. Casanova denied all knowledge of the business, but, as he explains without realizing the omen of the words for his later life, everyone said to him: 'Only you are capable of such an abomination; it's typical of you; only you would have dared to do such a thing'.

The local priest laid an indictment at the bishop's chancellery. The maybe-virgin sued for battery and rape. Bragadin, Barbaro, and Dandolo advised Casanova to leave Venice for a while. These things blew over. Meanwhile, flight was the answer. Sadly he took their advice and set off, under the name of Farussi, his mother's maiden name. It was January 1748, and he was nearly twenty-three.

In Milan he found Marina, one of Bellino/Teresa's sisters. In the course of protecting her from an unwelcome lover he met a pleasant young Frenchman, who introduced himself as Antonio Stefano Balletti, dancer. This friendship was to become one of the most important in Casanova's life. Balletti was not only *a* dancer, he was *the* dancer with whom Marina was to perform in Turin and other cities. The girl set out to captivate her partner. Casanova left them to it and went on to Mantua.

While he was wandering late, without either a special permit or a lighted lantern, a military patrol arrested him, for there was a war on (the war of the Austrian Succession) and he had broken the curfew. The captain of the guard introduced himself as Franz O'Neilan, baron, captain in the 57th Austrian Royal and Imperial Regiment of Infantry. O'Neilan's face brightened when he saw that fate had brought another young man of fashion to share his vigil. In no time the usual trimmings for a military guard of the period arrived – cards, punters, a banker, and a couple of ugly and raddled whores: but not ugly enough. Casanova got his fifth venereal dose. The acquaintance with O'Neilan ripened after Casanova's release the following morning. O'Neilan, Casanova notes with a kind of prim horror, was a very debauched young man. Tearing through Mantua at full gallop, his horse ran down an old lady and killed her. O'Neilan laughed. He had had ten venereal attacks and no longer bothered to cure himself. He liked to frequent the local bawds and not pay. His only pleasure was to see someone – anyone, but especially a woman – being hurt. Visiting a lady he saw some dates on the table, and ate them while waiting for her. When she appeared she asked where her dates were. He asked whether she wanted them back. When she said yes, O'Neilan, with a small effort, vomited them up on the carpet.

O'Neilan's most treasured jewel was a ring with a sharp spur on it. At the crisis of the sexual act, he liked to ram the spur 'betwixt and between', that is, into the woman's perineum. 'Do you think that tickles them?' he cried triumphantly. He was, at this time, nineteen years old.

Casanova was fascinated by him, without understanding why: that he was Casanova himself in a mirror, the one pathologically compelled to pleasure, the other to hurt, every woman he met.

Casanova spent two months in Mantua curing his disease and watching Balletti and Marina dance. He was on the point of leaving when a young man accosted him and told him he was wrong to have been so long in Mantua without visiting his father's natural history collection. Casanova politely went the next day.

They were called Capitani, and Casanova soon came to the conclusion that the father was off his head. It was an age of credulity. This man was not a peasant, yet even he really believed that a rusty knife blade in his possession was the sword with which St Peter had cut off Malchus's ear (John xviii, 10–11). Casanova took it from there . . .

Did the *signor* realize that the owner of this blade could possess all treasures hidden in the papal domains? If he had the scabbard as well, that is, for the blade had no magical virtue unless *in vaginum*. And not any old *vagina*, but *the* scabbard, St Peter's own. The Capitanis said they didn't have the scabbard. Casanova said he happened to know where it was. As the blade was useless without the scabbard they decided to work together, and share the proceeds.

Our Giacomo was off on the second major fraud of his career (as far as he admitted to them in his *Story*). He had advanced a long way from the grade-school chemistry and small-print phrasing which had served him in the mercury trick in Portici. He now used all his cabalistic knowledge to appear as a necromancer (at all times keeping a sharp eye open for the agents of the Holy Inquisition, who would burn him at the stake if they caught him practising black magic). He boiled up a boot sole to make a scabbard, and then aged it with sand.

He went to a library and made out a learned piece of nonsense as a clue to buried treasure. He wrote out one agreement between himself as Chief Magician and the Capitanis as owners of the sword, another with the peasant on whose farm near Cesena the 'treasure' was.

It is a long and not very amusing story, except for the involved machinations by which Casanova got the farmer's thirteen-year-old daughter naked into bed with him. To his own amazement he left her in the enjoyment, or at least the possession, of her virginity.

The climax of the charade came when Casanova frightened himself out of his wits with his own magic. It was necessary, before the cabala would communicate the exact location of the treasure, that he should spend the night in a barrel in the farmyard. It wasn't just a matter of finding a barrel and getting into it: black magic doesn't work like that. There had to be fastings and formulas and incantations. There had to be a magician's classical costume, and it had to be made by the hand of a virgin, a *clean* virgin (that was how he got the girl's clothes off; he bathed her).

When all was ready, Casanova got into his costume and the barrel, everyone else scuttled to bed and hid under the sheets . . . and the most tremendous thunderstorm burst. Exposed in his barrel in the farmyard Casanova was deluged, drenched, frozen. The thunder split his head, the lightning flashed on livid walls, casting weird momentary shadows. His own mumbo-jumbo, the white sheet, all the paraphernalia he had invented to terrify the peasants now terrified him. After standing it for two hours his nerve broke. He scrambled out of the barrel and fled to his room, exhausted and shaking with terror.

The charm of this story is that Casanova tells it; and that is, of course, the charm of Casanova, too.

Seeing the end of the game in sight, and fearing the Inquisition, Casanova sold his scabbard to the Capitanis for 500 scudi (about 350 dollars or £125) and with that as his only profit from all the amazing energy, imagination, and hard work he had expended, he made to leave Cesena. But during his very last night at the opera who should be there but Signor Manzoni, his lawyer-master, in company with the famous courtesan La Giulietta. Manzoni was her true love, some said, as distinct from the men she took for the money.

Through these two Casanova met General Spada, of the Imperial Austrian service. All very useful, but Casanova was again on the point of leaving Cesena when a fearful uproar from a room down the passage in his hotel made him pause. An elderly man in bed was yelling at the landlord in Latin. The landlord stood at the door, with police. From articles of uniform scattered about the room Casanova deduced that the angry old party was a military man of some kind, probably a Hungarian. The landlord explained that there was a second person in the bed – Casanova saw the hump under the bedclothes – and though the second person had also registered as an officer the Inquisition thought 'he' was a woman, and, furthermore, not married to the old Hungarian. Therefore, the Inquisition's police had the right to break in; indeed, he had opened the door for them. But payment of a few sequins would, of course, obviate all unpleasantness . . . otherwise, both would go to prison. Casanova saw at once that it was a put-up job between the police and the landlord, to soak the ignorant foreigner.

The captain kept roaring in Latin, the hump stayed put under the bedclothes, and Casanova swung into action. He dashed to the bishop's palace and demanded that the bishop call off his police. The bishop's secretary laughed in his face. Casanova, hugging himself with glee, dashed to General Spada, his new friend, and told him that an honest military man was being shaken down by the grasping clergy. The general notified the bishop that the Hungarian captain would stay in Cesena at the bishop's expense until the latter had publicly apologized, paid a fifty sequins fine, and punished his rascally police.

Casanova returned happily to the inn and invited himself to breakfast with the captain and his invisible friend. He waited . . . the bedclothes heaved, turned back, out came a tousled head, a lovely face. She wore her hair like a man, but there was no doubting which sex she belonged to. Her name was Henriette.

Casanova felt the usual stirrings of the heart. They were all invited to lunch at the General's. The girl, dressed in a fetching uniform that settled any lingering suspicion as to her femininity, was French, and spoke only her own language. The captain, who was nearly sixty, had only Hungarian and Latin, which he had believed all well-bred people spoke in Italy, as they did in Hungary. Curiouser and curiouser, thought Casanova. What was such a beautiful girl, adventuress though she obviously was, doing with the penniless old warrior?

At lunch the French girl stole the show, to the chagrin of La Giulietta, who was not used to being upstaged. Henriette shone not only by her beauty and the piquancy of her situation, but by her wit.

'It seems extraordinary,' commented La Giulietta, 'that you two can live together without talking to one another.'

'Why extraordinary, Madam? We get on perfectly together, as talking is unnecessary for our kind of business.'

44

'I don't know of any business that can be conducted without either talking or writing.'

'Pardon me, Madam, but there are some: cards, for instance.'

'Do you mean to say you only play at cards?'

'That's all we do. We play Pharaoh and I'm the banker.'

'But does the bank make much?' asked the General.

'What the bank receives is of so little consequence, it's scarcely worth talking about.'

As Casanova wryly adds, no one ventured to translate that exchange for the benefit of the old captain. He was not merely in love now, he was bewitched. The girl was obviously well educated as well as beautiful. He at once gave up his plan to go to Naples, where fortune and influential friends awaited him. Instead he would accompany the captain and the girl to Parma. He offered them the use of his carriage and his services as interpreter. The old man accepted with pleasure, so Casanova had to hurry out and buy a carriage, for he didn't have one. The journey began.

Casanova's love deepened. He was going out of his mind with desire to possess the girl carnally, but he was also beginning to worship her spiritually. She said she had fled to Rome to escape a hateful husband. Her father-in-law found her and tried to persuade her to return home. At this point the old captain, in Rome on some obscure Magyar mission, saw her in Civitavecchia with her father-in-law. His mind worked: old man, young woman . . . she must be a hussy. He sent over his servant with an invitation on his own account. She accepted, and became his mistress. Now she was accompanying him to Parma, whence they would go their separate ways. The captain had soon realized that she was no whore, and after that had clearly felt rather uncomfortable with the young lady, for he was not a gentleman by birth.

Casanova made up his mind. He must have Henriette. As a man of honour, he asked the captain if he could try to take her over. The worthy soldier agreed with relief. Casanova then confronted Henriette with an ultimatum. They were in Bologna, two stages short of Parma, where she had made the captain promise to leave her and make no further inquiries about her. Casanova now told her that he was deeply in love with her. He wanted her for himself. Completely. For ever. In Parma she knew no one, she had no money. What would become of her? He would flatly refuse to abandon her in Parma, as the captain had agreed to. He would leave her here and now, or never. Was he to come to Parma?

Henriette said 'Come to Parma.'

So began the most rewarding love affair of Casanova's life.

The girl herself fascinated him, and so did that piquant contrast, displayed at General Spada's, between her dashing present and her obviously respectable past. She was a lady, but she had certainly sold her virtue to the captain. She had been well brought up, so where did she get that indecent wit? She certainly had not offered much resistance to Casanova himself. What sort of a lady was she, then?

This is the moment to say that the identification of Henriette has been one of the chief objects of all true casanovists for over 140 years. Later in his *Story* Casanova describes rather closely where she lived in France, and other details about her. These clues, and much careful investigation have led Rives Childs to the tentative conclusion that she was Jeanne Marie d'Albert de St-Hippolyte. Born on 22 March 1718, she married a M. Fonscolombe on 4 February 1744, and had two children – a boy in 1744 and a girl in 1746.

Casanova probably found, as I do, that the clue to her piquant attraction lay in her nationality. The French have always been famous for their sexual freedom, though it was never as great as advertised, and should more properly be called sexual realism. Casanova himself was soon to remark on the noble French families who shared their wives; of others who raised their wives' children by lovers, with grace and no reproach; of the astonished giggles which greeted him when, on a young lady thinking she was pregnant, Casanova said he didn't know she was married. Henriette was Casanova's first French girl, and though he insists that she was four years younger than he, she was in fact thirty-one to his twenty-four – that is, a woman, not a girl, and mother and lover, both. The realistic hedonism of the species attracted him; and this was a lovely wild example of it.

He was like a man intoxicated, which he was – with love. As soon as they reached Parma he asked her to promenade with him but she refused to be seen there in her dashing military costume, which was, of course, a public notification that she was, for the moment at least, not respectable. He went out alone and without telling her what he was doing ordered fine linen enough for twenty-four chemises, cambric for handkerchiefs, dimity for petticoats. He enrolled a dressmaker and a milliner and seamstresses, and on the way back to the hotel dropped into one shop for silk stockings and another to bespeak the services of a bootmaker. He hired an egregious Belgian-perhaps-Jesuit called de la Haye to teach her Italian; and then sat back like an excited child while all these magicians, their mouths full of pins or tacks or irregular verbs, set about the business of producing a sophisticated *soignée* woman.

But she sent him out again when the clothes were at last ready. He walked round and round, like an expectant father outside the maternity ward, until the appointed hour when he could return. He rushed back; the old Hungarian captain was also there, waiting. Henriette made her grand entrance and the two men fell dumb before her grace, gentility, beauty and breeding. The Hungarian in particular trembled to remember that he had offered to buy this goddess for ten sequins – which she had accepted; but that last thought was too much for his limited understanding.

Now Henriette agreed to go out, but only on condition that they received no one and made no public splash. She was afraid that some of the French courtiers flooding the city in the train of the new French duchess would recognize her. So they went to the opera – twenty times, according to Casanova, for Henriette loved music passionately – but she sat well back in an unlighted box and did not, as was customary, use a wax taper to follow the score.

So the days passed, in a wonder of sensual and spiritual love; but they could not keep the world out for ever. Several people knew of her existence and by a trick one of them manoeuvred Casanova into taking her to what he thought would be an intimate little party. It turned out to be a musical soirée in honour of the chief singers of the opera, Filippo Laschi and Giovanna Baglioni, and there were many guests, including Frenchmen.

After the professional orchestra had played, Henriette took the cello – Casanova gasped – and asked the leader to begin the concerto once more – Casanova froze – she bowed over the instrument . . . Here again we stumble upon one of those little scenes which, more than any scholarly research, make Casanova alive and, for all his faults, lovable. He was terrified for her sake, he trembled, he did not dare to look, his palms sweated; and who has not known this terror when a loved one, child or husband or wife, gets up on the public stage?

She played wonderfully well. Casanova's panic overflowed in intoxicated relief. Her sardonic wit flashed again: she told the company that she had learnt the cello in the convent when a girl, but only at the request of her father, backed by a special dispensation from the bishop, for the abbess thought that in playing the cello a girl had to adopt an indecent attitude.

Casanova's bliss was only shadowed by a presentiment that fate must soon expel him from such a paradise. And sure enough the fatal serpent came along, in the person of the Chevalier d'Antoine, who saw Henriette when he was riding with the Duke of Parma, and thought he recognized her – exactly what Henriette had feared all along. He asked to see her. Distraught with fear, Casanova begged her to flee with him. She said she could not. She must see d'Antoine.

We do not know what was said at the interview, which lasted several hours. Casanova watched in the mirror from a room across the hall, the doors being left open. At last d'Antoine left. Henriette said she had given him a letter, and promised to await the reply here in two weeks' time. Meantime she wanted to get out of Parma at once. Casanova took her to Milan. His money was running out, for he had no time or inclination to make more by gambling or cheating, and Bragadin was holding his allowance for him in Venice. He gave Henriette the best time he could, but they spent hours merely holding hands, gazing at each other, and crying.

Two weeks later, faithful to her word, they were back in Parma to receive the reply to her letter. D'Antoine gave it to her. She dismissed him, and told Casanova, 'We must part.'

Without knowing for certain what she had fled from or what she was being recalled to, it is impossible to know why she took this decision. If Henriette *was* Mme Fonscolombe, then she had two small children at home. The husband she had run away from had perhaps agreed to a formal separation. There may have been an estate to inherit, or administer.

I think, too, that one reason lay not in the letter, or in her own situation at all, but in Casanova. She had now spent three months with him – in the most perfect bliss, he says. She may not have felt the bliss to be quite so perfect, for she was very intelligent. If she were a Catholic, and married, how could she marry Casanova? And – this is the question she must have put to herself, lying awake beside her lover – was Casanova the man to be anyone's lifelong partner, married or not? By now she knew him better than any woman except the perspicacious old Signora Manzoni ever would, and I think she decided with regret, with a real sorrow amounting to misery, that in the end there would only be disillusion and unhappiness for both of them. If the brutalities of a stupid husband had turned her into an adventuress, the caresses of a brilliant adventurer now turned her back into a wife, or at least a *grande dame*, bound to her duty; for Mme Fonscolombe lived apart from her husband after this year of 1749.

Casanova was to leave her in Geneva. They crossed into France by the Mont Cenis Pass, making the northern descent on sledges. After four days of hard going they reached Geneva, and took rooms in the Hôtel des Balances. Henriette found an opportunity to slip into his pocket five hundred louis (about 1,250 dollars or £500). Solemnly she charged him never to enquire after her and, if they met by chance, to pretend not to know her. She made him promise not to move from Geneva until he had heard from her.

Her carriage left. Casanova watched it out of sight with bursting eyes. Then he went to his room, collapsed on his bed, and abandoned himself to sorrow.

The coachman came back next day with a note from Henriette. It contained one word – *Adieu*. Casanova sank deeper into misery. This was the first time since childhood that he had really suffered. He had allowed Henriette to pass his protective guards. She cared for him as a person. And now he had lost her.

Dumb, blind with misery, Casanova went to the window. He stared out, unseeing, at the world beyond. Gradually, he noticed that words had been scratched in the glass with a diamond: *Tu oublieras aussi Henriette*.

4

The Grand Tour

Miserably, Casanova returned to Italy over the St Bernard Pass, feeling neither the cold nor the discomfort of a journey which in those days, and in bad weather, was an ordeal with which nothing in our ordinary life today offers a comparison. He arrived in Parma hoping for solitude in which to die; but in the next room he found one de la Haye, the man who had taught Henriette Italian.

Wearily Casanova faced the world. Nothing would interest him, nothing excite him again. But a stupid acquaintance, a man of no knowledge of the world, bet him that no one could obtain the favours of a certain actress under a hundred ducats. A wager? — a woman? Casanova put on hat and sword and went out, fire and spring returning at each pace to his step. He won his bet, and another dose of venereal disease.

Soon to Venice, accompanied by de la Haye and one of the latter's young protégés, Louis Saussure, Baron de Bavois. Through Bragadin Casanova got de Bavois a commission in the Venetian army. Through de la Haye's insidious, ceaseless propaganda he himself succumbed for a while to a sort of religious mania.

But here, in this serene city, from whose stones he gathered a kind of sustenance like a mother's milk, a sense of belonging — needed by all of us, doubly so by fatherless Casanova, whose mother trod the stages of the world — his head began to clear of sickly fumes. He saw that de la Haye was trying to supplant him with the three old men, and warned him with bloodcurdling directness to keep his fingers out of the pie. He shook off his attack of faith, and looked about him.

Gambling, theatres, balls, girls; he got one by a promise of marriage, which he later 'forgot'. The girl's mother complained, and one of the State Inquisitors, Zorzi Contarini dal Zaffo, a formidable old man of seventy, interviewed Casanova in private. Nothing more was said and Casanova had triumphed again, he thought. But they had merely put another line under his name in the black list of the Most Serene, but Most Vengeful, Prince.

Then, falling upon good luck in a lottery and at faro, he decided to make a Grand Tour. He set out for Paris in May 1750, travelling with his friend Balletti. The three main stops en route were at Ferrara, Turin, and Lyon. Each had its incident, and the three together remarkably illumine Casanova as a man, and, through him, the eighteenth century in which he lived.

At Ferrara the adventure was straight picaresque. A whorish actress called La Catinella, thoroughly bored at the inn, had caused the innkeeper's gawkish son to fall in love with her, and had promised to marry him. In fact she was waiting there only for the arrival of a German count, her lover. Being perhaps drunk when Casanova arrived, she greeted him as her cousin, and at once took him into a private 'family conference' about the ensuing marriage. Casanova had no idea what her game was – she doesn't seem to have had much idea herself – but he knew enough to raise her skirts and help himself as soon as the door closed on their conference. *Ooh là là*, you are a one, La Catinella cried in effect, offering no impediment . . . There is a sound of hoof-beats, impetuous male voices; and the count arrives. Casanova is shut into a closet. Through a crack he glumly watches the huge German's impotent attempts to repeat his own treatment of La Catinella.

After a time the lovers rode away. The innkeeper's lovesick son finally heard Casanova's yells and let him out of the closet. As he was a relative of the young lady, they gave him a free dinner. He assured the young man that La Catinella would certainly come back to marry him, and went on his way. *There's one born every minute*; and the interest of the story is in its epitomizing The Eighteenth-Century Plot: actress deceiving count, adventurer deceiving yokel, closets and petticoats and galloping horses; and, for moral, a proverb that was true until over a century later: *Honest folk stay at home.*

In Turin the affair was Chaucerian, which is rare for Casanova. The smells of the street were such that men walked with nosegays held to their noses, but Casanova never uses a direct peasant word. His ladies did not have what Chaucer called *queyntes*, but *charms*. He does not use any of the scores of available words for his own male organ, but calls it his *steed*. He describes sexual acts in indirect language. His adventures with women are romantic and charming (except when they give him gonorrhoea), and the animal facts of menstruation and defecation, for example, never intrude, although they were obviously much more obtrusive than they are today. It is as though the upper classes of the century, being unable to avoid seeing, hearing and smelling the bowels of life, sought to disguise them under Arcadian terms. The following century saw a full reversal of this attitude: Victorians secretly wallowing in the words and images which a prudish society, new privacy, and better plumbing had banished from day-to-day life.

In Turin, Casanova was restless. He hadn't had a woman for forty-eight hours or so. The chambermaid was a good-looking country puss, healthy and buxom, but careful. She whipped in and out of doors without giving anyone a chance to grab her; she did not bend over near the gentlemen; she kept her eyes down. Casanova, piqued by this challenge, lay in wait, cornered her at the foot of the back stairs, and pounced. Up with her skirts. With speed, and honeyed words, his steed at the ready – to work:

At the moment I penetrated her, a loud eruption rather cooled my ardour, so much so that the young girl covered her face to hide her embarrassment. Endeavouring to reassure her with a tender kiss, I started again. But a blast louder than before struck my ears and nose. I kept going, but with each thrust she exploded, as regularly as clockwork.

Casanova dissolved into helpless laughter. The girl ran off to hide her embarrassment and Casanova sat on the stairs for a quarter of an hour laughing; and was still laughing when he wrote. Chaucer would have liked him, after all.

In Lyon Casanova took the most consequential step of his life. He became a Freemason.

Freemasonry, as known today, emerged in the seventeenth century. In the Middle Ages a gentleman belonged to Christendom. Anywhere in it he could travel freely, be helped, be known. The device on an English knight's shield would be instantly recognized in Poland. Castles, cathedrals, and monasteries were the Lodges of the order. Its common language was Old French; its lord of the manor the Holy Roman Emperor; its parish priest the Pope. Then Christendom broke up into nations; and the barriers between peoples grew higher, denser, more permanent. The schism of the Roman Church completed the dismemberment, and inquisitions, witch-hunts, burnings, and religious wars buried the remains. There was no more Christendom; there was no more 'free society' in Europe, except the Jewish community, headed by its bankers.

In this situation Freemasonry was born, in Great Britain, although its origins are also associated with various medieval societies of craft journeymen in France and Germany. When real Masons accepted certain outsiders as honorary members of their brotherhoods, the latter gradually branched off to become what are known as speculative masons, or Freemasons. The official purpose of Freemasonry is simply 'charity', and in general it has held to that purpose, especially for its own members. Within this rather too-embracing definition 'each Masonic degree is an initiation rite ... the central theme of these ceremonies is the building of King Solomon's temple and legendary events associated with the work. At the heart of this Masonic mythology is the hero-figure Hiram Abiff, the principal architect of the temple, murdered by three Fellow Craft masons because he refused to part with the secrets of a master mason.' (James Dewar: *The Unlocked Secret: Freemasonry Examined*, 1966.)

Outside the central nave of Masonry there are several side chapels. One, credited to Chevalier Andrew Ramsay, tutor to the exiled Stuart princes, is known as the Ancient and Accepted Scottish Rite, and is rather more mysterious than Craft Masonry (in consonance with its obvious original purpose, to further Stuart intrigue). It was to a Scottish Rite lodge that Casanova was admitted – the Grande Loge Écossaise; Amitié, Amis Choisis.

The nineteenth degree of this rite is called Rose Croix of Heredom, and here Freemasonry makes a vague connection with another secret society, the Rosicrucians. The earliest Rosicrucian document is *Fama Fraternitas*, published in 1614. It describes the journey of one Christian Rosenkreuz to Arabia, Damascus and Fez in search of oriental wisdom; his return to Germany in 1402; his choice of disciples; his founding of an order to study and promote the secrets (such as the cabala) he had brought back with him – the existence of this order to remain secret for a century; the death of Rosenkreuz, in 1484, aged well over a hundred; the finding of his body in a vault, or arch, in 1604, with secret writings and symbols; the loss of the site of the vault immediately afterwards. From here, the course of those interested was plain – to join the society, and look for the vault and the secret wisdom.

There was an obvious similarity between Rosicrucianism and Freemasonry; many men belonged to both societies; the symbolism is very similar, and indeed another side-order of Masonry is called Royal Arch; but they are not and never were the same. As a broad generalization, Freemasonry is social and Rosicrucianism mystical in purpose.

Once started, Freemasonry spread like a brush-fire, because it was badly needed. It attracted some quacks and freaks and crooks, but its chief appeal at the time was to men of intelligence and curiosity, because it re-created a free society. Here Catholic could talk to Protestant, tradesman to aristocrat, Spaniard to German, merchant banker to master carpenter. It gave a refuge, the only one, from the narrow bigotries of Church and State, which many privately despised but few could, or would, publicly dispense with. For the next two hundred years it flourished mightily; it was a vital and important force in the eighteenth century, in spite of almost universal proscription, especially in Catholic countries. This did not prevent eminent Churchmen, including many cardinals and probably a few popes, from being Freemasons.

What Authority found so terrible about Freemasonry was that very transcendental 'brotherhood' which was its *raison d'être*. The secret gatherings at the Lodges hatched few plots, but they did provide a wonderful net of communication and information for plotters, as well as for true seekers after uncensored knowledge. Masons did not become traitors to their countries or their religions – patriotism and a belief in God are part of the unalterable Landmarks of the Craft. But, in this mid-eighteenth century, more than in any time before or after, in a society breaking away from aristocracy and not yet fallen into bureaucracy, the Freemason's grip, the secret word and cryptic phrase, would serve to open a thousand barred doors. This, Casanova, sharp and energetic but low-born and penniless, needed above all.

The two young men, rolling in a diligence which made Casanova sick, reached Paris in June 1750. Casanova stayed two years, during which he learned the language from the famous dramatist, Crébillon *père*, and made the acquaintance of many whores, actresses, and courtiers and of Francesco Morosini, the Venetian ambassador, who later played an important rôle in his life. For the rest, his life revolved around the Balletti family, particularly his friend's mother, Silvia, whom Frederick the Great rated a superb actress. Casanova says she was like a mother to him, and – most unusual in the profession – morally above reproach. The Paris secret police reported, later, that she was his lover. They were both probably right. There was in the household also a daughter, Manon, whom Casanova noted as a perfect beauty; but she was only ten years old.

In Paris the smart young man learned how really important capitals and courts function. He saw women teetering along the corridors of Versailles, looking as though they were about to fall flat on their faces at each step. To his astonishment they were wearing six-inch heels. But why? Fashion . . . just fashion. He met La Pompadour and the Maréchal de Richelieu. He saw Louis XV and his Queen, and could not contain his scorn, as a citizen of the great Republic of Venice, at the affected manners, the sheer waste of human dignity, at court. He has a marvellous description of the queen eating dinner, alone at a vast table, surrounded by standing courtiers. After a period of silent chewing the queen looked up and called 'Monsieur de Lowendahl'. The man addressed stepped forward three paces, bowing. The queen said she was of the opinion that the best kind of stew was a chicken fricassée. M. de Lowendahl, bowing again, thought so too. He stepped back three paces. End of dinner-table conversation. Lowendahl was a field-marshal.

On the sexual side Casanova had an affair with his landlady's daughter, who became pregnant. He wriggled out of trouble, but the case had gone to law, and now his name was written on the tablets of the Paris police as well as those of Venice, Parma, Padua, Rome. He passed a few pleasant nights in a high-style brothel and orgy barn called the Hôtel du Roule, in the Faubourg St-Honoré. Here the customers chose girls from the rack, and were served sumptuous meals, drinks, and all that man could desire, for exorbitant charges measured out by the madame with a stop-watch. She would burst into the bedrooms, regardless of the state of events at the time, watch in hand, and the customer either paid up for the next longer period or was thrown out.

And Casanova unwittingly became a pimp for Louis XV, though it is only fair to say that he would have done it wittingly if he had thought of it. The affair began when he accompanied a friend to supper with an actress named Morphy, of Irish descent. After his meal the friend wanted to stay the night. There was no bed for Casanova, so he tried to hire the bed on which the actress's thirteen-year-old sister slept. This turned out to be a filthy straw bolster set on boards, and Casanova changed his offer to the girl. He didn't want her bed, but he would pay three francs to watch her undress. She accepted the terms, and for an additional three francs allowed him unlimited fondling, in fact everything except the penetration of her virginal *con*; that, her sister had told her, was worth twenty-five guineas, and she was on no account to sell the privilege for less.

On seeing the girl naked Casanova thought she might be a beauty; but he couldn't tell because she was so dirty. He washed her with his own hands, a domestic duty that delighted him all his amatory life, and the next day he told his friend that the girl was a raving beauty indeed. He christened her O'Morphy, from the family name, because the word means 'beautiful' in Greek. He also paid a German painter, he says, to paint her in the nude, lying on her stomach, leaning on her elbows, and displaying her girlish hindquarters to the best advantage. The steatopygous portrait of the thirteen-year-old was seen by M. de St-Quentin, the King's chief procurer. It was designed to arouse the lust of any man with a fetish on female buttocks or female immaturity. His Divine Majesty Louis XV was obsessed in both these areas. St-Quentin at once sent for the actress, and told her to scrub her young sister again and bring her up to Versailles for inspection. In a pavilion in the park the King verified O'Morphy's virginity with his royal hand. To the swooning joy of her sister, and after the passing of money, she entered the King's harem.

That is Casanova's story . . . but the portrait he ordered was almost certainly a miniature, probably by Johann Peters, and probably copied from the famous Boucher painting of the O'Morphy. And official documents record that she was discovered for the King by one Lebel, not by Casanova. But who knows? Lebel may have been the middleman.

All this was as froth on a generally aimless existence. Casanova was drifting, but he had not yet fully made up his mind to do it professionally, as his career. His gambling continued, and he made his first serious essay at the 'cabalism' of women, that is, with women as dupes rather than as objects to be won. His first victim – 'patient' would be a better word – was the Duchess of Chartres, a cousin of Louis XV. She was twenty-five years old, a nymphomaniac, and president of the female Masonic lodges of France. (Some of the side-orders allowed for women in masonry.) It was the Masonic connection, of course, that led her to hear of Casanova, and to ask advice from his cabala.

The Duchess suffered from acne. Casanova's oracle ordered her to purge her bowels, eat thus and so (very little), wash the skin frequently in cold plantain water . . . in brief, go on a diet, take exercise, go to bed early, and keep her skin scrupulously clean. In 1752 these rules sounded like the advice of a mad necromancer, and were therefore obeyed with a rigid respect. The duchess's acne improved, Casanova's fame spread.

In the middle of 1752 he decided to leave Paris. Ostensibly the reason was to escort his brother Francesco to Dresden, but probably he was getting bored. This Francesco was the brother who he says was his enemy through life: he had come to Paris, probably on Casanova's invitation, to earn his living by painting private portraits, but he hoped to make his name as a painter of battle pictures, a genre then much in demand. There had been a disastrous showing of his work, and now he was fleeing to Dresden to learn his craft from the bottom up before attempting to return to Paris. So, in August, they left Casanova's favourite city, after one final typical fling. A day or two before going Giacomo dined at an inn and was grossly over-charged. He paid the bill under protest, adding a rude word to the hostess's name at the foot of it, and left to walk in the Tuileries gardens. A fierce little man ran after him, announced that he was by name the Chevalier de Talvis and by inclination protector of the innkeeper-lady. He called upon Casanova to fight for his life. Casa-nova soon wounded the manikin in spite of his huge sword, and proceeded on his way.

. . . to Dresden, and his mother in the flesh. Having installed his brother where he could study and copy the many battle paintings in the museum, and got himself a dose of venereal disease, he wrote a play called *La Moluccheide*. A humorous parody of a tragedy of Racine, it was performed at the Dresden State Theatre on 22 February 1753, and was very well received. The king laughed a great deal and gave Casanova a large present; and this is about all that Casanova, who devotes pages to a successful petty chicanery, has to say of this considerable, and real, triumph.

. . . on to Prague, and the dancer Teresa Morelli, who took care of him without giving him a souvenir. Perhaps he even did as much for her. To Vienna, where the atmosphere was oppressive even to a man brought up under the Star Chamber secrecies of Venice. The Empress Maria Theresa, obsessed by her lack of sexual charm and a consequent oppressive piety, had filled her capital with spies and stool-pigeons. Chastity police harried women in the streets and burst into private houses on suspicion alone. A woman could only protect herself from their molestations by going about veiled and carrying a prayer book, as though on her way to mass. One of these agents, finding Casanova urinating close against a wall, curtly told him to finish the job else-where, because he was doing it where a woman could see him. Casanova looked up, and 'sure enough, I saw in a fourth-storey window the face of a woman who, if she had had a spyglass, could have seen whether I was a Jew or a Christian'.

Here he met again the perhaps-Jesuit de la Haye, with yet another young male *protégé*; and Bepe il Cadetto, the villain who had cheated him at cards in the Pesaro guardroom, only now he called himself Count Afflisio, and had transferred from the Spanish to the Austrian service. In modern terms, this is like saying he had transferred from the Russian to the American army, but his real profession was not 'officer' but 'adventurer' and the change meant no more than a

Mississippi gambler's transfer from the *Robert E. Lee* to the *Dixie Belle*.

Casanova was in a circus, and the same people kept turning up because they were in the circus too: fashionable Europe. In the country, when night fell, there was no light and the tired peasants slept early and rose early. In the capitals a million candles burned and under them swirled the courtiers and the harlots, dukes, monsignors, oboe-players, Lords of the Bedchamber . . . Rome, Vienna, London, Paris, Venice, Naples, Warsaw, Prague, the same pimps and statesmen eddied through them, winning or losing according to their skill and luck, according as their protectors lived or died, according as treaties were made or broken. And the Freemasons went on for ever.

It was nearly time to go. The murmur of the mother-city disturbed his sleep, her image came between him and the upturned, expectant female faces below. He had been three years away from her breast.

He went, as always, with a flourish: via Pressburg (Bratislava), where the first person he saw was de Talvis, the angry manikin of the Tuileries gardens. The quarrel was not renewed. Instead they went to the palace, where the bishop, a true prince of the eighteenth-century Church, was running a very successful faro bank; the table in front of him was covered in gold. With episcopal unction he urged de Talvis to risk a card. De Talvis agreed – the stake to be the whole of the gold on the table. The bishop blenched but did not have the quickness of mind to ask to see the colour of de Talvis's money. He turned the cards, and lost. De Talvis swept up all the gold and left the city and the country without a moment's delay. Well, a moment's, for there was one person present who never lost his head, and whose brain worked very quickly indeed. While the bystanders gaped at the empty table and the plucked bishop, Casanova followed de Talvis downstairs and 'borrowed' a hundred ducats off him.

Four days later he slept in Trieste and, taking ship, he arrived in Venice on 29 May 1753. Bradagin, Barbaro, and Dandolo greeted him with joy.

5

The Path to the Leads

Every year on Ascension Day the Doge of Venice was rowed out in the great state galley, *Il Bucintoro*, to marry the Adriatic, in token of Venice's command of the sea. The wits said that one day the top-heavy *Bucintoro* would go down, and the marriage would at last be consummated, but it was the biggest day of the year in Venice, a day of noise and crowds, ceremonies and excitement. So Senator Bragadin stayed away if he could, and this year Casanova, like a dutiful son, took him to Padua for a week's peace and quiet and himself hurried back to Venice to take part in the festivities.

On the way a fast-moving post-chaise turned over in front of him, throwing its occupants into the road. One of them was a lady, or at least a woman, for there, set like a bud in the centre of the petals of the up-ended petticoats, she was displaying Casanova's favourite flower. He picked her up, shook down her clothes and went on his way, since she was accompanied by a young man in German uniform.

In Venice a little later a masked woman accosted him coquettishly, and revealed herself as the owner of the bud he had seen at Oriago. She was Maria Colonda, and he had known her at Padua when they were both children. Now she was in flight from her husband, and the officer with her was her paramour. His name was Pier Capretta, and, as it very soon appeared, he was a dangerous and unstable young crook. He thought he could rook Casanova through the wiles of his mistress, and Casanova did make a half-hearted attempt on the lady's virtue (if that is the right word), but was not sufficiently attracted to fall for Capretta's specious schemes. Capretta then thought of his sister, Caterina, known to all readers of the memoirs as C.C. With her Casanova fell genuinely, purely and passionately in love. He took her everywhere, and noted that her brother was going out of his way to give him opportunities to seduce her. But, virtuous from love and seeing himself as the guardian of the dear child's morals, he did not take his opportunities, for a time. He did, however, lend the brother money which he knew he would never see again, being willing to be duped for Caterina's sake.

He took her to the theatre and was annoyed when the profligate brother came to his box with La Colonda; still more angry that he had to accept the brother's invitation to a cosy little supper at the latter's private casino, or pleasure-villa; but much worse was to come. The drunken Pier assaulted La Colonda amorously, and she was giggling too much, being also drunk, to resist him. He ruffled up her petticoats to show Casanova what, as he disdainfully notes, he had already seen at Oriago, and handled since. Then the outrageous fellow lay back, pulled her down astride his rampant steed, and in that fashion did his business right before Casanova's eyes ... and before the eyes of little C.C. Casanova desperately drew her attention to scenes outside, to paintings on the wall, but the girl's eyes were glued to a mirror where she could see what her brother was doing. She blushed. Casanova was furious. In front of the innocent child! The brother apologized abjectly the next day – it was the drink in him, he said – but Casanova was not to be appeased.

Soon the mother and father went away for two days, leaving their little treasure in charge of Pier. Casanova took C.C. out to the gardens of Giudecca, hired a room, and formally relieved her of her maidenhead. Then he told Bragadin that he proposed to ask for her hand in marriage. He needed support, and a respectable job to match the 10,000 ducats the girl would bring as her dowry.

Let us for a moment leave Bragadin preparing to negotiate with C.C.'s father, and take note of a 'friend' who was to keep intruding into Casanova's life. He was Antonio della Croce, a young fellow of almost unmitigated vice and charm. Croce offered Casanova shares in a faro bank, which was to be manipulated to pluck fat chickens. Croce's wife acted as lure to bring the would-be roosters in. Later she had a baby girl, to which Casanova stood godfather. His signature appears on the baptismal register. But by then the father, Antonio, had been ordered out of Venice for open and unnatural relations with a patrician called Gritti.

Back to C.C.'s father, Christoforo Capretta. He came to the Bragadin palace, but Casanova was not invited to take part in the discussion. He was only the prospective groom; besides – though it never occurred to him – it is likely that Bragadin and Barbaro and Dandolo didn't intend to lose him any more than he intended to lose them. They may well have told the father he was a no-good, but kept talking to lull Casanova's suspicions.

Casanova waited in extreme anxiety for some days. Then he had his answer. The father had put C.C. into a convent. No one knew where it was except her parents.

It took only two days for C.C. to send him the information by a trusty washerwoman called Laura. She was in a convent in Murano (probably S. Maria degli Angeli), and would stay there for five years till she was twenty, when her father intended to marry her to a merchant. Would Casanova please get her out, and they'd run away together, and live happily ever after? Her room-mate was a *marvellous* woman of about twenty-two, rich and well born, who gave her all kinds of kisses and embraces which would certainly make Casanova jealous if the room-mate had been a man. Oh yes, and she was pregnant.

It is necessary to explain that in the convents of that time not all the inhabitants were dedicated or committed religious women. Many girls were incarcerated to get them away from unsuitable lovers, or to put them in a place of safety during the dangerous years of adolescence or to receive a little education. Some had taken vows, some had not. Supervision was sometimes strict, sometimes lax, and gold could accomplish most things. Nuns could and did get out of convents to all kinds of escapades. It was well known that some of the ladies behind the masks in Carnival were technically Brides of Christ, and all the more sought after because of it. An army of pimps, messengers, and gondoliers catered to this, as to all other tastes of a hedonistic society.

Casanova and C.C. communicated in a stream of letters carried to and fro by Laura. Casanova knew a great deal about what was called 'the Venetian vice' and certainly recognized that C.C.'s room-mate was a lesbian, or at least, as one might say nowadays, A.C./D.C. The room-mate, whatever her motives, stood faithfully by C.C. when the latter had a miscarriage, accompanied by severe haemorrhage. Unless she had hidden the bloody sheets until they could be passed out to Laura – who smuggled in fresh supplies bought by Casanova – C.C.'s condition must have become known. She might also have bled to death.

Casanova attended Sunday mass at the church on Murano where the nuns went, so that C.C. could see him at least once a week. After ten or eleven weeks he received a proposition, by letter. One of the nuns wanted to meet him, the more privately the better.

Casanova was in a quandary, of a sort. If he accepted this exciting offer, some pedantic fellow might construe it as disloyalty to C.C. whom he considered as his wife. If the obvious result came about, there were those who would say he had been unfaithful. It was a tricky problem.

Casanova accepted the offer, wondering whether the writer was C.C.'s room-mate. After a certain amount of fencing, and one of those misunderstandings without which no eighteenth-century love affair could reach a consummation, an assignation was arranged. She chose the place: a private casino on Murano. They met there, alone except for the chef and a serving-woman. From the furnishings and the books the casino clearly belonged to a rich and cultured man. From the meal and the pink *oeil de perdrix* champagne served it was a Frenchman (but, alas, the Frenchman was offering him a veiled insult: such champagne was only of second quality. Casanova should have remembered his own experience: 'I have always liked the French, but never the Spaniards ... nevertheless I have been tricked more than once by Frenchmen, never by Spaniards'). After suffering pleasurable tortures of self-reproach over his unfaithfulness to little C.C., he happily fell for this new girl, M.M. She was tall, pale, blue-eyed, beautiful, intelligent, and very randy. He goes to great lengths to hide her identity, but she was probably Maria Eleonora Michiel, daughter of a patrician family. Her mother was a Bragadin.

M.M.'s show of maidenly coyness wore thin very quickly because, as Casanova had never doubted, she was not a maiden. She had a lover, a rich man. Casanova, who knew Venice intimately, deduced that the lover was the French ambassador to the Republic, the Abbé François Joachim Pierre de Bernis. On that first night M.M. offered him her all, but did not let him take it. The way she did so, turning the couch in a certain direction and holding him off so adroitly that, although cleared for action, he could not fire, made him suspect that the young woman not only wanted justice to be done, but wanted it to be seen to be done. The performance, he deduced, was for the benefit of a voyeur hidden in the next room. The voyeur must be her lover, and the owner of the casino: de Bernis.

Casanova did not mind, and he was in any case used to threesomes with foreign diplomats. The English ambassador, Sir John Murray, liked him to be present when he was pleasuring his mistress, the raddled old courtesan Ancilla. He drew the line, however, at using condoms, which M.M. set out for him at their next meeting, to the surprise, perhaps, of the modern reader; but a preventive sheath, which he claimed to have invented, was described by the anatomist Gabriello Fallopio as early as 1564.

Putting aside the condoms with a well-turned extemporaneous French verse, Casanova set to with a will. First he wrapped his head three or four times around with a huge bandanna, giving himself the appearance of an oriental potentate. The sultan then *imperiously* took off the slave-girl's clothes, laid her down, and began to arrange her with the strictest regard for the unseen watcher's pleasure. He placed cushions under her buttocks and made her raise one leg, so that de Bernis could get an uninterrupted view of the furry portcullis. Then, as John Barrymore once described the consummation of an affair with an English duchess, he rode triumphantly through the main gate with pennons flying, drums beating, and horses neighing. I will not draw a veil over the ensuing combat, but refer the reader to Casanova's original. Suffice it to indicate here that they passed the night carrying out the sexual positions described by Aretino and drawn by Giulio Romano two centuries earlier.

The affair followed a predictable course. C.C. was drawn in, de Bernis came out from behind the arras, and sexual square-dancing began. Burgundy, strawberries, hare, ortolans, larks' tongues, more champagne (presumably still second-class) – nothing was lacking from the orgies at the casino on Murano, nor did Casanova omit to eat oysters from the ladies' breasts, a fetish of his as awkward as insanitary. The biggest surprise to the modern reader, however, will probably be Casanova's offhand reference to one of the up-to-date French words he had learned in Paris: *à gogo*.

As all good things must, the naughty idyll came to an end. De Bernis was recalled to help negotiate an end to the war between France and the Holy Roman Empire. He gave Casanova sound advice: be careful, end the affair with despatch, leave no loose ends ... To no avail, as he must have known. Casanova continued as before, at first in the ambassador's casino, then in another that he rented in his own name. C.C. was dropped altogether. M.M. became mysteriously ill, and he moved to Murano, to a cottage outside the walls of the nunnery, to be near her. His housekeeper here was Tonina, daughter of Laura the go-between. He was so worried that he could not eat, and even did not notice Tonina's charms until M.M. drew back almost miraculously from death's door and began to recover. Then his appetites returned, and he enjoyed Tonina and her soup with equal relish. As to M.M. he had promised to help her escape from the nunnery, and run away with her, and marry her, at the first opportunity. But sadly, during the days that separated their nights of love, he lost all his money gambling. What use was a beggar to a high-born, intelligent lady like M.M.? With keen regret he had to give up the idea of marrying her.

Meanwhile, back at the palace, trouble was brewing. Senator

Bragadin's elder brother, Procurator of S. Marco, had died, without sons. (There were nine elected Procurators; the senior three were responsible for the superintendence of S. Marco, including its enormous wealth; it was a very influential post.) The senator decided he should marry an old mistress, by whom he had once had a son, thus legitimizing the son and keeping the 900-year-old name of Bragadin alive. Casanova could think of nothing worse than a son, bearing the senator's name, intruding into their relationship. The prospective bride was a smart woman, and offered him a considerable bribe to speak in her favour . . . but Paralis was not to be suborned, and when consulted in the usual cabalistic way, spoke out firmly against the marriage. Bragadin gave up. Paralis had probably saved his life, he thought, and Casanova agreed.

It is time here to take a look at Casanova's story from the outside. This period, the sexiest of the whole book, is full of inconsistencies, mysteries, and false trails. Events that certainly took place in 1748 are mixed with others that can with equal certainty be dated 1753. Outraged churchmen have denied that de Bernis had any part in it; but there is independent evidence that he certainly played uncanonical games, and presumably it was not for nothing that Voltaire nicknamed him the *Bouquetière du Parnasse*. We will not be surprised, by now, knowing something of Casanova's needs, to learn that dear sweet virginal little C.C. turns out to have been thirty-one, or three years older than Casanova. My own opinion on the whole period described is that he did have such affairs as he describes, but they were probably not so concentrated, nor so high-toned, and that de Bernis was involved.

The lights are about to dim, so let us call the roll of the Venetian ladies: C.C. – gone, M.M. – going. Another Murano nun who had once been Marta Savorgnan, his first true little wife – dead. Tonina – sold to Sir John Murray. A mysterious pale girl of eighteen, Anna Maria del Pozzo (only she was really twenty-eight) who had never menstruated and in consequence had been bled 104 times: Casanova thought he had a cure for that, and it worked, but the family sent him packing. His surgical interventions never were properly appreciated . . . Tonina's little sister, Barberina, a minx: she offered to get him some figs from the top of a tree if he would hold the ladder. He did, she shinned up, presenting him with a clear view of at least one fine fig, just ripe. So fine, indeed, that he swore to love her always. But fate had other plans for him.

Now the supporting players began subtly to move, toward the wings. The audience sees what destiny has in store, but the actor holding centre stage, enamoured of himself and his boundless energy, notices nothing.

In the lengthening shadows Casanova's enemies took substance, animated by his unending indiscretions, follies, and arrogance. First, Senator Bragadin's uncle took it into his head that Casanova was responsible for Bragadin's absorption in the cabala. This was not true, for the folly ante-dated Casanova. But the family would have heard how he had prevented Bragadin's marriage and so ensured the end of the name. They were out to get him.

Second, Signora Memmo, the mother of three of Casanova's patrician contemporaries and companions, decided that he was corrupting her sons and turning them into atheists and Freemasons. Hundreds of eminent Venetians were Freemasons, but the State Inquistors didn't like it made public; that would bring in the Church Inquisitors, and the Most Serene had managed extremely well in keeping the Church's nose out of its affairs.

Third, Casanova had leaped with both feet into a literary squabble then shaking Venice, as to the relative merits of the playwrights Zorzi and the Abbé Chiaria, a Jesuit. Casanova came down on Zorzi's side, perhaps because he found Signora Zorzi an agreeable lover. Unfortunately the Red Inquisitor at the time (the one appointed by the Doge, who wore a red robe) was Antonio Condulmer, a leader of the Chiari faction.

Fourth, the Countess Lorenza Maddalena Bonafede tried to borrow money from him, failed, and took to tearing off her clothes and running naked through the streets of Venice, calling out Casanova's name. They shut her up as a madwoman, but it must have caused comment.

Fifth in the mounting indictment against Casanova there was the backlog – the mass rape of the weaver's wife; the breach-of-promise case; the beating-up of the young whore; the affair of the corpse's arm; the assault on Razzetta . . . a long garbage-strewn trail of fights and flights, seductions and blasphemies. And the fellow had now deeply insinuated himself into the lives of several patricians. That was bad, and could be dangerous.

Finally, he continued to prove that all the allegations, all the bad tales and evil rumours, were true, or ought to be. His dealings with the Church, the governing aristocracy, and the honest bourgeoisie, were one long cocked snook.

The Establishment put spies on him, notably a jeweller called Giovanni Manucci. Manucci flattered Casanova with inquiries about cabalism and Freemasonry: doubtless he had a magnificent library of rare tomes on the ancient wisdoms? Casanova swallowed the bait, showed the spy his library and even lent him the books, which were taken to the Inquisitors and examined at leisure. When they were ready, the Inquisitors struck – but it was a blow deliberately aimed at space.

Messer Grande, the chief of police, broke into Casanova's lodging, informing the landlady that he was looking for contraband salt which he believed to be hidden there. Casanova was at Bragadin's palace. He was furious. Of course he had no salt! What right had Messer Grande to break into his lodging? He would complain to the Three, it was an outrage . . .

Signor Bragadin really loved Casanova. History should take note of this gentle old man, wise and foolish, who saw in the appalling scoundrel an unfilled capacity for affection, and gave him a home and a father, preserving the young man's real talent as a liver of life when he might so easily have sunk and died unnoticed in the gutter. Bragadin now tried, for the last time, to save Casanova from the consequences of his unwisdom. In the presence of Barbaro and Dandolo he spoke to him earnestly, with all the love he could summon. He had himself served as an Inquisitor, he said. He knew how these things were done. The Three would never send Messer Grande to look for a sack of salt. It was not salt they wanted, but him – Giacomo Casanova. But Messer Grande had spies; he would never go to a house when the man he wanted was out. So the search of the lodging was meant as a warning: *Leave Venice*! Messer Grande had announced that he would return the next day: interpreted, the words meant that Casanova had twenty-four hours in which to get out. Weeping, Bragadin begged Casanova to go.

Quem Juppiter vult perdere, prius dementat, as Casanova, with his penchant for quoting Latin tags in and out of season, would have been the first to murmur. Casanova refused to go. He begged Bragadin to stop crying, as he could not bear it. The senator controlled himself, and they said goodbye. The old man said he did not think he would ever see his 'son' again. Nor did he.

Next day, 26 July 1755, at dawn, Messer Grande arrested Casanova in his lodging. Casanova's fear and sense of outrage were not lessened, but his self-importance was much soothed, when he saw that Messer Grande had thought it necessary to bring with him no less than forty police. They took all his books and papers, and for four hours kept him shut in a room in Messer Grande's house. During this time he slept fitfully, getting up on the stroke of every fifteen minutes to urinate. He filled two large chamber pots in the process, although, as he says wonderingly, he had not eaten or drunk. Then they took him to the Doge's Palace.

The Secretary of the Inquisitors, at this time a man called Domenico Maria Cavalli, took his name and formally handed him over to Lorenzo, the chief jailer of the prison, to be put in the cells high under the roof of the palace, and hence, because the roof was coated with lead plates, known as the Leads.

Lorenzo took him up several flights of stairs, past a garrotting machine, and into a cramped cell barely five feet high. Casanova, who was six foot one-and-a-half inches tall, had to crouch. The door slammed. From outside, the jailer asked him what he wanted to eat. Casanova didn't know. He hadn't thought about it. The jailer went away.

He was alone, under the Leads, from which no prisoner had ever escaped, not knowing what he was charged with, nor how long he would be kept there.

6

The Great Escape

Prison's first effect on Casanova was total constipation, which lasted fifteen days. At the end of this period his bowels overcame what must have been a severe psychosomatic stricture, and he had a movement. It was so powerful that it nearly made him faint, and did give him a bad case of piles, from which he suffered for the rest of his life.

During this early period he terrified himself out of his wits once when, waking from sleep, he touched a hand beside him. He seized it, found it cold and thought they had put a corpse in with him. When he pulled at the hand, he realized that it was his own: he had been sleeping on his arm, and thus numbed the hand . . . shades of the practical joke which had led to his first flight from Venice!

On 1 November 1755 he saw the great beam supporting the roof slowly turning on its side, then turning back. The floor moved under his feet and he knew it was an earthquake. Driven to madness by ninety-seven days of solitary imprisonment, he could believe that the fall of the Doge's Palace would somehow free him – over eighty feet up inside it – alive. He raised his hand and screamed, 'Another, my God! another, even stronger!' This was the shock that destroyed Lisbon, in one of the worst earthquakes in recorded history.

From the middle of November he was seldom without cell-mates, none of whom was interesting or helpful. Lorenzo, the head jailer, fed him reasonably well. For reading matter he was given *The Mystical City of God*, a religious work of inordinate length and stunning boredom by the Spanish nun Maria of Agreda, which gave him acute melancholia. Then, through the pleas of Bragadin, he managed to get something better. He was now allowed to exercise in the main attic farther along under the Leads, and there he found chests full of paper, uncut pens, accounts of old trials, some dating back for centuries, a piece of polished black marble measuring one by six by three inches, and a straight iron bar as thick as his thumb and eighteen inches long. He secreted the marble and the iron bar in his cell, not knowing, he says, just what use he could ever have for them.

He soon thought of something. Using his spittle to ease the work, he began to sharpen the iron bar by honing it on the marble. It cost him a month, a stiff arm, and a huge blister, to make it into a pointed spike, which he hid in the armchair the benevolence of the Tribunal had allowed him. With the spike as his only tool, he began to bore through the floor, which he reckoned was the roof of the big chamber where the Inquisitors held court. In order to hide his progress he had to prevent the cell being cleaned, and this he did by feigning chest pains and bronchia *before* he began work. The good Dr Bellotto came, and supported Casanova's contention that the dust from the cell must not be disturbed, or it would kill him.

Slowly, week by week, he worked through wood, then marble terrazzo (he used vinegar from his salads to soften this), then more wood until, toiling stark naked in the oven-like heat of midsummer, sweating face-down in his hole, he heard the bolt squeak in the outer door. He hurled his spike into the hole, swept the wood splinters after it, pulled his bed over all, blew out the lamp (which he had made himself, and was not supposed to have), and lay down just as Lorenzo entered with a new prisoner. Lorenzo commented on the smell of hot oil, but said no more. The new man was in only a week, and then Casanova could return to his task. He finally reached the ceiling below, only to find that he had come out so close to a big beam that he could not enlarge the hole toward that side, and so could never get his body through. He therefore began again, a foot farther over. Now he had to make sure that no dust or debris fell into the chamber below, and be careful at night that no light from his lantern showed through the hole to astonish any watchman.

When his hole was big enough he determined to make his escape on 28 August 1756. He had sound reasons for choosing the 28th: it was the day before a festival when the Inquisitors held court on the mainland. The chamber below would be empty, and the servants and jailers busy getting drunk. Exactly at noon on 25 August, as he thanked God for allowing him to bring the work to completion, once more the bolts squeaked, and Lorenzo came in, beaming, to bring good news. Through the intercession of Senator Bragadin, Casanova was being moved to a better cell, in fact a *good* cell, two windows, light, air, a nice view, everything. Casanova, nearly fainting from shock, feebly protested: he did not want to move; he liked it here; these rats were his personal friends; too much fresh air was bad for a man in his condition. Lorenzo thought he was mad, brushed aside his protests, and led him along the passage, assuring him that all his effects would be brought along at once.

That was what Casanova was afraid of. The chair came first. A quick look showed that they had not discovered the iron bar. Piece by piece, the rest followed. Last, foaming with fear and rage, came Lorenzo. He threatened all kinds of death and torture if Casanova would not tell him how he had obtained the instruments by which he had made the enormous hole in the floor of the other cell. For a long time Casanova did not answer, then he said merely, 'You provided them to me.'

This was a shrewd counter, its relevance less pointed now than then, when jailers were not civil servants but men themselves on the fringe of the underworld, as ready as their prisoners to make money, and not much more finicky about how they made it. (This particular man, Lorenzo Biradonna, for instance, was condemned to ten years for murder, the very next year.)

Casanova's hint that, if questioned, he would say he had bribed Lorenzo, added to the ruthless secrecy of the Tribunal, prevented Lorenzo from doing what any modern jailer must have done: tell his superiors of Casanova's attempt, and have steps taken to prevent another one. What he did, as the other jailers later told Casanova, was to swear them all to secrecy and then have the damage repaired at his own cost, saying nothing to the Secretary of the Three. Yet the Three probably did get to hear of it, for the next prisoner to be put in to share Casanova's cell, his new one, was patently a spy. His name was Soradaci. On the plus side, Lorenzo had undertaken to exchange books between Casanova and another prisoner. Casanova soon found a way to communicate with this other man: he wrote a message on the fly-leaf of the first book exchanged, rather romantically sharpening his little finger nail and writing in the juice of some mulberries he happened to have by him. His little finger nail was of inordinate length as he had let it grow to serve as an earpick.

The other man was a renegade priest and patrician, Father Marin Balbi, and he also had a cell-mate, Count Andrea Asquini. Balbi was in the Leads for fathering three children on three girls. Casanova, more determined than ever to escape, decided to use him as his accomplice. Every day the jailers sounded Casanova's cell on all sides except one – the ceiling; because it was impossible that he could make a hole right through it in one day, and a hole partially bored there could not be concealed. Balbi's cell was adjoining, but the jailers did not sound its walls. Let Balbi make a hole in his ceiling, therefore, covering it (and indeed the whole cell) with large pictures of the saints. When that was done, Balbi could climb up into the attic space above both cells. From there he could make a hole in Casanova's ceiling, but not actually break through till the moment came for full escape.

Balbi agreed to the plan, and now Casanova had to pass him the iron spike. This he achieved by a singularly complicated procedure involving a huge plate of *gnocchi*, so much butter that it spilled over, and a vast folio Bible to hide the iron spike. Lorenzo had to carry the *gnocchi* balanced on the Bible, his attention so concentrated on seeing that the butter did not spill over that he would not notice that the Bible contained the spike.

But the trick worked; and Balbi set to. He soon reached the attic and began to dig in the ceiling over Casanova's cell, listening for the latter's code of warning signals. Casanova, now furiously impatient, had to think of a way of getting his own cell-mate, the spy Soradaci, to keep quiet about what was going on. He hoodwinked the man into betraying him in a small matter, though under oath to the Virgin Mary, and with this as his weapon, began to play on the fellow's superstitions. First, kneeling in Soradaci's presence, he prayed to the Virgin to punish with the most awful tortures the man who had broken his vow to her. He reduced Soradaci to gibbering terror, and meanwhile warned Balbi to be ready to finish the work in a hurry, as cabalistic means had informed Casanova that he would escape between the end of October and the beginning of November. This could only mean the night of 31 October/1 November. Casanova, who was as superstitious as the spy, though he never admitted it, intended to make the attempt that night.

Precisely at two o'clock, Casanova told Soradaci, the Virgin Mary would send an angel to begin working to free him, and to free or punish Soradaci according as to whether he helped or betrayed Casanova. Soradaci, naturally, did not believe this story ... until the hammering began in the empty attic above, exactly at two. Then Casanova dropped Soradaci to his knees with a swingeing blow in the ear, and kneeling himself, bade the angel welcome.

The mumbo–jumbo continued, day by day, until on the evening of 31 October, to the accompaniment of more abracadabra, Father Balbi completed the hole through the ceiling, and dropped into Casanova's cell. Now the truth was out. Casanova flatly told Soradaci they were going to escape, and he was coming with them: so also was Count Asquini.

It was not so easy. Asquini was old and very fat, and could never drop from ceilings, swing from chandeliers, or slide down banisters in this d'Artagnan-like adventure. Soradaci did not want to go, and foresaw that his only hope of saving his head was to pretend that the desperadoes had overpowered him with threats on his life. So, at noon on 31 October 1756, having got rid of the unfit and the unwilling, the Great Escape began, with the punctual appearance of the angel/monk Balbi through the roof of Casanova's cell.

Soradaci by now knew that Casanova had duped him but he could not raise the alarm with the two rascals standing over him with the murderous spike, and – this is what in the end made escape possible – nothing would happen if he did. The cells could only be reached through the chambers used by the Inquisitors when in session. Most days, therefore, the jailers had to do their work before the Inquisitors arrived. They then locked up and went home, or to other trades and avocations. The walls were thick: a man might scream but no one would answer, no one would report. In secretive Venice, in the secret centre of the most secret tribunal of all, few would dare to hear.

Being thus sure that no one would interrupt them until about seven the next morning, the escapers had nineteen hours in hand. First, Casanova made Soradaci, who was a hairdresser, cut their beards with scissors Balbi had brought. Then he spent an hour testing the roof of the Palace with his spike, stopping when he saw that it would only take a few minutes more work to get through the rotten wood. Then he returned to his cell and spent four hours cutting up sheets, coverlets and bedding, and carefully knotting the strips until he had about two hundred feet of 'rope'.

Returning to the attic, he quickly broke through to the lead sheets of the outer roofing. With Balbi's help he prised one of these sheets loose, and bent it back whole. Through the square aperture they looked at a bright crescent moon. Casanova instantly decided that nothing more could be done until the moon set, for as they explored the roof it would send their elongated shadows to perform antic evolutions on the Piazza S. Marco, arousing much unwelcome interest. It was now eight o'clock; the moon would set about eleven-thirty.

So, back to Count Asquini, and an hour spent in trying to borrow thirty sequins (67 dollars or £27) from the old miser, who could only be persuaded in the end to part with two. (Prisoners were allowed money, as they could enjoy certain comforts and delicacies on payment.) It was now nine o'clock. From nine to ten-thirty Casanova talked with Balbi and Soradaci, and divided the rope into two equal coils. At ten-thirty Soradaci was sent up, like Noah's dove, to scout the weather. He came back with a report that the moon was nearly down and there was a thick fog. Casanova wrote a last sad, firm letter to the Inquisitors and allotted the bundles of clothing.

Soon after eleven he climbed through the hole and onto the sloping roof of the Doge's Palace, Balbi following. Balbi took hold of Casanova's waistband. By jabbing his spike under the edge of the lead plates Casanova worked up to the ridge of the great roof, dragging Balbi behind. On the way Balbi dropped a bundle, which rolled into the gutter. The packet contained valuable documents he had found in the Palace attic, the aggrieved monk said. Casanova, restraining an impulse to push his companion over the edge, told him it didn't matter. Balbi then lost his hat, which fluttered all the way down into the Rio di Palazzo.

Casanova left Balbi sitting there in the fog, and spent an hour pulling himself along the ridge in an exploration. He found no way down, and decided that their only recourse was to get back inside the building at some point where it was not a prison, and then walk out when all was opened in the morning. To effect this re-entry he chose a dormer window projecting from the roof about one third of the way down from the ridge, on the side of the Rio di Palazzo. (This was therefore somewhere directly above the Bridge of Sighs.) He slid carefully down the roof to the dormer, sat astride it, and looked over the front: entry was barred by a window – and an iron grating.

His nerve failed him. He had not eaten or slept for two days. He had been a prisoner for fifteen months, and his temperament, very far from phlegmatic, temporarily reached its limit of endurance. He sat, miserable, afraid and baffled, on the dormer roof, ninety feet above the canal, unable to think or act.

The thunderous clangour of a sound both familiar and challenging threw him out of his despair – the clock of S. Marco striking midnight: *the* moment between 31 October and 1 November. Nothing had changed, except his spirit . . . but he attacked the grille with his spike and in fifteen minutes had prised it loose, in one piece, to be carefully set down on the roof. Then, he broke in the window (cutting his left hand) and went back to Balbi.

Balbi was cold, frightened, and very cross. He had been alone, not daring to move, for an hour and a half. Casanova led him to the dormer, tied him firmly onto a rope, and lowered him through the window until he reached the floor of the room below. This turned out to be a drop of twenty-five feet.

Casanova set out to find something he could tie his own rope to.

In a further exploration of the roof he came across a barrel of mortar and a ladder thirty-six feet long. Tying his rope to a rung he dragged the ladder to the dormer window and set about inserting it, with the intention of climbing down it. He could, as he points out, more easily have set the ladder across the dormer, tied his rope to a central rung, and so gone down; but he had an obsession about leaving no exterior traces of their route, so the ladder had to be got inside the Palace.

Manoeuvring long ladders through small windows on slippery sloping roofs ninety feet up in dense fog is highly specialized work, in which Casanova was a mere beginner. Struggling to get enough of the ladder through the dormer so that its weight would tilt it down, he lost his footing and slipped over the parapet, as far as his chest. Slowly, carefully, he put up first one knee, then the other, and dragged his body up after them. He lay for a while racked with cramp and exhaustion, unable to move. The nearly fatal effort had pushed the ladder in far enough. It slid easily the rest of the way. Casanova blithely threw down the remaining rope and bundles, and holding only his magical spike scrambled quickly down to join Balbi.

They drew in the ladder and explored the room. It was about ninety feet by thirty, had windows showing the stars, and large barred doors. It was 1.30 a.m. Balbi ranted and raved, but Casanova arranged the rope as a pillow, and went to sleep.

At five o'clock Balbi awakened him. This time they found a door at the opposite end to the barred ones. The spike soon dealt with the small lock. From here on the escapers were in the giant deserted halls and galleries of the Doge's Palace. They passed through a succession of rooms, galleries and chambers, and down four separate flights of stairs. Some doors they found open, others they opened with the spike, and one they bashed a hole in – a noisy business – and dragged each other through, getting severely cut and torn by splinters in the process.

At last, near six o'clock, behind an unbreakable, unopenable door in a passage on the courtyard side, near the Giants' Staircase, they reached the limit of their own efforts. They opened the bundles, and dressed in the only clothes they had, the ones they had been arrested in. Casanova was wearing a 'dress made for love-making in August', and a wide-brimmed Spanish hat trimmed with lace. If one didn't look closely enough to notice the blood seeping through in half a dozen places he might have been an unseasonably summery all-night reveller, 'a man who has been to a ball and has spent the rest of the

74

night in a bawdy-house'. Casanova's gorgeous cloak hid Balbi's rags; but then, that made one certain that Balbi had stolen the cloak.

Thoughtlessly, Casanova opened a window. A passer-by in the courtyard saw the apparition in the lace-trimmed hat, and hurried to tell the doorkeeper that he must have shut some great personage inside the Palace. The doorkeeper came out with a key, slowly opened the door, and paused in astonishment. Casanova went firmly by him, and walked fast down the Giants' Staircase. At his heels Balbi cried 'To the church!' But in Venice churches had not been sanctuaries for years. Casanova ignored his companion, went to the gondola jetty and called 'To Fusina, at once!' This required a second gondolier, for Fusina is five miles across the lagoon, at the mouth of the Brenta Canal. In a moment they were away, soon round the Custom House Point, and winging down the canal by the Giudecca. Now Casanova could change his destination from Fusina to Mestre; but any witnesses on the jetty would have heard only the order to go to Fusina.

As he looked back down the lovely reach in the opal morning, the sun soaring through the rim of the horizon, only themselves and the young gondoliers and the gliding boat alive in all the world, realization burst upon Casanova that he was free, and with it a full appreciation of the terrors of the escape and the horrors of the long imprisonment. He broke down, and for a while tears and sobs racked him. He was free – and going into exile from his beloved Venice.

Three-quarters of an hour later they reached Mestre, still in the territories of the Most Serene Republic. Here Casanova ordered a carriage to take them to Treviso, and set off in a fever of impatience, to realize that Balbi was not with him. He went searching for him. The brutish monk, whose only real talent was lifting servant-girls' shifts, was back at the old stand; Casanova found him in a coffee-house, ogling the waitress. Casanova dragged him out, determining to rid himself of the incubus as soon as he could, and ran into a man called Tomasi, whom he suspected of being an agent of the Tribunal. He asked Tomasi to step aside for a private talk, grabbed him by the neck, and drew his spike, intending to kill him then and there. Tomasi jerked himself suddenly free and ran off across the fields, but turned to blow Casanova kisses, meaning that he wished him well. Casanova staggered back to the carriage, realizing how close fear and frustration had brought him to unjustified murder.

At Treviso they were still in Venetian territory. Here Casanova ordered another carriage, but this was to put the inevitable pursuers off the scent. In fact they left the town on foot, walked into the flat, featureless country, and struck out across the fields towards foreign territory. They were still many miles from safety when Casanova collapsed from hunger, and could not go on until he had sent Balbi to get food from a nearby farmhouse. (Balbi, he remarks viciously, was stronger than he: thoughts of caution or honour never troubled him, and he was a monk!) After eating they tramped on for three more hours. Then, drained by nervous and physical exhaustion, relief from the dangers overcome, and fear of those yet to follow, Casanova could go no farther.

Resting under a tree, he explained his plan to Balbi. They must separate, because police and spies would be looking for the two of them together. No one would necessarily connect any single man with the two fugitives, nor could a doubtful hazard at the identity of one be cross-checked against the appearance of the other. They would therefore part here, go different ways, and meet again at the first inn on the left in Borgo di Valsugana, the first town over the border in territories belonging to the Sovereign Bishop of Trento. To prove his goodwill, he would give all his remaining money to Balbi: which he at once did.

Balbi refused. Casanova had promised to lead him to safety and that was that. He would stay with him. Casanova rose wearily, measured the monk for a grave, and began to dig with his faithful all-purpose spike. After a little time the message sank in. Balbi went off.

Casanova bestirred himself, found a shepherd, and made enquiries about the houses he could see dotted over the countryside. One of them, the shepherd said, belonged to the local chief of police. It was to this that Casanova, directed by one of those unexplainable inner certainties to which he was prone, now directed his steps.

A woman opened the door to him. Her man was out, searching for a monk and a certain Signor Casanova who had escaped from the Leads. Casanova spun a cock-and-bull story . . . he had been hunting, lost his way, fallen down a cliff. The woman fed him, her mother tended his cuts and wounds, and he fell asleep.

He slept for twelve hours. Then, dressing quickly, he slipped out of the house, and continued on his way; but when he saw a church he could not pass it until he had given thanks for his freedom. It was now 2 November, the Day of the Dead, and mass was being celebrated. Here he saw Marcantonio Grimani, of the S. Polo branch of the clan (Casanova's guardians were of the S. Maria Formosa branch), and Casanova tried to borrow some money. Grimani refused him with the kind thought that monks along the route would provide.

Casanova, expressing his sarcastic gratitude, went on his way. Now he was in the foothills where the Piave comes out of the mountains. He walked seven hours, till sunset, and begged shelter at an isolated house. Once again the master was away, but the housekeeper gave him food and a bed, and asked no questions. Next morning he crossed the toll bridge over the Piave, promising to pay when he came back (he didn't have a penny), and kept walking.

This day he did five hours, ate at a Capuchin monastery, walked again until four in the afternoon, and at last reached his goal for the day, the house of a man on whom he had some claim. He asked the man for a loan of sixty sequins, but panic fear of the Inquisitors far outweighed any sense of obligation the fellow might have had. He refused the loan and begged Casanova to leave his house at once. Casanova was in no temper to brook such a refusal. He drew his spike and said that he would have the money, if not as a loan, then by force. He took only six sequins, and went on.

He spent that night on straw in a peasant's cottage. Next day, astride an ass, wearing an old overcoat and a new pair of shoes, he came to the Venetian frontier post at La Scala, in the high valley of the Brenta. The guard did not look up. Casanova passed into safety.

7

High Summer in Paris

It would have been churlish to check a raconteur like Casanova in the full flood of his best story; but now that we are safe in Borgo di Valsugana, the infant Brenta prattling between the houses, and Casanova is in bed recovering his strength, we must examine the thrilling tale with a more critical eye.

It is full of improbabilities and question marks. There must have been cells in the attic, under the eaves, but they were certainly not like the one which privileged visitors are now shown, alleged to be Casanova's. The interior geography of the escape, which I have tried to follow on the spot, is so confused as to be untraceable. He was a strong resourceful man, but imagination boggles at the idea of him dragging a thirty-six-foot ladder along the sloping roof, down to a dormer window only a few feet from the gutter, and trying to insert the one into the other. He also says that the setting moon would cast the escapers' shadows onto the Piazza S. Marco, but the moon sets in the west and the Piazza S. Marco is on the west side of the Palace. There is an inordinate amount of happy coincidence and clever contrivance throughout. It does not read like truth, but as though Casanova had thought up all conceivable obstacles and shown how a brave, clever man could master them. This impression is the more remarkable, to me, in that he says nothing of other, real obstacles which he must have overcome. In tracing his escape, for example, I was struck by the fact that the road he took runs right through the middle of an imposing frontier fortress at Posterno, which guarded the descent into Valsugana. Passing here must have been a truly dangerous moment, but he does not mention it.

All in all, one cannot quarrel very vehemently with the sceptics who insist that the Great Escape was a Great Fiction; that he bribed himself out, with Bragadin's help. Palace officials of today say that he escaped through connivance, on the night of a great ball, let out by some lady. On the other hand, the bills for repairing the damage the two did in the escape are still extant, and Lorenzo was definitely imprisoned. The doorkeeper who opened the final door was called Andreoli, and he gave evidence that Balbi and Casanova knocked him down (which would have been his story in any case). There is plenty of evidence that Casanova's story was never doubted by Venetians themselves, and in Venice it would have been impossible to hide the suspicion, let alone the fact, of such a famous suborning. Nor is it easy to explain why Casanova was allowed to bribe himself out when there had never been a hint that such was possible; and over the centuries there must have been prisoners with a hundred, a thousand times Casanova's *piston*.

My opinion, coloured by a romantic willingness to believe the more picaresque of conflicting possibilities, is that although many details, measurements, directions and personalities have been worked and reworked to his advantage, and much has been distorted in memory, overall Casanova did escape much as he says he did.

And now he is on his endless journey once more. But prison has changed him, as it changes most people. He went in as a vain, self-satisfied, talkative coxcomb, essentially boyish and amateur in his misdeeds. He came out in the prime of manhood, no longer young, or light-hearted, but professional, criminal and dangerous.

Pausing only to get rid of Father Balbi, for whom he found a place in a monastery, he set off for Paris, *mighty Paris*, his magic city. He arrived there on 5 January 1757, on the day and almost at the hour when Robert Damiens, a discontented and perhaps unbalanced servant in the Jesuit College in Paris made an attempt on the life of Louis XV. The Ballettis greeted Casanova like the long-lost and wayward prodigal he actually was. Nothing had changed except that the mother, Silvia, was obviously ill, and little Manon, whom he remembered as a child of twelve, had turned into a dewy and desirable seventeen: a virgin, he thought, but in some ways more sophisticated than older women, for she lived among actors.

Casanova was now thirty-two, tall, dark, brilliant, her adored eldest brother's closest friend. Manon fell in love with him, and through all the adventures and grotesqueries of the next three years, we should remember her, waiting for him at the house in the Rue du Petit-Lion-St-Sauveur, crying when he neglects her, writing endless letters, gradually, through sorrow, growing up to see him for what he was – lovable, impossible.

Next, to get a job, or, more accurately, some money. In those days someone in Casanova's position did not study the Situations Vacant columns; he went to the most influential man he knew and asked what the other could do for him. The 'patron' would help as much as he could, because it paid him to have men beholden to him. (The system nowadays is called politics, but in Casanova's time it was more honestly called patronage.) Casanova had an extremely powerful acquaintance in Paris – his playmate of the Murano casino: de Bernis, recently appointed Foreign Minister of France. So one day Casanova set out for Versailles two hours before dawn (official work started early, and finished early: there was much pleasure to be got through in the evening hours) and had an interview with de Bernis. The Minister promised to do what he could, advising Casanova meanwhile to think of a way to increase the revenues without raising taxes. That would be a sure way to fame and favour, de Bernis said, as politicians had said a thousand times before and have repeated a million times since. With that he introduced Casanova, as a brilliant financier, to the Comptroller-General, Jean de Boullogne.

The meeting with Boullogne went the way of many such in Casanova's life. He knew what he wanted, and he knew what the other needed. Moving on light feet, all his antennae out, he took advantage of every hint to improve his own position. Boullogne told him about La Pompadour's military cadet school. She had founded it sixteen years before, but though she was the king's mistress she had the sense not to ask him to finance it: that was Boullogne's job – without taxation. Twenty million francs was needed.

The superintendent of the school, Joseph de Paris-Duverney, and the Comptroller himself – everyone, indeed – depended for his position on royal favour, which meant the whim of La Pompadour. It was easy to imagine the desperation with which they would try to save themselves from her wrath. So, when Boullogne and Duverney mentioned twenty million francs, Casanova said he knew of a method to raise a hundred million. Having no such method, nor any ideas, he was struck with secret hilarity when Duverney said keenly that he knew what the method was; it had been tried before. There were obstacles to be overcome, were there not? Casanova looked mysterious. Duverney thought they must discuss it further with the full board. Casanova shrugged. Ah, naturally it was necessary for men of finance to hold their counsel. Casanova looked out of the window.

A meeting was arranged with the wizards of the Treasury. They talked technical finance. Casanova didn't understand a word, so held his tongue and looked grave. After a good meal Duverney took him into a private room where another man was waiting with a large folio book. Duverney gave Casanova the book and said with a smile,

'That is your plan'. Casanova glanced at the title page and said, 'Yes, that is my plan'.

Duverney told him that he had been forestalled: the plan was this gentleman's. He introduced Giovanni Calzabigi, then about forty, who in turn introduced his elder brother Ranieri. They were both what we would today call 'operators' but, unlike modern operators, they were also artists. Ranieri wrote the librettos for Gluck's *Orfeo ed Euridice* and *Alceste*. Casanova has a vivid description of him:

He looked unattractive, as he was covered in a kind of leprosy; but this didn't impair his appetite, his writing, or his physical and intellectual capabilities; he talked well and amusingly . . . he was frequently seized by an irresistible urge to scratch himself all over the place; and since scratching is socially unacceptable in Paris, whether you do it through sheer necessity or just by habit, he preferred the luxury of being able to use his fingernails to the pleasures of society.

No trumpets sounded at the meeting, but the Calzabigi brothers had lit the beacon which would guide Casanova for the next ten years. It was not a steady light, but it was a powerful one. It was the same that has beckoned like a vision to so many finance ministers ancient and modern, seeming to solve the riddle de Bernis set Casanova: raise money, lower taxes. It was the idea of a State lottery.

The Calzabigis explained why their plan had never been put into effect in France. Casanova undertook to show the full council how all objections could be overcome. A meeting was set up for two days later. He now had forty-eight hours to think up answers to problems he had never before heard of. This he did by listening to the Calzabigis, while pretending not to.

It was not a straightforward 'raffle', but a 'Genoa lottery', based on an old custom in Genoa which was exported all over Europe at about this period. In Genoa new magistrates were chosen every week by *lotto*. Every eligible patrician was given a number, and all the numbers were put into an urn. Each week five slips were drawn out, and the men whom these numbers denoted became magistrates. The populace betted on the outcome. The State soon took over the betting as well as the actual election, and guaranteed the size of the prizes. In the lottery for the French military school the number of tickets to be put in the urn – that is, the number of numbers – was set at ninety. A man drawing any one correct number got back his stake multiplied by a certain factor which gave a small advantage to 'the house'. If he linked three correct numbers on a single ticket it was a *terne*, and he received 8,000 times his stake. Four correct numbers was a *quaderne* and earned 60,000 times the stake. A *quine* – all five numbers – made the winner a multi-millionaire.

Over a long period 'the house' always won, but a number of lucky draws could cause a temporary heavy loss, and such a loss would bankrupt small promoters if it came early in the life of the *lotto*, before they had had time to build up a reserve. It was this chance of the temporary loss which made rulers nervous and in general led them to farm out the rights to run the *lotto*, at a certain fixed percentage of the take, rather than run it themselves or back it with the credit of the state. Hence men like Casanova and the Calzabigis ran the big risks and took the big gains.

In this form the lottery was approved, and Casanova was allotted a certain number of sales offices. He put in clerks to run them, and collected the considerable profits. Financially secure, he plunged into the high-life of Paris. He made hundreds of acquaintances – many of them Freemasons – but only two are of particular remark. One was Count Maximilian Lamberg, traveller and writer, who became his friend for life. The other was a character who styled himself the Comte de Saint-Germain, claimed to be several hundred years old, to know all knowledge, and never to eat. No one knew where he really came from but it was said that he was born in 1706 in Bayonne, the result of a liaison between the wife of King Charles II of Spain and a Portuguese Jew. (Note again the Jewish theme in anything to do with the occult.) Whatever the truth, he was famous all over Europe and is Casanova's principal rival as an adventurer and charlatan. His chief dupe was Louis XV, who provided him with a castle and huge sums of money to pursue his researches.

But most of Casanova's affairs in Paris were, naturally, affairs of S-E-X. The first emphasizes once more the extraordinary lack of privacy in which sexual contacts were made . . . It began with Eduardo Tiretta, who was twenty-three, came from Treviso, and was a Count; but now he earned a nobler title in bed with a not-so-young *demimondaine*. Casanova called on them the next morning and the lady said that the young man's name should be Count Six Times. Tiretta, eager to show how he had earned the soubriquet, made it a seventh time on the spot. Casanova observed that his compatriot was equipped with credentials which would guarantee him the entrée to all female Paris.

Casanova and Tiretta met a beautiful young virgin, Mlle de la M., and her aunt, whom he calls Mme X.X.X. Aunty was fat, ugly and gossipy; she had bad breath, poor teeth, and a sad miscellany of other faults; but she was rich. As for Mademoiselle, a marriage had been arranged for her with a merchant from Dunkirk. Casanova was immediately captivated by her. While the rest of the company played piquet he talked to her about Tiretta's feats and equipment. Finally, by way of illustration, he showed her his own rampant steed. The girl – she was seventeen and only just out of a convent – went to watch the game of piquet but soon came back to him. Casanova continued his demonstration, and set her hand upon the swelling object of interest. Delighted by her astonishment at its size and the manifest stirrings of her sexual interest he ended the lesson by delivering an appropriate offering into her hand. She then bent – unwise virgin – to put more wood on the fire. Casanova whipped his hand up her skirt and felt her sex in sufficient detail to confirm that she indeed *was* a virgin.

These public proceedings are frequent in Casanova's narrative. The fascination to us is not in whether they did or did not happen, but that Casanova expected to be believed when he said they did. In other words, the behaviour he describes was sufficiently commonplace to arouse no particular disbelief. As the ladies' dresses were always floor-length, and the men's breeches fastenings quite complicated, the actual exchange of 'favours', tremendous or trifling, was much more difficult than similar attempts would be today. One is left with an almost unbelievable picture of the eighteenth-century drawing-room. Yet every painter of the period has corroborated it. Look again at those lovers' meetings, those kisses snatched in statue-strewn grottoes, those Arcadian fondlings in ornamental groves: the central action is almost never shown *in deserto*. There is always something going on in the background – haymaking, cardplaying, dancing, often simple voyeurism. The lovers are enjoying a rapid but not particularly private ecstasy in the middle of the ordinary affairs of life.

. . . Or of death, which stood more closely then at life's elbow. Damiens, the man who had tried to murder Louis XV, was to be publicly executed on 28 March, in the Place de Grève (today the Place de l'Hôtel de Ville). The ladies demanded a good view, and Casanova hired a window for the spectacle. Damiens' flesh was torn with red-hot pincers, molten lead and boiling oil were poured into the wounds, and finally (the Church praying over him) his limbs were torn from his body by four powerful horses. The performance lasted several hours, and the victim's shrieks would have caused queasiness in the most hardened, except that everyone felt so much horror at the man's unspeakable crime (nicking Louis XV in the arm with a small knife) that there was no room left for any softer feeling.

83

The window that Casanova hired was rather narrow, there being room for only three people to stand in it side by side; so Mlle de la M., Aunty, and another woman stood in front, Casanova and Tiretta directly behind them. As they were all perched on the narrow step, it was necessary and proper for the gentlemen to raise the ladies' skirts a little in order not to tread on them. As Damiens' agony filled the air, Casanova noticed that Count Tiretta was drawing up Aunty's skirt considerably higher than was necessary to save the hem from being trodden on ... high enough, indeed, to enable him, once he had unstabled his own steed, to set upon the great work, dropping the ample skirts back over the whole. Casanova quickly moved into a position where his body shielded Mlle de la M.'s susceptibilities from the exercise going on next to her, and awaited some kind of outcry from Aunty. Nothing of the sort. Aunty merely looked pensive. So, throughout Damiens' long dying, Count Tiretta performed sexual gymnastics on the aunt, while Casanova stood amazed at his friend's nerve.

There is a famous picture of the execution of Damiens. The reader of Casanova's *Story* can never look at it without examining those massed figures in the windows opposite, trying to find the pensive Aunt and, perhaps just visible over her shoulder, the hardworking expression of the majestically equipped Count Six Times.

It turned out later that Tiretta had treated Aunty in the Italian manner and after it was all over she had taken umbrage. Everything came out all right in the last chapter but one: Tiretta again called on Aunty, this time using the front door; Aunty was so pleased that she hired him, at a good salary; Mlle de la M. surrendered her virginity to Casanova, and begged him to save her from the Dunkirk merchant by marrying her himself. In the very last chapter, of course, Casanova backed out, handing the angry girl over to the merchant. Count Six Times honourably filled the post of house stallion for Mme X.X.X. until she died. He later emigrated and became an architect in Bengal. Manon Balletti, now dim, now bright, in Casanova's heart, according as he was about to mount another woman or had just done so, kept nagging at his conscience. There was definitely an understanding of marriage between them, which had caused the annulment of a previous understanding of the same sort whereby she was to marry Clément, her clavichord teacher.

Now Casanova, to oblige de Bernis and perhaps to get away from Manon's reproachful silences, went on a secret mission to Dunkirk. We know from one of Manon's letters that his dates for this visit are wrong; he may have gone twice – but there is much that is mysterious about this period in his life, and it seems certain that he was engaged upon more espionage than he allows. On this mission he was to report on the warships in the harbour – their condition, guns, state of morale, etc. The ships, it must be emphasized, were French. Why the government in Paris found it necessary to hire a spy of any kind, let alone a runaway Venetian, to bring them information on their own ships, is hard to understand. One explanation lies in the fact that the word 'government', as used above, did not mean what it does now. De Bernis was the official Minister of Foreign Affairs, but the ships in Dunkirk were part of the King's navy, about which the Foreign Minister needed to know but about which the King felt no obligation to tell him anything, certainly not the truth. Another possibility is that Casanova was now a French citizen . . . but more of that later.

He did his spying expeditiously and returned to Paris, *en route* involving himself, quite needlessly, in two fearful quarrels with various city officials. In telling of them he seems to be making a conscious effort, after the tale of his successes, to show his warts, to provide a darker background against which the triumphs would shine more brightly. And his first story after his return from Dunkirk is a very funny one, and is told against himself. One evening the young Comte de La Tour d'Auvergne offered him a ride home. The third passenger in the carriage was the Count's mistress, a little bit of fluff called Babet. As the carriage was rather narrow, Casanova and the Count sat side by side, with the girl upon their laps. Casanova's blood began to heat, and he had a notably low boiling point. Soon he stealthily put out his hand, took the girl's and pressed it onto his breeches.

Thinking that her hand could not refuse to do me such a sweet service I . . . But just at the crucial moment: 'I really am most appreciative, my dear chap,' said La Tour d'Auvergne, 'for your typically Italian courtesy. I don't think I deserve it; I hope it's not intended to show your contempt.' At these alarming words I stretched out my hand and felt the sleeve of his coat. Presence of mind was no good in a situation like this . . .

Next the Count fell ill and Casanova pronounced that what ailed him was not sciatica but evil humours, which he offered to cure by cabalistic means. Casanova invented a nostrum, and invented the spells and incantations to go with it. He knew that all were equally worthless; yet, when it was over, after they had spent hours at the mumbo-jumbo, the Count stood in awed silence, and Casanova himself felt that he had performed some marvellous feat.

The cure worked – at any rate, de La Tour d'Auvergne got better

– and as it had been effected by the cabala, he told his aunt about it. This aunt was, to use a gross meiosis, 'interested' in occultism. She was in fact one of the great nuts of all time. Born Jeanne Camus de Pontcarré in 1707, she was married in 1724 to the Marquis d'Urfé. While her husband still lived (he died in 1734) she was a mistress of the Duke of Orleans, Regent of France during Louis XV's minority. The d'Urfés were a notably eccentric family, and in Jeanne de Pontcarré they had picked a lady guaranteed to strengthen the strain. Now in her fiftieth year she was the very archetype of the slightly unhinged rich woman who is destined to have her money taken from her by one kind of charlatan or another. Usually, at her age, it would have been gigolos or fashionable doctors. Mme la Marquise d'Urfé was fated to go down in history as chief victim of the most notorious snake-oil salesman who ever lived.

Casanova achieved his domination over her because he had a powerful and courageous personality, a first-class brain, and the nerve to carry through the most ridiculous impostures and pretences. Perhaps an even stronger reason was that, deep in his bowels, behind his scorn for the whole business and his sneers at those who believed in it, he himself was a believer.

With Mme d'Urfé he began cautiously, for she was not unintelligent, she was merely mad. Invited to her house, he saw that she had spent huge sums of money on acquiring a cabalistic library. She had built a laboratory with all the correct properties – alembics, chemicals, retorts, matter which had been boiling for years. At that first meeting it was she who was probing Casanova. With her wealth and her high position in the aristocracy, she must have been besieged by cut-rate practitioners of quackery. She had only recently rid herself of one of them, Jean Paul Lascaris, who had traded on being a relative. So she went cautiously, leaving openings for Casanova to make a fool of himself. Casanova may not yet have learned much about necromancy, but instinct and observation had taught him a great deal about rich lonely widows. He was careful, controlled, and inquiring. He was not here, he implied, to teach Madame anything – or to show her marvels: far from it – he only dared hope that she would teach him.

The pas-de-deux went on through two or three visits. Gradually she bared her knowledge. Skilfully he made use of his own small stock of cabalistic learning to feed the flames of her interest. At last, by sneaking a quick look into some of her magic recipe books when her back was turned, he was able to tell her something she believed no human could possibly have known. His wit and intelligence and his sheer attractiveness as a male animal completed the work. The old lady became his disciple and slave. Since women, by occult law, could never reach the ultimate secrets, she needed a man anyway, and now she had a learned and virile one. As Blacksnout he was an initiate in the mysteries of the Rosy Cross, and his avatar in the Inner Council was that most powerful and advanced spirit Paralis. Why Paralis should sojourn on earth linked to this Venetian Giacomo Casanova was a whim of the Inner Ones, which she was too earthbound, or perhaps too female, to fathom.

The Seven Years War had begun, and the finances of France were in a bad way. Boullogne commissioned Casanova to see how much cash and non-French exchange he could get out of the Amsterdam bankers for French Government paper to the face value of twenty million francs. Casanova set off confidently, armed with a side commission from Mme d'Urfé to sell sixty thousand francs' worth of shares she owned, on which she had not been able to collect dividends for years.

Casanova's stay in Holland was an unqualified success. He sold the government paper for foreign exchange at only eight per cent discount. Through Benjamin and Samuel Simons, bankers, he sold Mme d'Urfé's shares for 72,000 francs. This was on 5 December 1758: the transaction is on record. On cabalistic information he persuaded the Dutch banker Thomas Hope to insure a ship generally believed to be lost at sea. When the ship turned up safe Hope made several millions profit, gave Casanova a part, and urged him to stay in Holland, marry his daughter, and go into partnership with him. The daughter, Esther, was equally fascinated by him and his cabala. In fact, the sun shone, the brilliant Casanova shone, everything was coming up roses. And in the telling he does not forget that slanting side-light which shows that the hero is only human after all: he very comically describes his first day on ice skates, his innumerable falls, explains how he is the butt of everyone's jokes.

What he does not explain is that Thomas Hope in fact had no daughter, only a son. So this Esther may have been an illegitimate daughter, or perhaps a niece living in Thomas's house.

In Amsterdam – an important encounter – he met Teresa Pompeati, née Imer, who had been showing him the mysteries of female exterior plumbing eighteen years earlier when old Senator Malipiero discovered them. Teresa now made her living off men and by singing in theatres, accompanied by her five-year-old daughter as a tearjerker. It was only five years since Casanova had spent some delicious nights with her in Venice, and as he chose to see his own features reproduced in the little Sophie, he decided that she was his child, and offered to take her off Teresa's hands and bring her up himself.

Teresa refused. She wanted to keep the girl for her old age, when Sophie's charms would replace her own as principal bait for rich admirers.

But she did offer Casanova her twelve-year-old son, Giuseppe, instead. At first Casanova did not think much of the idea, and still less of the youth, whom Teresa had brought up to be a calculating little devil. Casanova liked open hearts, tears, passions, affections. Then he recalled that Mme d'Urfé wanted to be reborn as a man. According to the best authorities, she would have to die and then be reborn into the body of a young, half-celestial male. Giuseppe would fill the latter part admirably.

Forgetting Esther Hope, Casanova returned to Paris with Giuseppe. Mme d'Urfé was delighted with the youth, who now claimed he was of the noble Spanish family of Aranda. So 'the divine madwoman', as Casanova often styles her, gave the youth that title. As Count d'Aranda she sent him off for special tutoring, and the tutor's daughter taught him what her father couldn't.

Soon after his return from Holland Casanova went to the theatre. He was astonished to see, still more astonished to be hailed by, a Mrs Wynne. She was the daughter of a Greek merchant, and as a girl had been procured as mistress of an English visitor to Venice, Richard Wynne. Casanova had met her in Paris six years back, and again in Venice, when she had shown a distinct unpleasantness toward him. With her past, she could spot a roué at a mile, and she had suspected Casanova and young Andrea Memmo of designs on her daughter, Giustiniana. Casanova was too low to be a husband for the girl, and Andrea was too high. The Memmos were Twelve Apostle patricians: that is, the family had taken part in the election of the first Doge in A.D. 697. There was no possibility that a Memmo would be allowed to marry the daughter of a Greek girl's liaison, even though it was later legitimized.

This Miss Wynne, whom Casanova calls Miss X.C.V., was with her mother in the theatre, and he went over to them, happy to let bygones be bygones. Mrs Wynne's motive in making up to Casanova is not clear, unless we accept his own theory, that he was now rich and well connected in society, while in Venice he was a scapegrace ex-fiddler. She may have felt, too, that there could be no risk now as Giustiniana was being assiduously courted by a very rich old man indeed, Alexandre de La Pouplinière, one of the men to whom the King farmed out the right of collecting taxes. These Farmers General paid vast sums for the privilege, and it may be imagined that they made sure they did not lose by it. They were among the richest and best-hated men in France.

88

Casanova was now embarked on another remarkable amour, this one better documented than any other from independent sources.

He began to pay court to Miss Wynne (leaving little Manon Balletti to pine, and her mother Silvia to die, alone). Giustiniana had the skill to let him believe she would not resist very long or hard. Her mother looked on benevolently, sure that Casanova now presented no danger to her plans. To mothers in her position 'danger' meant, and means, pregnancy. Mrs Wynne was quite correct. There was no danger of Casanova making Giustiniana pregnant. She already was.

About the time when Casanova thought that his courtship would soon pay a dividend, she sent him a desperate note, and begged him to help her. Nowhere does she say so, and nowhere does Casanova say so, but she knew, and he knew, and we know from other evidence, that the man responsible was Andrea Memmo, who had evaded all her mother's barricades and become her lover before she came to Paris. Andrea was a patrician, a Freemason and a personal friend of Casanova's. These facts, as much as the girl's touching trust, led Casanova to act, and take considerable risks, on her behalf. The fact of her turning to him for help seemed very flattering to him, but we can hear the undertones he chose not to (*who of all my acquaintances is likely to know about abortions?*).

First he found out how far gone she was: six months. Next, she had to dress and act in a manner to conceal her condition. How could this be done? They arranged to leave a midnight ball by devious means, and go together to a woman who would advise. The woman turned out to be a grubby abortionist who told them not to beat about the bush. Hide the condition indeed! They wanted to get rid of it, didn't they? Well, it would cost a hundred guineas, half down, half afterwards, and no questions asked. Casanova took the girl away at once. He knew that abortion was much too dangerous at this stage of her pregnancy.

He obtained drugs for her, and poor Giustiniana made herself ill swallowing them. She jumped up and down, took cold baths, gave herself diarrhoea, tried all the other well-known specifics to bring on an early delivery – without success. She grew desperate, and threatened suicide. Casanova shared the desperation, and asked Mme d'Urfé if she knew of a remedy. He probably meant, could she help him hush it up, as was done for many daughters of royalty and nobility every year. One of his troubles with Mme d'Urfé was that she regarded any request of his for help or advice as an obscure jest on his part, for as Paralis was all-knowing and all-powerful, how could poor little

Mme d'Urfé help? In this case, she reminded him of the aroph of Paracelsus. That would do the job without fail, she said.

Casanova found the appropriate place in the manual of practical necromancy. His eyes widened. The aroph of Paracelsus was certainly a remarkable medication, if that was the right word for it. It was a sort of pasteball made of honey, myrrh, beeswax — a few simple items like that — used to bring on menstruation. It had to be applied to the mouth of the uterus when the latter was in a state of sexual excitement. H'm. But it would be no good just putting the ball in there in any old way, as on a teaspoon, or by the fingers. Surely it should be applied on the end of a columnar object six to seven inches long, covered with a very thin integument of human skin. If such an object were worked back and forth in the vagina, it would impress the aroph against the excited cervix.

Casanova thought he had just the instrument with which to apply the aroph. He broached the subject to Miss Wynne. Giustiniana was under extreme nervous strain, but she wasn't mad yet. She burst into such peals of laughter that she almost achieved her desire on the spot. Casanova said no more about the aroph. It had been worth trying . . . But now what on earth could he do for her? He was a very determined man, especially when such a flattering trust had been placed in his powers.

A few days later poor Giustiniana, who had tried everything else, agreed to try the aroph. Casanova, in a frenzy of expectation had to bring the Wynnes' maid and manservant into his confidence, and use plenty of gold to ensure their discretion. With their help the attic next to Giustiniana's bedroom was made into an operating chamber. Casanova crept into the house after dark. Soon the girl came and joined him on the attic bed. With solemn deliberation, the lamp casting a yellow glow in the little room under the eaves, the narrow streets of old Paris silent below, she prepared herself to receive the aroph. Casanova's instrument stood ready for the application . . . And then the humour of it struck them both. For a time he did not think he would be able to do what he was supposed to do, for laughing.

He recovered himself. The aroph was ridiculous, but here was a lovely young woman, on her back, her thighs spread for him. He entered her, and for the rest of that night, and the succeeding nights, they made love, hardly bothering to keep up the fiction of the aroph. But it was no use, and Giustiniana, now in her seventh month, said that their exercises seemed designed more to create than to destroy: what was to be *done*?

Casanova turned to his contacts with the aristocracy. He might have done best to go to La Pompadour, who had promised to be his patron, but the lady he did go to turned out to be just as useful and probably more discreet. This was Constance, Countess of Rumain, a woman of his own age, a Freemason, a dabbler in cabalism, and a notable loose-liver. From her letters it seems possible that Casanova was her occasional lover, but he never even hints at this. To her he told the whole story. The Countess said it would take her a day or two to fix matters; in the meanwhile neither he nor the girl must take any other action.

Two days later she gave him his instructions. Miss Wynne was to run away from home, giving as her reason her absolute determination not to accept the arranged marriage with de La Pouplinière. Changing cabs two or three times, she was to go to a Benedictine convent at Conflans. The abbess, an extremely well-born lady, would be expecting her. They would take her in, and care for her through the birth of her child. They would farm the child out, and she would never see it again. When she was fit the princess-abbess would give her a warrant of good conduct, certifying that she had arrived on such a date, seen no one, done nothing untoward. With this, she could return to her family.

So it was done, Casanova gave Giustiniana exact instructions, he was up at dawn to observe, from hiding, that she carried them out. Her carriage disappeared and he returned to bed, well pleased with himself. One more gentil Ladye had been rescued from dragons by the parfit Sir Giacomo.

Thus, more or less, Casanova on l'affaire Miss Wynne. There are, as I said, most interesting side-lights from other sources. The Farmer General who wanted to marry her was very rich, and very prominent. Rumours of Giustiniana's pregnancy were sufficiently widespread for him to ask, and get, permission for a police officer to place his hand on her belly to prove the thing one way or the other. Seeing that she was then actually five months gone, we must credit the police officer's intense embarrassment and her own cool nerve for the fact that she passed the test.

But de La Pouplinière's heirs-presumptive and other relatives were ready to go any lengths to prevent his marrying again. They un-earthed the abortionist, Madame Reine Demay (Queenie, a singularly apposite name), and hired a scoundrelly pimp of a marquis called Castel-Bajac to bring Queenie forward. Queenie told the police that Casanova had brought a young woman to her and tried to get an abortion, which was of course illegal. This deposition was made on 1 March 1759. Later, after Giustiniana had fled, her mother charged

Casanova with abducting her. The girl had vanished and there was plenty of reason to think she was dead: de La Pouplinière's heirs had threatened to poison her; she might have tried an abortion after all, and died. The charge against Casanova would have been murder. Things would have gone hard with him but for the influence of the Countess of Rumain, and probably other Freemasons. Also, he was able to prove that he had been acting only as a friend, and was not responsible for the girl's pregnancy. These events are supported by documents in the official records in Paris.

For a time fashionable Paris talked of little else. Then, gradually, the gossip died down as the Wynnes moved on and other scandals displaced it. It took the redoubtable Mrs Wynne a couple of years to salvage her daughter's future from the Paris disaster, but then she married her off extremely well, considering – to Count Philip Joseph Orsini-Rosenberg, ambassador of the Holy Roman Emperor to Venice. He was a matter of forty-six years older than his bride and had a son who was twelve years older than she. For forty years she kept up a correspondence (it is all in existence) with the only man she ever loved: Andrea Memmo. And – this is one of the strangest truths about a strange, true business – she never told Memmo that she had had his baby. He may have guessed, but he never knew, and this is clearly shown by his letters to Casanova at the time, and later.

Giustiniana's young brother Richard settled in England, became a parson of the Church of England, and died in 1799 as rector of Ayot St Lawrence. In 1759, at the age of fourteen, he was borrowing money from Casanova to get himself cured of gonorrhoea ... his third dose: another true son of the century.

8

Dreams and Debauchery

Lèt us take good note of these brief months in Paris, when he had gold in his pockets and Miss X.C.V. in his bed, because it is a small plateau at the summit of his fortunes. *Facilis descensus Averni*: from here the way is down hill, though at first the decline is hardly visible and right to the end his courage can summon a fitful brilliance from the shadows.

Casanova sold his lottery offices and started a business for the hand-block printing of silk, which might have succeeded if the process had been waterproof, if there had been no financial chicanery, and if he had not employed thirty-five girls for his pleasure rather than his profit. And, there was the complaisant wife of a small haberdasher to help the thirty-five seamstresses keep his mind off his work. He spent many pleasant hours with this last woman, Mme Baret, at his country retreat, Cracovie-en-bel-Air (about where the Gare St-Lazare now stands), and she is one of the few women whose charms he describes with modern clinical precision. Her pubic hair was of a fine texture and the colour of gold, he records, and she was an expert in the art of making love, in spite of being a virgin, owing to her husband's incompetence, when Casanova seduced her.

Not surprisingly, the silk business ran into trouble. Casanova borrowed money to set it on its feet. Then the plant was robbed, creditors seized the business, sued Casanova, and had him thrown into the For-l'Evêque prison. Manon Balletti sent him her diamond ear-rings, with which to buy himself out, but it was not poor faithful young Manon who freed him but the equally faithful besotted Marquise d'Urfé, who obtained his release merely by asking for it.

Casanova left Paris under several dark clouds. Although no one had proved anything against him in l'affaire Miss Wynne he had certainly visited an abortionist with *some* wretched girl. Louis XV had summarily dismissed de Bernis from office. Casanova admits to having made several enemies, and the truth would probably multiply his score by three. The police records show that a number of counts were pending against him on charges of forging bills of exchange. His brother Francesco and his friend Antonio Balletti were involved in some of these cases.

His departure from Paris *en route* to Amsterdam is a romantic and vivid scene. The carriage leaves Paris in driving snow. Casanova leans back and draws out a book of philosophy. In the glow of the lamp he begins to read, and as he reads composes sentences of judicious criticism. The horses' silent hoofs pad across the great city. But at the end of the journey, and of every journey now, it is not the young and the eager and the innocent who await him, but the middle-aged, the evil, the calculating: self-styled counts and whole-time crooks, pimps, travelling whores, confidence men, gamblers, crooked police chiefs and ageing dancers . . .

In Amsterdam Casanova returned to the Hopes, and came close to seducing Esther. He was always skilful at drawing a women's attention to the area of combat. This time, noticing that Esther had a mole near her lip he bethought himself of ancient folklore correlating various parts of human anatomy (e.g. girls with big hands will have big feet, and gentlemen with large noses should look for ladies with large mouths), and he made his cabala write that she had a similar mole near her vulva. She didn't believe him, and naturally had to look. As the mole was far down and well back, she had to perform contortions to see it, even with the aid of a mirror. But it *was* there. To make sure, Casanova thought he had better see it . . . and, alas, that was all.

The lubricious and faintly comical scene fades, suddenly overlaid by a letter. It was from Manon Balletti, sadly breaking off their engagement and returning his portrait and all his letters. Writing thirty-five years later, Casanova painted a vivid picture of his absolute *bouleversement*. Why was this? Was it that for once a girl had rejected him, before he, by whatever devious means, could ease out of the relationship? Had he genuinely loved Manon? Could he really have believed that one golden day he would return and marry her and settle down? I don't know, but his grief and rage were still with him when he wrote; and he ignored her request to return her letters, for he had them by him when he wrote.

It was now early in 1760. He left Esther and Holland for Cologne and an affair with Mimi von Groote, the burgomaster's wife, although the lady already had an official *cicisbeo* in the person of General Kettler, the Austrian military attaché with the French army, which was wintering in Cologne after its defeat at Minden the previous summer. The affair with Mimi cannot be documented, but it is on record that a scoundrelly 'Baron' Wiedau, whom Casanova had met in Holland, now arrived in Cologne and charged him with uttering forged bills of exchange. Casanova was arrested, tried, and acquitted, whereupon Wiedau sued the city of Cologne. It is hard to imagine why Casanova omitted so juicy a story, particularly when it was creditable to him.

It is also on record that General Kettler distrusted Casanova so much that he sent a long secret letter to the Duc de Choiseul, the new Foreign Minister of France, warning him that this man was a dangerous spy. Choiseul seemed very unalarmed, and took no action, which has strengthened scholars in the belief that Casanova was a French citizen, and that if he was indeed acting as a spy at this time, it was for Choiseul.

Casanova moved on to Stuttgart where the Grand Duke of Württemberg kept high state, paid for by the money he received for allowing France to quarter an army on his soil. The city was full of old friends: La Binetti, a dancer he had known in Venice, now mistress of the Austrian ambassador; La Vulcani, an actress he had slept with in Dresden, now wife of Balletti *le Cadet*, younger brother of his friend and elder brother of Manon; La Gardela, daughter of a pimping Venetian gondolier and now titular mistress of the Grand Duke himself; La Toscani, to whom he had made love only the day before in Coblenz on his way there; and her little daughter, whom she was bringing along to sell to the Grand Duke as a virgin. Everything looked bright and clean and wonderful.

It was in fact a bad scene. He insulted the Grand Duke on the day of his arrival, and the Duke's mistress a few moments later. Then, when leaving La Binetti's house, he was courteously picked up by three military officers and invited to a debauch. The ensuing tale of complaisant ladies, drugged wine, and gambling for huge amounts 'on note of hand alone', is laughably familiar to us; to Casanova too, but he was under one of those spells which made him step into trouble, even though he recognized it.

When he escaped to his inn, the Bear, he owed 100,000 francs. He possessed this amount, but decided he would not pay. His efforts to escape payment are a fascinating study in the *mores* of the time. He did not go to the police but to the Austrian ambassador, La Binetti's lover, who told him to lay the matter directly before the Grand Duke. But the Grand Duke Charles II Eugene, whom history knows as a first-class cad, had been got at already; or perhaps had told some of his officers to organize the whole affair to teach a lesson to the loud-talking Venetian who snubbed him in his own theatre. Casanova did manage to present his petition, but it was disregarded. The officers pressed for payment. Casanova was placed under arrest in his inn, and a sentry put over him.

He determined to escape. His theatrical friends took his valuable clothes and jewels away under their cloaks every time they visited him. To gain time for his arrangements he told the officers that he was willing to come to terms with them, but naturally they must all three be present at the agreement. As they were in military service it might be some days before all were available at the same time.

Casanova's faithful Spanish servant Leduc arranged for a carriage to meet him outside the city walls, and on 2 April 1760, his thirty-fifth birthday, Casanova slipped out of his room while the sentry was not looking. In his bed he left a dummy head, wearing a night-cap. Later Leduc came, spent some time in the room and then left, telling the sentry that Casanova had gone to sleep. The sentry, as was his custom, locked the room door and went away. Meanwhile Casanova had reached the Ballettis' house. They lowered him down the city wall on a rope, and after struggling across a heavily ploughed field he found the carriage waiting. Three hours later he was safe at Fürstenburg, in the Margraviate of Baden.

Next morning he fired a salvo of furious letters back into Württemberg, the most offensive being addressed to the Grand Duke. Some days later Leduc turned up with all his belongings. Three hours after that he was on his way once more, through Schaffhausen, and so to Zürich, where for the first time he used the self-given name by which he was usually known for the rest of his life – de Seingalt.

The adrenalin which had coursed in a heady, frothing flood through the whole Stuttgart episode now died away to a trickle, and finally disappeared. He had faced murderous ruffians, escaped from sentries, slid down walls, galloped by night through sleeping towns, uttered death and defiance to the loathsome Grand Duke, toyed with La Toscani's young daughter even in the act of reading the fearful summons from the police ... and suddenly nothing mattered. For one of the three times in his recorded life he was without the one quality he had in superabundance: his demoniacal energy.

He lay in the inn thinking of the past, of what he had done and what had been done to him. He knew that all that had befallen was his own fault. He had just escaped from a trap garnished with bait which would always catch him – women and cards. He went to bed and dreamed:

I saw myself in tranquil solitude, surrounded by peace and plenty. I seemed to be master of all this beautiful countryside, where I enjoyed the freedom one seeks otherwise in vain. I was obviously dreaming, but even in my dreams I kept telling myself that these were not dreams. A sudden awakening at daybreak immediately contradicted me. I was so excited by this imaginary happiness, that I was determined to realize it. I got up, dressed quickly, and went out on an empty stomach, not knowing where I was going.

There is here a remarkable subtlety of phrasing. Although he specifically states that up to a certain point he was dreaming, after that point he was not, yet the reader is cajoled into ignoring the act of awakening. The dreamlike story continues dreamlike.

After some hours his wandering feet brought him to the Benedictine monastery of Our Lady of Einsiedeln, founded in 934. Since 1274 the Abbot of Einsiedeln had been *ex officio* a prince of the Holy Roman Empire, and also had a dispensation allowing him to eat meat on Friday. This Abbot, Nicholas II Imfeld, was delighted to meet another man with the same dispensation (Casanova had asked it of Pope Benedict XIV, the first time he kissed the Fisherman's Ring), and they passed an agreeable, civilized time together.

The life of the monastery enchanted Casanova in his weary state, and I am not surprised, for the Einsiedeln he saw is the one that still stands. It is enormous – a gorgeous splendour of baroque, the interior of the great church shimmering in white and gold, the monks' chanting like the murmur of eternity from high dim galleries beyond the altar.

> Fade far away, dissolve, and quite forget
> What thou among the leaves hast never known,
> The weariness, the fever, and the fret
> Here, where men sit and hear each other groan;

And did his heart ache and a drowsy numbness overcome his senses? I think so . . . Let the world look after him for a change. Here he would be allowed to eat what he liked, read what he liked (the second dispensation he had asked from Benedict XIV), and in this luxurious peace live another of those lives for which he was suited – the life of a scholar. He saw the rich and the learned and the well-born (particularly the well-born) beating a path to Einsiedeln. He could hear the whispers in the salons of Paris and Dresden: *Have you visited Father Giacomo at Einsiedeln? . . . a marvellous intellect . . . his 'Reflections on the Cosmic Fallacy' is quite the most brilliant thing published this century . . .* Since this was a Benedictine establishment there would be epicurean feasts; titled ladies would beg to be shown his private library, alone ... *just five minutes will do, they say, and by God it always does, even though he's a hundred and seven now* ...

Casanova applied for admission to Einsiedeln as a monk. Abbot Nicholas told him he would give him his answer in a fortnight. Casanova returned to his hotel in Zürich ... where four ladies were just getting out of a post-chaise. One of them was very pretty. Casanova stopped as though he had been shot. He had been without women for perhaps four days, a drought he had not known since his tenth year, except in prison. The endocrine juices flowed again, he straightened his back, he squared his shoulders, he puffed out his chest, and fixed the pigeon with a look calculated to set her in crouched readiness on the spot. The Abbot-Prince of Einsiedeln was never to number Casanova among his monks.

The lady of the post-chaise was Marie Anne Louise, Baroness de Roll von Emmenholtz. Ludovika was her pet name, and she was young and recently married to a much older man. An intrigue began, but in order to gain access to her Casanova had to pay perfunctory court to her lame friend, a woman of about forty-five. As the affair progressed the Lame Lady became jealous and, in Casanova's eye, the possessor of all the horrible attributes he could think of, from bad teeth and sagging breasts to falling hair, dandruff and halitosis. Casanova took a house in the country. The Lame Lady invited herself for a visit of several days, and settled in, over Casanova's furious insults. Ludovika and her husband came to stay. Since her husband never made love to her two nights running, she cajoled him into the act on a certain day, so that Casanova could have her the next day. She would be waiting for him at one o'clock in the morning. Casanova crept along at the promised hour. She was there in an anteroom, in the pitch dark, hushing him to silence. They fell upon the sofa. . . . what transports! How many times was not the combat renewed, kisses showered on beauteous breasts, not to mention other charms. And so back, exhausted and happy, to bed.

In the morning there was a note from the Lame Lady, who had left the house in a hurry. She thanked Casanova for his efforts of the night before, she said. He was quite a man! Now perhaps he wouldn't be so nasty about her physical attributes, since he had mistaken them for those of his beloved Ludovika. And if he should happen to notice a little sore in a certain part, well, she'd had that trouble for ten years and she was afraid it was catching. And she certainly wished she could be present when he explained it all to his lady-love ...

The guile of the sensible housekeeper, Mme Dubois, rescued him

98

from the worst of the difficulties, and then naturally she got into his bed, which was more than Mme de Roll ever would. (She lived till 1825, and is therefore one of the very few people who could have read of themselves in Casanova's *Story* first published in 1822.)

He set off again. Mme Dubois was succeeded, or accompanied, by some strapping lesbian bath-house attendants; Sara Muralt-Favre, a thirteen-year-old; and three nymphs on whom he performed for the pleasure of an old voyeur. In his rôle as Eminent Philosopher he visited the famous Dr Albrecht von Haller, a Swiss botanist, poet, and metaphysician. There is documentary evidence of this; but none of his other contention, that on several occasions he held brilliant discourses with Voltaire. Voltaire only mentions a visit by 'ce Ca . . .', with no further details.

These events took place in Berne and Geneva, where Casanova went after saying a last goodbye to Mme Dubois. Dissolved in tears, he took a room in an inn and went up at once. Looking sadly out of the window he noticed some words scratched in the glass: *Tu oublieras aussi Henriette*. His hair stood on end. He began to tremble uncontrollably. Where were the years? Where was Henriette, whom he *had* forgotten?

It was a beautiful curtain, the best of his whole career.

He shook off the *frisson*. On to Aix-les-Bains, and the usual army of whores, pimps, and card-sharpers. But there was something special, too: a nun, eight months and twenty-eight days pregnant. As she passed she raised her veil and Casanova lost his senses; she was of the same Order, she wore the same habit, she had the same appearance . . . as M.M.!

It was not M.M., but another girl who looked just like her, indeed had the same initials and an equally catholic libido, but apparently very little judgement. She had allowed a fifty-four-year-old hunchback dwarf to shin over the wall of her convent in Chambéry, and impregnate her in the garden. Finding herself *enceinte* she got permission to take the waters at Aix 'for her health'.

Casanova took charge of the arrangements. The baby was born and disposed of, and they settled down to sex. The first intercourse took place three days after the birth of M.M.2's child. All good things must come to an end, and too soon M.M.2 had to return to her convent. By then Casanova had come to love her with all his heart and soul. She was beautiful, accomplished, passionate, beyond compare the most wonderful woman in the world (and, in my opinion, quite imaginary). Dissolved in sorrow he cut off a lock of her pubic hair, and, standing beside the road with the fur piece pressed over his heart, watched as she passed, head bent, her glorious face hidden under the cowl. She walked on and away, down the road, out of his life, into the sunset . . .

On to Grenoble, where his cabala advised a Mlle Roman-Coupier to go to Paris and become the king's mistress, and his libido advised him to try the doorkeeper's two daughters and niece. All projects went according to plan.

Avignon, and two Italian actresses, one of them cursed with two disfiguring humps and an excitingly misplaced vulva. Marseille; the great seaport induced a strong attack of homesickness for Venice, but a girl called Rosalie and the re-enactment of a favourite dream helped assuage it. The dream − for all its folly, an endearing one − was Pygmalion's. Rosalie was not the first Galatea he had tried to sculpt into a lady. He had never succeeded before, but that did not discourage him. He set about buying her clothes and teaching her the ways of society; and he quickly removed her from Marseille so that her past (whatever it was) and her humble background would not handicap her.

And so to Genoa; but soon, goodbye to Rosalie, hullo to Veronica and Anna Maria. To Florence . . . he was not going anywhere he had not already been, now. It was a treadmill: the same places, the same faces. For here was Bellino/Teresa, now Signora Calori, just married to a younger man. After brief lovemaking for old time's sake, she directed his lust toward a lesser actress of the company, La Corticelli. She was a chit from Bologna, which apparently occupied the same position, in then-current Italian folklore, as Wigan in England or Hohokus in the USA today; the inhabitants didn't have to *act* funny, they *were* funny. Casanova says she was fifteen, but actually she was twenty-three. She was a little tramp, and Casanova recognized it at the time, but he was fated, he says, 'to fall in love with her skin'. Besides, she made him laugh. Few people or events had the power to do that for him nowadays. At her request he had the theatre manager beaten up, for allegedly going back on some promise he had made to her.

He now began to develop the strange fancy that 'the authorities' did not like him, whoever they were, wherever he was. It began here with the Auditor-Fiscal (state chief of police) summarily banishing him from Tuscany. He says it was because he refused to accept responsibility for a forged bank draft that had passed through his hands, but in truth he was being watched now, always. There are in existence several letters which the Auditor-Fiscal wrote about him to the judge of Pistoia at this time. The spies watched him because he kept disreputable company, but could only report that in himself he was a quiet, well-educated man who lived decently and paid his way – a tale which would have surprised some of his friends. It was the beating-up of the theatre manager which probably gave the police the opening they wanted to still their unease.

Casanova left Florence in a tearing rage and went looking for his youth. To Rome: a little girl in bed in the front hall of the Albergo di Londra; another called Mariuccia; and a call on the new Venetian Pope, Carlo Rezzonico (Clement XIII), to beg him to use his influence to have Casanova allowed back into Venice. No success there, so on to Naples, and the impotent Duke of Maddaloni, whose duchess could explain better than he how he had a son.

The Duke also had a mistress called Leonilda, and was at pains to show that his relations with her were quite platonic: he examined some pornographic designs in company with Casanova and the girl, and then exhibited his pendant instrument. By a rare chance Casanova was in the same state at the moment, but Maddaloni would not believe him, checked the matter with his ducal hand, and found that Casanova had told the truth. But now Casanova urged the girl to give him her hand, and to look into his eyes and nowhere else. Passionately kissing her hand and gazing into her eyes, under continuous excitation from Maddaloni, Casanova rapidly rose to the occasion and beyond, liberally besprinkling the ducal and definitely homosexual hand. The sweet young girl saw, or at least pretended to see, nothing, and Casanova who was no fool where the ladies were concerned, guessed that he could make further progress with her if he played his cards right. Unfortunately, on this occasion he really seems to have fallen in love, and instead of getting the girl into bed he wandered about like a moonstruck calf, thinking of marriage.

Finally, he asked for her hand, and she agreed. Her widowed mother was sent for hot-foot to oversee the transfer of her person from the impotent duke to the potent adventurer. The mother appeared, veiled. She lifted her veil . . . Casanova fell back, dumb with astonishment. It was Lucrezia, whom he had first fondled in 1744 in Marino to the sound of drums, shots and collapsing beds; and then covered a hundred times in Rome.

She took him aside and told him all. Their love affair took place seventeen years ago, when her husband had already given up performing the marital rites with her. He knew of her adultery with Casanova, and on that account had the baby christened Leonilda Giacomina. Leonilda was now sixteen and a few months.

Casanova's bride-to-be was his own daughter. The wretched man's grief knew no bounds. To lose his loved one on the very verge of a long–delayed and throbbingly awaited consummation . . . It was too much! Even after passing the night with Lucrezia, in a thousand embraces (perhaps the sexiest night he ever spent, he recalls), he could not really console himself. He had to give up all idea of marrying Leonilda, of course, and it was with some difficulty that he could even find it in himself to make love to her; but with Lucrezia's encouragement, he did manage that.

Everyone urged him to stay in Naples. His luck had always been good there and his genius obviously suited the local moral climate. Lucrezia said she would live with him, with or without a marriage tie, if he would stay. But what respectable fame could a man earn in *Naples*? Sadly, he left, northbound.

To Rome again, and a debauch organized by James O'Bryan, Earl of Lismore, an extremely wild young Irishman. The debauch has the same dreamlike quality of much that happens in this period, and contains several of Casanova's favourite voyeuristic spectacles, also some of those homosexual practices which he despised but never failed to observe and record. Casanova describes the company:

There were seven or eight girls, all very attractive, three or four *castrati* who played women's rôles in the Roman theatres, five or six abbés, husbands of any wife and wives of any husband, who boasted of their perversion and dared the girls to be more brazen than they were. In fact the girls were not common prostitutes but were well versed in music, painting and the art of lust. You can guess the kind of company when I say that in the middle of them I felt a complete novice.

After various coupling demonstrations and a sexual recognition test, Lismore began some simple exercises in elementary buggery, forcing his attentions on everyone present, especially a smallish French poet, Poinsinet de Noirville. When Casanova mentions this man he appends the Homeric strophe, *drowned in the Guadalquivir five years later*; but at this moment the poet's peril was not drowning but pederasty, and he barely escaped with his rectum intact. After a dinner at which twenty-four people drank a hundred bottles of wine, the jollity surpassed all bounds, culminating in Lismore's offer of his valuable watch to the first person present who should cause himself or Poinsinet to ejaculate in public. All present, except Casanova, set to with a will. Casanova noticed that only the abbés tried *fellatio*; none of the girls used that method, for fear, they said, of being thought to be lesbian in their private tastes, but really for fear that their ministrations might fail. The miseries of little Poinsinet (*drowned in the Guadalquivir five years later*), standing shivering without his breeches in the reeking hall, were compounded by the Earl's solemn promise that if he caused him to lose this watch he would personally sodomize him on the spot, before the lecherous multitude.

It disturbed Casanova to think that if Lismore had attacked him with his ready organ, he had nothing to defend himself except his sword, and what would that have availed him against so many? He left the orgy in pensive mood, determined to avoid such profligate companions for the future . . . especially as he was now a Knight of the Golden Spur and an Apostolic Protonotary *extra urbem*. The Order, created by Pius IV in 1559, had fallen into disregard. Where once the Pope awarded it to the Catholic great, now a host of Eminences presented it to their pimps. Pope Clement bestowed the order on Casanova in lieu of making any effort to arrange his return to Venice. Casanova would have preferred Venice, but . . . well, there it was, a handsome cross and an imposing ribbon. Better yet, when the insignia arrived he was staying with Rafael Mengs, so the famous painter witnessed his ennoblement; and could reflect that he, Mengs, had had to pay ten pounds for *his* Golden Spur. Casanova lost no time in asking another friend, Winckelmann the archaeologist, where he could get his cross set with diamonds and rubies. He knew better than to show off the bauble in Rome, where its worth was exactly known, but it would be a different matter in the outback.

So it was a proud peacock, the Chevalier de Seingalt, Knight of the Golden Spur, wearing his ignoble star, illegally embellished and improperly mounted on an incorrect ribbon, who arrived once more in Florence. The Auditor-Fiscal saw through the disguise, and ordered Casanova to report to his office first thing next morning. Pausing only to abduct La Corticelli, he went straight on to Modena.

The Chief of Police ordered him out of Modena . . .

He went to Turin, and was soon invited to attend on the Deputy Superintendent of Police, a man of sixty, who covered half his nose with black cloth to hide a malignant ulcer. This official ordered him out of Turin. His Masonic connections manoeuvred him back in, but his supposed business in Turin – a vague hint that he would represent the King of Portugal at a political conference (which no one believed would ever take place) was now patently a chimera, and he moved on, dreaming, gambling . . .

To Chambéry, in France, where he called on that broadminded convent which sheltered the broadminded nun, M.M.2, recently a mother, of whose pubic fleece Casanova still held a specimen next to his heart, unless he had mislaid it somewhere. M.M.2 was as desirable at ever, but she no longer needed Casanova. She was quite happy with a twelve-year-old novice who gave her a lot of pleasure, and peace of mind, too. This novice, when M.M.2 brought her down turned out to be a female Napoleon of sex. A low wall and a barred grill separated the nuns from the visitors. The little one soon told Casanova not to waste time standing there, where the height of the sill of the grating above the floor made their mutual lust in vain, but to hoist himself and kneel on the sill, holding to the bars; whereupon she expertly used her lips and mouth to 'suck the quintessence' of his heart and soul. French novices, unlike Roman whores, were apparently quite shameless about their sexual tastes.

But what he was seeking was not in Chambéry. On to Paris.

9

Gambler's Hazards

After visiting Mme d'Urfé, he began at once the fretful round that was the undercurrent of this whole period. Where were his friends? Where were the youth and beauty and wealth he knew before? Where, in a word, were his own strong, good times?

They were not here. His friend Balletti was going to Vienna, for good; the Cadet to Stuttgart, where he later taught dancing to the infant Schiller; de Bernis, gone; Silvia dead; the Duchess of Chartres dead of debauchery at thirty-three ... His brother Francesco was here, having learned to paint better battles, though a nasty critic pointed out that his horses were always in the rearing position, like the dummy in his studio, and that clouds of billowing cannon smoke always hid details which Francesco was too inexpert or too lazy to paint. But Francesco was still in debt, and still impotent (this was the same brother who was the only member of the gang not to enjoy the weaver's wife during that wild prank in Venice fifteen years back). His poor wife had been doubly deceived because he was a splendid, powerful physical specimen, and Giacomo had a hard time restraining himself from showing her that all Casanova males were not like her husband.

The company Casanova kept became increasingly brutal and brutish. Someone stole his ring and Casanova ran him through with his sword, left him for dead, and had to get out of Paris. He headed for Augsburg, on business for Mme d'Urfé, but since he had to go in such a hurry he left one of his servants, Costa, to bring on jewels and gifts with which Madame was supplying him for his negotiations on her behalf with the Inner Ones. In Strasbourg his other servant Leduc awaited him, also a dancer called La Renaud, and together they went on to Augsburg, and from there to Munich.

Here once more, and for perhaps the worst time, the roof fell in on him. He gambled heavily, and lost heavily. La Renaud possessed herself of his clothes and jewels and in return gave him a severe case of the venereal disease which had been ravaging her for years. Costa did not turn up from Paris and it became clear that he never would. He had decamped with all Mme d'Urfé's presents. To cap all, the nightmare of his life came true: he saw the waning of his strength. As is so often the case, and so appallingly true to life, Casanova's weakness did not come where he had expected it. Ever since his youth he had dreaded the approach of sexual impotence, the inability to move erect and desirous upon any and all women. What befell him now in Munich was flaccidity of the will. He knew La Renaud was cheating him, he knew he must get treated for the disease, he knew he must stop gambling, he knew he must *go*. But for three long months he did nothing.

Then at last he gathered together the remnants of his will-power and broke free. He fled Munich and returned to Augsburg determined to be cured of his disease or die in the attempt.

At that time, it was even money as to which came to pass. Doctors could not distinguish between the three diseases now officially labelled 'venereal' – syphilis, gonorrhoea, soft chancre – until towards the end of the century when Benjamin Bell published the results of his experiments on medical students; and forty more years passed before the individuality of the diseases was generally accepted.

In fact gonorrhoea is a urethral inflammation caused by a bacterium, the *gonococcus*; syphilis is a severe general disease originating in the genitals and caused by another micro-organism, *treponema pallidum*; and soft chancre is an ulceration caused by a bacillus which thrives especially in uncleaned crotches. Each needs very different treatment but in Casanova's time the treatment the patient got was, like the outcome, a toss-up.

Syphilis could not be adequately cured until after Paul Ehrlich introduced salvarsan in 1910. Before that mercury was much used, with indifferent results and many severe side-effects, because the dose needed to cure was very close to the dose sufficient to poison. Most syphilis sufferers went through the first two stages of the disease: hard chancre (usually painless) on the genitals, glandular inflammation, rash etc. A proportion eventually developed symptoms of the tertiary stage, such as severe and disfiguring ulceration, of the skin, bones, and mucous membranes (gummata), eventually dying of aneurysms, arterial disease, locomotor ataxia, or general paralysis of the insane.

Gonorrhoea usually had to cure itself, but before it had done so it could spread to the testicles, producing painful inflammation, and might cause severe damage to the male urethra, resulting in urethral stricture. It could also cause a disabling arthritis and, if it spread to the fallopian tubes in the female, sterility.

Soft chancre, very rare nowadays, was common in the highly insanitary conditions of the age. It caused painful genital sores, severe inflammation of the lymph glands, and abscesses and ulceration in the groin.

Cleanliness, rest, a bland diet and a large intake of fluid would help gonorrhoea. When combined with local dressings such a regimen would also help soft chancre. Most doctors, however, believing syphilis and gonorrhoea to be the same disease, favoured the use of mercury, sometimes by inhalation, sometimes by pill, often by inunction, that is, by mixing the mercury with a fatty base and rubbing the resultant paste into different parts of the body. Mercury did little to cure any venereal disease; it only caused ulceration in the patient's mouth so that his teeth dropped out, it 'rotted the guts', and it had a disastrously toxic effect on the kidneys, resulting in the patient's passing blood in his urine.

These appalling conditions, enough to frighten a modern man into total sexual incapacity, have to be seen against the general background. Venereal disease could kill you painfully, yes, but so could childbirth, dirty water, a cut finger, a broken bone, malaria, measles, tuberculosis, and innumerable other unrecognized and untreatable maladies. It was a brave man who toyed with the tarts in the eighteenth century – but he didn't know it.

The disease Casanova caught from La Renaud seems to have been aggravated soft chancre. Wasting away to nothing, suffering from two large inguinal tumors, he allowed his doctor, Salomon Kephalides, to operate on them. Kephalides did so – this was before anaesthetics, of course, and the pain Casanova endured is almost unimaginable – and broke into the wall of an artery, causing a dangerous haemorrhage. Casanova's life was saved by another doctor, Francesco Algardi of Bologna, physician to the Prince-Bishop of Augsburg.

Now he learned that Leduc, his faithful young Spanish servant, had robbed him too. He was too low-spirited to act. He could only suffer, and try to struggle free of the mishaps, follies and evils threatening to strangle him.

Dr Algardi's regimen consisted of a mild laxative pill taken morning and evening, a glass of milk and water, and a bowl of barley soup. This stark diet cured Casanova in two and a half months, but left him ravenous. He set to work to rebuild himself. All his appetites had always been enormous but now he ate so that his cook Annamirl and Gertrude, the landlady's pretty daughter, feared disaster. He reassured them by making love to both of them together. Being well on the mend, he took over a bankrupt theatrical company, mainly because it included at least one pretty girl. There was an orgy, and this was a good one, as though he had sworn to outdo Milord Lismore. A simple party turned into a fornicatory free-for-all, the room full of naked drunken nymphs and satyrs, fondling, romping, singing, thrusting. Only the pretty girl's fiancé did not join in, but sat staring into the fire, his head in his hands, his back to the revelry. Nothing that anyone could say would cheer him up. There's always one wet blanket.

But Casanova had for the time being reached the end of his nerve. He did not want to gamble. He did not want to go on the hunt, bold for prey, whether the purse was lined with dry gold or wet silk. He wanted a sure thing, a chance to use his charm, not his nerve: something simple and easy . . . like, for example, turning old Mme d'Urfé into a young man. He set out for Paris. He spent three weeks there, in the rooms she had reserved for him in the Rue du Bac, not making the scene in any way, as he wanted her to believe that he had come to Paris only to start the divine work. However, the preparations for Mme d'Urfé's rebirth make so complicated a tale that I will not tell it here, but complete, in itself, in the next chapter. It is necessary to know now only that she once again provided Casanova with ample means, and that he once again set off eastward, this time to meet an angel without whose participation the magical ceremonies could not begin.

For this rôle Casanova chose La Corticelli: inexplicably, because her characteristics were not those of an angel, but of a sexy Bolognese *gamine.* She met him at Metz, as ordered, but spoiled the act by her behaviour, and he had to get rid of her, telling Mme d'Urfé that she was a bad angel, and another was on the way. Meanwhile, on to Aachen. Here Casanova fell into bad company, as he says; and one is permitted to wonder what *they* fell into. More gambling, more women, more violence, and on to Sulzbach, joined now by Mme d'Urfé. Here there was a pretty Mme Saxe and her extremely jealous lover, M. d'Entraigues du Pin. Casanova didn't like jealous lovers at any time, and especially not when they were also stingy card players. This d'Entraigues would beg him to play at piquet and then get up as soon as he had won a few louis. Casanova finally refused to play with him. D'Entraigues protested and Casanova goaded him into agreeing to play with side stakes of £50 each, which were to be forfeited by the first man to leave the gaming table.

Giacomo Casanova and Pierre Louis d'Entraigues du Pin, adventurers both, sat down at this rather obscure spa – frequented at that time of year only by a few professional gamblers and light ladies – at three in the afternoon. The game was piquet, at five pounds the game. At nine p.m. d'Entraigues suggested they break off for supper. Casanova refused. Everyone else went off to eat, came back to watch the marathon, and about midnight trailed off to bed.

At six the next morning (hours are early in a hydro) people began coming down again, to find the two men still sitting, in their silks and satins, at the green baize table. Mme d'Urfé and Mme Saxe persuaded them to have some chocolate at the table, and they agreed that either could absent himself for up to a quarter of an hour, presumably to relieve himself, but must not take or ask for food.

The game continued. At noon the spectators went to dinner, the players played on. At four p.m. of the second day, having played for twenty-five hours, they took some soup. Casanova felt fresh, his opponent 'resembled a disinterred corpse'. Mme Saxe begged Casanova to give up, saying he had made his point, but Casanova meant to frighten the wits out of d'Entraigues; and he would also have been very much aware that the great piquet duel would soon become talked about all over Europe, greatly enhancing his reputation . . . if he won. Trusting to his iron constitution he played on, aided by superb gamesmanship from Mme d'Urfé. The divine madwoman, who naturally believed that Paralis Blacksnout was invincible when he chose to be, kept murmuring to d'Entraigues with obvious sincerity, 'O Lord, I pity you, sir!'

They played all through the second night, unwatched now. D'Entraigues grew distraught, played the wrong cards. Casanova picked a quarrel with him for no reason. The man came near his last gasp. Casanova, who up to this point had not noticed whether he was winning or losing the actual game, now saw that he recouped all his earlier losses and was beginning to win.

At nine o'clock in the morning the ladies came down again, and again Mme Saxe begged the men to split the stakes and call it quits. Casanova fixed her with the last remains of his lust and said he'd do anything, even that, to please *her*. Stung, d'Entraigues swore he'd go on till he dropped; which after taking a dish of soup, he at once did, keeling over unconscious on the spot. Casanova took an emetic, slept a few hours, and was down at three p.m. for a large dinner. D'Entraigues did not show up till the following day. They had played for forty-two hours.

Bâle, Geneva . . . fresh game: a girl called Hélène, and her cousin

Hedwige. Hedwige was a blond bluestocking. No one could confound her in philosophical or theological discussion, though she was only twenty-three. She was big-busted and pretty too, and Casanova suspected that like most bluestockings she was dying to exchange her toga for a frilly nightie. Hélène was a brunette, and much less complicated. Casanova decided that the education of these two must be carried out simultaneously, since 'if one girl permits the smallest favour, to spare her blushes her friend is obliged to agree to a much bigger one'.

He describes the twin seduction:

In a flash, while philosophizing about shame with theological wisdom, I presented myself to them as naked as Adam. Hedwige, blushing, perhaps fearing she might lose favour in my eyes by wasting time, dropped the last veil of her modesty, while quoting St Clement of Alexandria, who said that shame was rooted in the shirt. I extravagantly praised her beautiful figure with the aim of encouraging Hélène, who was undressing slowly; but when her cousin reproached her for her sham modesty, this had more effect than all the praise I heaped upon her. At last this Venus was naked before me, covering one of her most secret charms with one hand and a breast with the other, and painfully aware of everything she was unable to hide. Her embarrassed confusion, this struggle between dying modesty and heightened sexuality, delighted me . . . Little by little she became bolder and we spent some time admiring one another, and then we went to bed. Nature spoke out imperiously to us and we had to satisfy its demands. Wearing a protective sheath which I had no fear would burst, I elevated Hedwige to the rank of woman, and when the sacrifice was over, she told me, covering me with kisses, that the moment of pain was nothing in comparison with the pleasure.

Hélène, who was six years younger than Hedwige, now had her turn; but the most beautiful fleece I had ever seen offered some resistance. Jealous of her cousin's success, she opened it with her two hands, and even though she could only be initiated into the mysteries of love-making by enduring great pain, she only breathed sighs of happiness, responding to my efforts and almost outdoing me in tenderness and passion. Her charms and her participation cut short the sacrifice, and when I left the sanctuary my two beauties saw that I needed rest.

The altar was cleansed of the victims' blood, and we washed together, delighted to have served one another.

The whole episode, beginning in one of those ornamental gardens where Casanova found such elegant uses for gazebos, stone peacocks, ornamental urns and the like, and including more *tableaux vivants*, after Aretino, sparkles with a singular light, dry voluptuousness, like a Roederer *cristal* of a good year.

But he had to move on, of course; Turin (a dancer called Agatha, and her mother); Pavia (another dancer); Milan ... dear me, in Milan it seems to add up to six ladies. None of them are important, but one of the affairs well illustrates the atmosphere in which Casanova breathed and lived.

Trying to make love to the Countess Attendolo-Bolognini (the Count had sold him the right, for an expensive gown), Casanova failed because he had just been playing with one Zenobia, who was not a wasteful girl: and because he was now thirty-eight. So he did not come up to the Countess's reasonable expectations. After vain striving the Great Stallion of Europe had to admit defeat, furl his flaccid guidon, and slink out with his tail, in the curiously apt expression, between his legs. He expected Spanish tantrums from the Countess (née Teresa Suazo y Ovalla Zamorra), but nothing happened, except a laughable incident when she gave him sneezing powder by mistake, and both their noses started to bleed and she quickly got a basin and they put their heads together over it, so that his blood and her blood fell together into the basin ... drip ... drip ... drip.

He stopped laughing, suddenly, when a Capuchin monk warned him under the secrecy of the confessional that his life was in danger. To save himself he must go to a certain house, find a certain old woman, and demand of her 'the bottle and everything that depends on it', using money to grease her palm.

Casanova followed the monk's orders, got the bottle and learned that it contained his own blood mixed with the Countess's. 'Everything that depends on it' was a wax figure of himself, made with enormous sexual organs. The Countess had hired the old woman, a witch, to revenge herself on Casanova. The witch was making ready to bathe the wax figure in the mixed bloods and then throw it onto burning coals. What would have happened to the living Casanova was not stated, but it would certainly have been painful and perhaps fatal.

In the ending of this story Casanova again reveals the fascinating truth about himself. The Countess's plot should have brought forth a philosopher's condescending smile. Far from it. Just as he had terrified himself out of his own wits in the spell-casting near Cesena fourteen years earlier, so now, at the sight of the manikin adorned with the Golden Spur and the huge balls, he broke down in uncontrollable hysteria; and was not ashamed to say so, thirty years later.

As even more indicative of the times, note that the Christian monk explicitly believed the nonsense, too.

His second – perhaps his chief – pleasure in Milan was the organization of extravagant fêtes, dinners and masques, whose only purpose was to show the Chevalier de Seingalt as a big spender. The details bore the modern ear and eye, stirring only a vague astonishment that so many adult people should be willing to spend so much time and money on such childish amusements. This emphasizes how the world has grown up since Casanova's time, not in wisdom, but in the ordinary meaning of sophistication. The élite of Casanova's day were like the peasants of Spanish or Italian hill towns in, say, 1900 (before radio became general, at least) – that is, hardheaded in what they knew, gullible in what they did not, easily taken out of themselves by magic, buffoonery, the crudest of fiestas. It is through such eyes, the eyes of a shrewd child, that Casanova's ostentation, and his cabalism, are to be seen.

Such were his pleasures. His business, his passion, his mania, was gambling. He lost £40 one night, £500 the next, £700 more a few nights later – all at faro. He recouped a little by going into partnership with a man he knew to be a 'Greek', that is, a card-sharper. Still he lost. He had the true gambler's superstition, and next time went to the faro table masked and dressed in such a manner that no one could recognize him. In his own mind he had in fact *become* this new person, leaving his ill luck with the other fellow, the man the world knew as Seingalt. Armed with a hundred Spanish gold pieces (about 1,500 dollars or £650), he began again. In under an hour he had lost it all. He got up. The crowd expected to see him leave, but instead he opened another purse, took out 300 Venetian sequins (about 700 dollars or £280) and began once more. He put a hundred of his sequins on a card, going *paroli*, *sept et le va*. He won, and went on playing all night. As dawn broke, so did the bank. Casanova had won 34 lbs weight of gold, to the value of 2,856 sequins or £2,700. A few days later he won again, 2,500 sequins this time.

Yet, overall, he lost more than he won during this stay in Milan. In addition the fantastic expenses of his way of life were bankrupting him. Mme d'Urfé awaited him at Marseille. It was obviously high time to connect up his purse once more to the inexhaustible reservoir of her gullibility and wealth.

He set off on 20 March 1763, taking with him a girl, Crosin, whom he had found abandoned in Milan by that Antonio della Croce, crook, pimp and pederast, to whose daughter he was a rather undutiful godfather. In Genoa he picked up the man he had chosen as his chief assistant in the rebirth of Mme d'Urfé, a third-rate pornographer and poetaster variously called Aspagona, Pogomas, and Passano. Then just as he was again on his splendid way, a strange and unwelcome reminder of his background intruded on his plans. A dirty, slovenly monk arrived, declaring himself to be Casanova's youngest brother, Gaetano. Casanova never liked any of his family very much, but this posthumous Gaetano he positively detested. And here he was, broke, snivelling, and with a girl who had run away from home for him; rather, for his fine talk of marriage, and the money they would get from his rich brother Giacomo. Giacomo's fury was tempered by the observation that the girl, Marcoline, was a real, fiery Venetian beauty. His brain raced. He had to go on to Marseille; but why not take the girl with him? And if absolutely necessary, the impossible brother too? No sooner said than done, and the little group continued its journey by sea – Casanova, Crosin, Marcoline, Gaetano and Passano.

They went ashore at Mentone where the girls fell into bed to recover from seasickness, while Casanova paid a call on the Prince of Monaco, whose territory it was then. The Prince, whom Casanova had known well in Paris, sent him to introduce himself to the Princess. She was playing the clavichord in another room. While they exchanged stilted platitudes, the Prince raced through in hot pursuit of a servant-girl. The Princess frigidly ignored the incident. Casanova left in disgust. The Prince of Monaco had a miserable palace and miserable manners, he commented.

On to Marseille, enjoying Crosin and Marcoline simultaneously, while the two young ladies also enjoyed each other, for Marcoline was as strongly lesbian as his M.M.s 1 and 2 from earlier days. At Marseille, after a period of necromancy with Mme d'Urfé, on to Lyon, because the rites had to be repeated in another place. Near Aix-en-Provence the carriage in which he and Marcoline were travelling broke down and they had to spend the night as guests at a large house set back from the road. Casanova never saw the face of the lady of the house, for out of doors it was hidden in a great cloak and cowl against the blustery wind; and then she sprained her ankle and went to bed. The party all went to her bedroom to eat and chat, as the custom was, but the thick curtains baulked Casanova's natural curiosity, which became more urgent when he noticed that Marcoline and the half-hidden hostess were fondling each other in unmistakable love-play. He was therefore rather put out, but not surprised, when Marcoline told him that she had been invited to share the hostess's bed for the night (the lady was a widow) while he was to sleep elsewhere, alone and uncomforted.

He was not a man jealous of lesbianism. Apart from the mental pleasure to be had from seeing or thinking of two tumescent females instead of one, it almost invariably meant that he enjoyed both women later. The next morning Marcoline's satisfied expression showed that she had passed a good night in the exercise of her Venetian skills. The only women as strongly and indiscriminately passionate as the Venetian, Casanova notes sagely, are those of Provence.

This voluptuous hostess, a Provençale, gave Marcoline a note for her to give to Casanova at the next stage – not before. The note read: 'To the nicest man I have ever met – Henriette.' Casanova fell back thunderstruck. Henriette! He must go back, find her, beg her to marry him . . . But of course he didn't. He went on to Lyon.

The business with Mme d'Urfé continued its shady course behind drawn curtains. Front and centre in Casanova's bright memory was his disposal of the wonderful Marcoline. George III had ascended the throne of England some years earlier, but the Most Serene Republic liked to be sure of its facts and had only recently sent ambassadors to offer the new king its congratulations. These men were now on their way back to Venice. One of them was Francesco II Lorenzo Morosini, the same Procurator Morosini who was Casanova's irritated protector most of his life. Another was Tommaso Querini, whose valet was Marcoline's uncle. Going along with the mission at his own expense, for practice and fun, was Andrea Memmo, Casanova's long-time playmate and the father of Miss X.C.V.'s baby. All this being so, it was child's play to arrange for Querini to become Marcoline's guardian, take her back to Venice, and undertake to find her a suitable husband.

But Marcoline asked him sadly why he wanted to get rid of her. She didn't want to go. He had rescued her from his unspeakable brother; he had taught her love; he had (she must have implied) provided her with an inexhaustible stream of girls for her Venetian passions; they had enjoyed each other, body and soul. So, why? Poor Casanova couldn't answer because he didn't know himself, except that he had to go on . . . He was also, as the next chapter will relate, near the end of Mme d'Urfé's gullibility, and the law was closing in on him.

They parted. Marcoline returned to Venice with the ambassadors – if she existed and if this encounter ever took place. There is doubt. The ambassadors actually reached Lyon on 11 July 1763 and left again on 14 July. But an extant letter from Casanova to a Venetian friend proves that he reached London on 14 June of that year. Therefore he could not have met the ambassadors in Lyon. As for Marcoline, she seems so much the mirror of his favourite imagined lusts that one doubts her reality. Yet, in my opinion, Marcoline was a fact, the meeting with the ambassadors a myth.

Casanova headed for London via Paris and a girl in black drawers. The ambassador Morosini, a notable skirt-lifter himself, had given him a letter to be given to a Mlle Charpillon if he saw her around. It was only to say he was sorry he had not been able to say goodbye to her. No, it was not important.

It was early June, 1763. Casanova had last left Paris in January 1762. Since then he had been to Metz, Nancy, Pontcarré, Brussels, Liège, Aachen, back to Liège again, through the Ardennes, Metz once more, Sulzbach, Bâle, Geneva, Lausanne, Turin, Geneva again, Chambéry, back to Turin, Pavia, Milan, Lodi, Genoa, Mentone, Antibes, Marseille, Avignon, Lyon . . . He had made love to at least twenty-three women, God knows how many times. He had won and lost at least 20,000 pounds sterling. He was ready for the richest and most profligate city in the world – London.

But before following him across the Channel let me relate the whole story of his dealings with the Marquise d'Urfé, which at this point in time came to an end.

IO

Miracles for Mme d'Urfé

To understand the lunatic logic of the affair of the rebirth of Mme d'Urfé, it is necessary to understand something of the lunatic logic of the cabala.

A fundamental belief behind the cabala, or keb-ali as Casanova sometimes called it, is a very ancient one – that some words, symbols, or ciphers are not merely representational of God; they *are* God. Cabalists believed that when they had written down one of these magical symbols, God became present in the letters or figures. The symbols (God) contained all knowledge, past, present and future. To learn what you wanted to know was only a matter of putting the question into God's (cipher) language and interpreting His (cipher) answers.

The usual method, the one used by Casanova, was to give each letter, first, an equivalent figure. Thus, a 21-letter French alphabet would be

a	b	c	d	e	f	g	h	ij	k	l	m	n	o	p	q	r
1	2	3	4	5	6	7	8	9	10	11	12	13	14	15	16	17

s	t	uv	x
18	19	20	21

Let us suppose that we are, like Casanova, working in French. An anxious lady asks him, 'Why has my husband gone to Marseille?'

Casanova writes it out in French, thus: *Pourquoi mon mari est-il allé à Marseille?* Then he writes down the number of letters in each word, thus:

8	3	4	3	2	4	1	9

Next, he writes out the question in the magical pyramidical form, using not the words but the figures he has just obtained, thus:

```
                8
            3       4
        3       2       4
    1       9
```

That is as far as the actual question went, but the cabalist needs more figures than this to work with. He needs a pyramid of six rows, so Casanova completes the pyramid as follows:

```
                8
            3       4
        3       2       4
      1       9       1       9
    1       5       6       2       5
 19     20      9       7       8       9
```

He produced the extra figures thus, doubtless gabbling out the formula at high speed: 'starting after the first 9 in the fourth row,' he chants, 'repeat the Mystic Line. Add the left outside diagonal, 15, 1 and 5 . . . Add these sacred figures together: 6 . . . Add the right outside diagonal, 25, 2 and 5 . . . Begin the Fatal Line by adding together the fifth 19, then the Mystic Fourth, 20, then the third, 9, and the second, 7, and the Holy Beginning, 8, then add these . . . 19 and 20 and 9 and 7 and 8, is 63; is 9.'

If Casanova had seen that figures he might need in extracting the answer were not readily available, he would have used a different patter, to get what he needed. (This particular pyramid was made up by the present writer.) He would also give himself more leeway by writing down at the side, say:

```
    O   S   A   D
    6   3   3   9
```

– the letters representing the initial letters of the four Prime Intelligences of the Overworld, and the figures the number of letters in the mystical name of each.

Here comes a divergence between charlatans like Casanova and deluded seekers who really believed in the cabala. The believer works according to a set pattern, and tries to make sense out of what he gets. His own researches and experiments might make him believe, for instance, that each figure pointed to the next. Thus, in my pyramid, the 8 at the beginning means, take the eighth figure from here, which is 1; then the third from the 3, which is 2; then the fourth from the 4, which is 1; and so on . . .

```
1    2    1    1    1    9    9    10    9    5
```

This, when transliterated, reads

a b a a a i i k e

. . . which may be clear in Polynesian, but not in French or English. So, back to the drawing-board, to devise a means of having God use the higher numbers . . . or select numbers on a ouija board; all this in deadly seriousness.

The charlatan, on the other hand, has already worked out the answer that the inquirer is to be given. To the question asked here, let us suppose it is to be:

I	L	V	I	S	I	T	E	U	N	E	B	O	N
9	11	20	9	18	9	19	5	20	13	5	2	14	13

N	E	A	M	I	E
13	5	1	12	9	5

(The figures are the numerical equivalents of each letter, as in the key on page 116: the message means, in English 'He is visiting a girl friend'.)

The cabalist, having worked out in his head ways to reach the figures he wants, now speaks fast, in a cloud of incense. It sounds as though he is using some divine formula, but actually he is ad-libbing to get already selected results, and remember that he is free to 'read' double figures any way that suits him; e.g. 18 can be seen as 1 and 8, or 9, or 7, or 18.

One of the innumerable ways in which he can read my pyramid in order to answer the question as he wished is:

Take the first and the third and subtract the second
8 plus 4 minus 3 gives . . .   9 = I
Add the first and the second
8 plus 3 gives . . .   11 = L
Add the first five together
8 plus 3 plus 4 plus 3 plus 2 gives . . .   20 = V

. . . etc., etc., with incursions into the sacred letters and figures as desired. It may look silly when read in cold print in a well-lit twentieth-century room; but given the superstitions of the age, a general belief in either holy miracles or unholy occultism, the surrounding mumbo-jumbo and the state of mind of the person inquiring . . . well, people were swallowing much more every day. Above all, the speed and skill of the cabalist had a shattering effect. Few women could read or write in those days, fewer still could do advanced arithmetic. When a woman saw Casanova form such a pyramid, or perhaps formed it herself on his instructions, and Casanova started spouting figures so fast that it seemed impossible any mortal man could have worked them out, and the transliterated figures made such sense, what could possibly be responsible except some magical power inside the cabala?

It was this cabala, worked in more or less the method described, which was Casanova's chief – but not his only – tool in the d'Urfé affair. At her earliest meeting with him she had regretted that she could never speak with the spirits, because she was a woman.

But, she added meaningly, there *was* a well-known process by which an adept in the mystical secrets of the Rosy Cross could arrange for a woman to be reborn into the body of a male child. The male child had to be one born of sexual connection between a human man and a semi-divine woman. To produce such a child and perform the rest of the tricky operation was surely not beyond Casanova's powers, she hinted. Indeed, as he had reached the highest levels of mystical knowledge, nothing was beyond him.

Yes, yes, of course, Casanova answered. Then, she implied, what is stopping you? Casanova could only sigh, and look out of the window for fifteen minutes, with his back to her. When he turned round she saw tears in his eyes. She was much moved. She thought that Casanova wept because he knew that the rebirth of the spirit necessarily meant the death of the present body. She, the Marquise d'Urfé, must die.

Casanova's tears were in fact tears of bafflement. The old lady was immensely rich. She had the total gullibility of the very shrewd. Cabalism and the Rosy Cross were not matters of opinion to her, but matters of fact. Given this attitude, which enshrined a determination to make a desired sense out of the responses of the cabala, Casanova was the answer to all her prayers.

And she to his. Her position and wealth would be of incalculable value. But the operation that she had set her heart on was a dangerous business. The subject's spirit was supposed to leave its present abode after taking an overdose of 'the poison which killed Paracelsus' (probably laudanum). Suppose she survived; then she'd know that she was still a woman, and that the operation had failed. At best, she would find another cabalist and dismiss Casanova as inexpert or an impostor. Suppose she really died: it would have to be very carefully handled indeed, to keep the police and relatives out, and to ensure that her money came to him.

So in these early stages (Paris, 1757–8) Casanova played for time.

He would do anything else that Mme d'Urfé wanted, and he promised to perform the Great Operation later, but it would take time. Male children born of immortals did not grow on bushes, *tu comprends, chère Madame. Patience!*

When Casanova went to Holland early in 1759, it will be remembered that he met Teresa Imer, now Pompeati, with two children, a girl called Sophie and a youth of twelve, Giuseppe. Casanova wanted to take Sophie away from the whorehouse squalor he found her in, but had to accept Giuseppe instead. A few days later Mme d'Urfé wrote that her genius had told her Casanova was bringing back to Paris the magic youth into whose body her spirit was to pass.

Thus Casanova's notoriously unreliable chronology. To my mind it is much more probable that the two events came in the opposite order. First, Mme d'Urfé told him about her 'dream', then he decided to make it come true, and bought the use of the boy from Teresa.

A little later he returned to Paris, taking Giuseppe Pompeati with him. From the beginning he cordially disliked the youth, whom he describes as a tightlipped little monster, always aware of the main chance, wilful, vicious, cold and cunning. Mme d'Urfé was naturally overjoyed to meet the youth whom she was to become. She insisted that Giuseppe live with her, while she arranged for him to go to school to learn French and good manners. His departure for school was somewhat hastened when the rash dame took him into her bed the first night at her house. Giuseppe, with his mother's example before him, could only think of one reason why a woman would want a youth in her bed, and acted accordingly. Casanova quickly warned Mme d'Urfé that all would be spoiled if she did not wait for the boy to attain full puberty. He was then packed off to M. Viard's school, with new clothes, a new station in society, and the new name he chose for himself – Count d'Aranda.

Casanova was not pleased. He had no moral reasons against a change of name, in itself; indeed he was about to start calling himself Seingalt: but the real Count de Aranda was Prime Minister and Chancellor of Spain, under the King. He was also the Grand Master of Spanish Freemasonry. Don Pedro Pablo Abarca de Bolea, Ximenez de Urréa, 10th Count de Aranda, First Class Grandee of Spain, was not likely to be overjoyed to learn that his name was being used by a whorish dancer's son, for some unknown but certainly vile purpose. Casanova reduced Giuseppe to tears, but the boy swore that he would run away if they made him renounce the title. It served him well in a boarding-school like this, he pointed out, and Casanova had to agree. He returned to Paris in a thoughtful mood. He had given

Madame something to play with, which would keep her busy for a time. But he saw dangers ahead, and the character of the Count d'Aranda was one of them.

He now got into the trouble that I have described over his silk-printing process, ending up in jail. Madame wanted to hire lawyers to fight his case, but he had other plans for her money, and settled with his opponents out of court; then he left France (September 1759). Here began the long and apparently aimless circumnavigation of Europe which started in Amsterdam with Esther Hope, continued through the Stuttgart flight, Mme de Role, M.M.2, Leonilda, Lucrezia, and countless others until it ended in Paris once more, in mid-summer of 1761.

As soon as he had arrived he sent his servant Costa with a note to Madame, to find out 'whether she was dead or had come to her senses, which would have amounted to the same thing to me'. On Costa's return he narrowly examined him on the manner in which the Marquise had received the note. Costa answered: 'She looked at me in the mirror, mouthing some words I couldn't understand; burning incense, she walked round her room three times, then she gazed at me attentively with a haughty air; at last, with a very sweet smile, she told me to wait for an answer in the ante-room.'

Casanova heaved a tremendous sigh of relief. People had such malicious tongues. Madame might have heard all kinds of slander about him. But all was well. She was as crazy as ever; crazier, in fact. When Costa saw her she had still been wearing round her neck the large magnet which she believed would one day attract lightning, causing her to soar up to the sun. The scientifically-minded Casanova had always longed to tell her that when she reached the sun she would be no higher up than on earth; but he wisely held his tongue.

She harped again on her wish to be reborn as a man. It was difficult, yes, but not impossible. The steps to be taken were clearly laid down in the text-books – proper sacrifices, clean virgins, careful calculations, exact times. But Casanova had little desire for the work at this moment. Perhaps he still had enough money. And he did not want to make one great killing out of the old lady; he wanted a steady, respectable position as Charlatan by Appointment. As he told himself and the readers of his *Story*, time and again, repeating the words of his great contemporary Robert Clive – 'I stand amazed at my own moderation'. He could have taken so much much more, and frequently refused the gifts Mme d'Urfé tried to shower on him. He might also have seen very clearly that the great work of turning Mme d'Urfé into a young man was likely to be the last he could undertake with her. The time was not yet ripe.

But it was over two years since he had brought the Count d'Aranda to Paris. The old lady was getting, if not impatient, at least uncomfortably eager. Something had to be done. He told her that he was now ready to take the next step. For it, he needed the help of Querilinth, one of the three Chiefs of the Rosy Cross. But Querilinth's earthly avatar had been put into a dungeon in Lisbon by the infamous Inquisition. He, Casanova, would arrange for Querilinth's release: not by going to Lisbon – that would have been boorishly simple – but at Augsburg, thirteen hundred miles away. For this he would require beads and knives for the natives, only the natives of Bavaria wanted watches, jewels, snuffboxes and the like. He would also need a sizeable credit to live on and to bribe unbelievers, Jesuits, and inquisitors ... Mme d'Urfé was delighted at the prospect of activity, but pointed out that the Congress of Augsburg had now been postponed till September (it was then July). Casanova said, correctly, that the Congress would never meet at all, as such, but that many delegates would be there. In any case, if he could not succeed in Augsburg, he would go on to Lisbon.

This insistence on Lisbon (he could easily have said that Querilinth was in Madrid, Rome, anywhere) is one of several examples of Casanova's mystical belief that something marvellous awaited him. Mysterious Portuguese abbés offered him clandestine missions ... when everything else failed, there was always Lisbon ... several times he was on the point of going there ... or would have, if ... But in fact he never did go, and so, writing at the end of his life, he could still place the end of the rainbow in Lisbon.

Casanova left Paris in a hurry. This was the disastrous trip which cost him the last of his young man's really rude health, which went with the soft chancre and the inguinal tumours La Renaud gave him in Munich. It also cost him most of the fortune which Mme d'Urfé was going to give him, for, as we know, Costa skipped with it. So Casanova was broke and badly in need of help when he reached Paris once more on 31 December 1761. His first act was to dismiss his servant Leduc there in the middle of the street, without a reference, ostensibly for some peccadillo in Augsburg, but in fact, I am sure out of *Weltschmerz* and a feeling that he could trust no one.

In Paris he spent three weeks in the luxurious rooms Mme d'Urfé had reserved for him in the Rue du Bac, hardly going out, in order to convince her that he had come to Paris with no other intention than to begin the great work. They spent the time, he and she, in making the proper devotions to the seven planets, each on its appropriate day. (The planets are *Saturn*, guarded by Arelim; *Jupiter*, guarded by Chasmalim; *Mars*, Seraphim; *Sun*, Shinanim; *Venus*, Tarsishim; *Mercury*, Benei Elohim; *Moon*, Ishim.)

He now had a complete plan, and in these days expounded it to Mme d'Urfé. The exercises with the planets were intended to give him the spiritual contacts who would help him find the maiden required for the next step. The maiden had to be the daughter of an adept in the Rosicrucian Mysteries. Once found, Casanova was to impregnate her with a male child in a special manner known only to the High Brethren. The impregnation had to take place under the full moon of April, May, or June; but if it were to take place in France, only the April moon would serve.

When the child was born nine months later, Mme d'Urfé would take it straight from the mother's body and keep it in bed beside her for seven days. At the end of the seven days she would pass her soul and spirit to the child by a mouth-to-mouth kiss. She would thus 'die'. Her useless body being disposed of (no one says how), Casanova would look after the seven-day-old boy until he was three years old. Up to this point the boy would contain Mme d'Urfé's intelligence, but would not be aware of it. It would cause comment, obviously, if a two-year-old baby boy chattered on about 'his' daughter, 'his' fortune, and 'his' love affairs with the great Regent of France forty years ago. When the boy was three, the spirit inhabiting him would begin to be aware that it was really Mme d'Urfé, and the boy would gradually become Monsieur d'Urfé ... and then Casanova could begin to teach him/her those ultimates of necromancy, the Philosopher's Stone and the Elixir of Youth.

'Oh yes, and one more thing' (across the centuries I can hear Casanova speaking softly) 'Madame must make a will in favour of the magically-born child,' appointing Casanova to be its guardian until its thirteenth year. Otherwise her money and estates would go to others at her 'death'.

In the privacy of his rooms after the sublime madwoman had gone home, he must have sat back and mopped his brow ... again and again. He had thought that the threat of death would make her pull back, at least delay; but not a bit of it. She was in a hurry. Why not? She believed. He must play to her determination, then. He had three months to find the virgin; then there would be nine more before the birth of the child – a full year at Mme d'Urfé's expense, and the expense could be made very considerable. What must he do when she was supposed to die? Well, he'd cross that bridge when he came to it. She might, of course, really die at any moment from natural causes. Provided the child had by then been born, and named, he would have thirteen years at the money.

What seems odd in Casanova's tale here is the loss of the Count d'Aranda, who was to take a major part, but now is not included. My guess is that the youth was turning out too smart and too unscrupulous to play the rôle Casanova would have alloted him.

He now (January 1762) went off in search of the angelic virgin. His choice, we know, fell on La Corticelli, and we also know he could not easily have made a more foolish one. She had been at Prague for the last nine months, as actress, dancer and mistress of a local count. But she accepted Casanova's suggestion without hesitation, and came with her mother to meet him at Metz. The mother, Signora Laura, was a terrible snob, and refused to pose as La Corticelli's governess. The fact that she had travelled as the girl's mother had to be concealed from Mme d'Urfé, for the girl was of divine origin on the maternal side, and Signora Laura was all too earthy. In ten days' hard work at Nancy, Casanova transformed the girl from Maria Corticelli, dancer and whore, to Countess Lascaris, descendant of a famous family which had provided several Eastern Roman Emperors. (Lascaris was also a name in Mme d'Urfé's heritage.) With more difficulty, Casanova turned the energetically protesting Signora Laura from the Countess's mother into her personal servant. All being ready, the party set off to meet the Marquise at her estate of Pontcarré.

She greeted them in the grand manner. Pontcarré was a fortified château, with crenellated towers, a moat and battlements. Mme d'Urfé caused the drawbridge to be lowered for their entry, while she awaited them in the great entrance arch, surrounded by hundreds of servants, lackeys and tenants. The Countess Lascaris was embraced, ushered into the castle, and besprinkled with perfume; she managed to keep a straight face. Old Signora Laura grumbled and growled and Casanova at once arranged for her to be given a separate room, where she stayed except to go to mass.

They spent a week defending themselves against the fierce gnats of the region while they waited for the April full moon. That night Mme d'Urfé led the virgin Lascaris, heavily scented and dressed only in a transparent veil, to Casanova's bed, and then stayed to watch the impregnation. She took a natural interest in this, as it was herself who would be born of the act nine months later.

At the end of the moon period Mme d'Urfé asked the cabala whether the Countess Lascaris had conceived. Casanova had done his best, but he wanted to draw the business out, for the reasons we have seen; so his cabala answered that the girl had not conceived, and the fault was Count d'Aranda's. The rascal had been watching the impregnation from behind the screen. This story, which was quite untrue, achieved its main object, and also got rid of d'Aranda, who was banished to one of Madame's estates near Lyon, given an abbé for a tutor, and told not to show his face for a year. He was pleased to go and Casanova was pleased to see the back of him. The Countess Lascaris, forgetful of her divine origin, had been visiting him in his room. Casanova was having enough trouble with her and Signora Laura already; they had done their part, now they wanted to be given their money and set free.

So Casanova had two angry and vengeful women on his hands, beside the anxious Mme d'Urfé, as the party moved on to Aachen to repeat the impregnation there. (It will be remembered that at the May or June moons the ceremony had to be performed outside France.) In Aachen La Corticelli began to kick up her heels, and not metaphorically. At a great ball she danced so professionally, kicking and pirouetting and showing her legs up to *here*, that any astute observer, and there were plenty, must have known she was not a countess, but a chorus girl. Casanova was furious, but Mme d'Urfé, delighted with the girl, gave her a casket full of jewels worth 60,000 francs (about 6,250 dollars or £2,500). Casanova at once took possession of it, to prevent her, as he says, 'going off without my leave'.

Corticelli/Lascaris bided her time until the May full moon and then the poor girl was suddenly smitten of a fierce fever, which caused her to writhe and twist on the bed in such pain that the husbandman could not insert his dibble. The magic hour, three minutes past four, passed with no entry. Poor Mme d'Urfé was in tears. Her rebirth had miscarried before conception.

Casanova turned to his cabala, and after long consultations found the cause of the Countess's strange fit: she had been sexually defiled by an evil genius. A purer virgin, or rather, a virgin under the protection of stronger spirits, must be found. This one was no good. Mme d'Urfé smiled again, and Casanova went to La Corticelli in her bedroom. She told him waspishly what he already knew: that she would go on having convulsions until he gave her the casket of jewels. Casanova refused. There was a scene – there must have been many glorious scenes between these volatile, passionate, extrovert charlatans. La Corticelli screamed that she would tell Mme d'Urfé all. Here Casanova could afford to smile. Tell her, he said; see if she believes you.

He returned to the cabala and shut himself up with Mme d'Urfé and the magical numbers. After much calculating, the Upper Ones informed the seekers that instruction on the rebirth would come from the Moon. Mme d'Urfé was to write and ask for them.

One of the delightful things about being a Rosicrucian, or an adept in the mysteries of the cabala, is that you know the proper procedure for any eventuality, however curious. Is there a gryphon casting a spell on your asparagus? You have only to look up the correct formula in the proper *grimoire*. Has your husband been cohabiting with vampires? Vol 11, page 587, see under *Anaemia*. Write to the Moon? Why, that's in . . .

Mme d'Urfé was delighted. She knew the formula. She would attend to the matter on the first possible date. Posts for the Moon went only in the first phase of the new moon. Meanwhile, as the unhappy Countess Lascaris was possessed by a devil-gnome, nothing said was reliable, except that one could rely on its being false and defamatory.

Leaving La Corticelli and her mother grinding their teeth and Mme d'Urfé drafting her letter to the Moon, Casanova settled down to serious gambling. He lost heavily to the French and Germans, and had to turn to the English. Whenever he gambled himself into financial trouble, he could rely on English pigeons to get him out again.

Back at the castle, La Corticelli told Mme d'Urfé all: who she was, where she came from, what Casanova's game was, everything. The good lady nodded and smiled and took no notice.

The correspondence with the Moon was managed thus: while Madame was writing her letter to the Moon, Casanova was secretly writing the Moon's reply. He used silver ink on green paper, and signed it 'Selenis' (the spirit of the Moon). Then a bath was filled with warm water, appropriately perfumed. After burning incense and scattering more perfume, he and Mme d'Urfé took off their clothes and punctually at one o'clock in the morning entered the bath. Casanova held Mme d'Urfé's hand in one of his; in the other he held, hidden, Selenis's reply. In the bath, they burned Mme d'Urfé's letter in an alabaster cup full of spirits, and she saw the words flying up to the sky. Ten minutes later Selenis's reply magically appeared, floating on the water. Madame reverently placed it on a silken cushion to dry.

After they had dried and dressed themselves they read the missive. Madame's face saddened when she read that the great work must be delayed until the arrival of Querilinth. This was the same Querilinth whom she had given Casanova a great deal of money to rescue from Lisbon the year before, to no avail. But now he was free, and would come to her in Casanova's company, at Marseille, the following spring. Selenis also confirmed that the Countess Lascaris was dangerous and must be got rid of. Casanova packed her off to Turin.

The action now calmed down somewhat. Casanova had gained a breathing space to find someone better than La Corticelli for the next phase. After the great piquet marathon at Sulzbach, and a stay in Berne, he parted with Mme d'Urfé at Besançon, he to go to his theological exercises with Hedwige and Hélène in Geneva, she to her estates at Bresse, near Lyon, to see the young Count d'Aranda, of whom she had grown very fond. Casanova called on her there, and told her that he must go to Turin, there to meet Frederick Gualdo, head of the Rosy Cross. It is not clear whether this Gualdo was the same Querilinth who was to accompany Casanova to Marseille the following spring; or a Being who would put Casanova in touch with Querilinth; or the mysterious Gualdo, or Walter, Rosicrucian adept who was supposed to have lived in Venice and disappeared from there in 1680, *then* aged ninety. It made no difference to the sublime and soft-hearted madwoman. She was delighted to give Casanova 50,000 francs and three rich dresses for the poor, deluded gnome-infested La Corticelli/Lascaris. Count d'Aranda clamoured to be taken to Turin, too, probably realizing that Uncle Giacomo was going to roll in fields of female charms; but Casanova ominously says, 'It may be imagined that I succeeded in putting him off'.

Casanova duly went to Turin, where he could not avoid La Corticelli; but he did not give her her dresses, or her casket of jewels. He used the jewels to further his suit with a dancer and at last got La Corticelli off his back by surprising her in bed with another man. The other man thus became responsible for her. The girl had a last try at revenge, by telling the whole story of her relations with Casanova to the Countess Vignati di S. Gillio, who ran a salon and counted herself patroness of the Turin stage. (James Boswell met her here two years later.) The Countess arranged for the tale to be published. Casanova got hold of a copy, and says that although it was in the main accurate, it did him no harm. That may be so; or it may be that the story, read on top of a hundred other reports and rumours, was at the root of much of his troubles with the authorities in northern Italy, then and later.

On to Milan, where La Corticelli's dress bought him admittance to the fierce Spanish lady's bed, and so eventually back to Genoa with La Crosin. Querilinth was waiting for him there in the person of Passano the pornographer. A little later his brother the renegade priest Gaetano turned up with the lesbian nymphomaniac, Marcoline. Casanova does not make clear in his *Story* when he decided to incorporate Marcoline into his plan, but at some point he found reasons beyond plain lust for taking her with him to France. Passano and

Brother Gaetano now assume the rôles just given up by La Corticelli and her mother – traitors, malcontents and spongers dogging Casanova's footsteps and whom, in spite of his masterly stratagems, he never seems to be able to get rid of.

On arrival in Marseille he hid Marcoline and took Passano and Gaetano to the Hôtel des Treize Cantons to meet Mme d'Urfé. The old lady went mad with joy at seeing Querilinth. Gaetano went mad with frustration at not knowing what had become of Marcoline, Passano, who knew nothing of the subject, went mad trying to field Rosicrucian and cabalistic queries of staggering complexity. Was he not Querilinth, a Grand Master of the Order?

Once more Casanova and Mme d'Urfé began the preparations for her rebirth. She had already collected presents for Querilinth, and now asked Casanova (under his new cabalistic name of Paralisee Galtinarde) whether they were suitable for that august spirit. The gifts were seven pounds of each of the precious metals associated with the seven planets: that is, lead for Saturn, tin for Jupiter, iron for Mars, copper for Venus, mercury for Mercury, silver for the Moon, and gold for the Sun. There were also seven carats' weight each of the seven precious stones: that is, diamond, ruby, emerald, sapphire, chrysolite, topaz and opal.

Casanova took one look at this and decided that on no account should Passano lay his hands on any of it. He told Madame that the gifts must, of course, be consecrated before they were presented to Querilinth. The consecration was a tricky business, which had best be left entirely to Paralisee Galtinarde. The cabala also thoughtfully ordered Casanova to go to the country for seven nights and to sleep with no mortal female during that period in case Querilinth couldn't perform his impregnatory functions and Casanova had to substitute for him at the last moment. Casanova now had a reason for his absences from Mme d'Urfé, and time to enjoy Marcoline; which he did, having first sent his brother away because the snivelling wretch had traced Marcoline to her lodging and was pestering her.

When Casanova returned he found Passano/Querilinth, who was sixty, in bed with venereal disease. Passano had also somehow found out about the precious metals and jewels intended for him, and when Casanova refused to give him any of it, he demanded £1,000 hush money.

Casanova returned to Mme d'Urfé and told her he feared there was something fishy about Querilinth. He was acting oddly, and he had contracted this unmentionable complaint. Mme d'Urfé was horrified. She had never heard of a spirit from Beyond getting a social disease. And to think that in a few days he had been going to impregnate her! Casanova agreed: it was most upsetting.

The cabala was consulted, Casanova pulling out the numbers and Mme d'Urfé turning them into letters. The message was quite unequivocal. Seven salamanders had transported the real Querilinth to the Milky Way. The sufferer next door was the (transmogrified) Comte de Saint-Germain, the quack and adventurer they both already knew. As for the syphilis, he had got it from a female gnome, whose intention was that he pass it on to Semiramis (Mme d'Urfé), thus causing her to die before her pregnancy came to term. Madame could trust Blacksnout (Casanova) to rid her of the false Querilinth and make contact with the true one. There would be worship of the Moon for seven nights, and on the fifth of these Casanova himself would impregnate her, after they had both been bathed by a water sprite.

Thus *The Story of my Life*. It is clear enough that Casanova himself was now going to have sexual intercourse with Madame, though the cabala called them Galtinarde and Semiramis, their cult names. What is never made clear is, what happened to the old plan? What happened to the tried and trusted system wherein a virgin of divine parentage was to be impregnated, and Madame's rôle was only to take the newborn babe at birth and cradle it for seven days? After the defection of La Corticelli there is never any attempt at finding another virgin. If he thought of Marcoline as the replacement, he nowhere says so. Instead, suddenly, it is Madame who is to become a mother, and the divine spirit is relegated to the rôle of usherette and lavatory attendant. Marcoline's real function was in fact neither of these, but the more challenging one of standard-raiser. Casanova admired and liked Madame d'Urfé, but it was a very long time since she had set the Regent of France's blood on fire. Casanova doubted whether he could do his duty by her unless Marcoline was also present to put his phallic limb into fighting trim.

He was now attacked from the rear by the ungrateful and syphilitic Passano, who wrote a long letter to Mme d'Urfé detailing all Casanova's villainies. The good lady gave Casanova the letter, saying she found the dialect so strange that she couldn't understand a word. In fact, she probably read it, and saw that the beastly gnomes had poisoned the false Querilinth's mind as well as his body. Casanova reacted quickly. He got an order on a banker in Lyon, took it to Passano, and gave him an ultimatum: either go into hospital, or leave for Lyon within the hour. He didn't care which. In any case Passano was dismissed. Passano decided to go to Lyon, though he was really much too ill to travel, he said.

Casanova went off to instruct Marcoline in her part for the coming rites. Broadly speaking, she was to stand naked behind Mme d'Urfé's shoulder, where Casanova could see her as he embraced the old lady. Also, under pretence of washing their sexual organs, she was to start *fellatio* (the Venetian kiss) on Casanova, to bring him three times to the starting slit.

By now the metals and gems had been consecrated. Casanova and Mme d'Urfé delivered them to Selenis (who could be trusted to forward them to the real Querilinth at his new address on the Milky Way) by throwing them into the sea, with due religious ceremony. Only, Casanova did not want any harm to come to them from the damaging effects of sea water, so the box that he threw into the sea contained fifty pounds of lead, while the box which contained fifty pounds of precious metal and jewels stayed dry in his room. He did not burden Mme d'Urfé with this knowledge.

The great work began – again. The calculations and oracles common to all forms of magic enjoin a very strict attention to detail if results are to be obtained. All had been done, correctly. On the stroke of the ordained hour, Marcoline appeared, dressed in green velvet jacket and breeches, silver lace gartering, and green stockings. Her hair was bound in a green net and fastened with a silver brooch. She gave the old lady a note, written in invisible ink. When Madame dipped the letter in the bath, the message became apparent: the green girl was a water sprite, unhappily deaf and dumb, come to perform certain ceremonial bathings.

Here begins another of the more comical and touching sections of the *Story*. There is a sense of a charade, of a wildly funny but also sexy ritual being performed; there is a transmitted awareness of the various emotions present in that room – in Casanova, of cupidity struggling against shame and distaste, of desire being transmuted from the seen secrets and voluptuous attitudes of Marcoline into action in the Marquise's aged flesh – of the lady's raptures, sacred and profane, for she appreciated a good man as much as any woman – of Marcoline's bi-sexual voyeurism and, probably, her sympathy with and understanding of the old lady . . .

It was a long night, and everyone came out of it with honour. Casanova actually made love to Mme d'Urfé once, and pretended to do so twice more. What Casanova did not give Madame in the way of thrills, Marcoline's lesbian skills did. The Marquise went to her bed exhausted, and stayed there 107 hours on the orders of the cabala. Casanova crept into the closet where Marcoline had hidden, and then, carrying the chest full of precious metals, they went to

Marcoline's rooms, ate, drank, slept, and made love for fourteen hours on end.

When Casanova went to visit Mme d'Urfé in bed next day he found her radiant, but worried by an unusual problem. She was, she believed, pregnant with a son who would eventually become herself again. But she was a widow, so the boy would be born a bastard, and her property would go to her relatives. It was very difficult . . . but she had thought of a solution. Casanova should marry her. He would thus become legal father and guardian of the child, who could of course then inherit her property.

Another question – where and how was she actually to give birth?

And, she said, she felt pretty mannish already. As soon as she reached puberty in boyish form, she wanted to try out her male equipment on Marcoline.

Casanova thought he had better get her out of Marseille at once, for she was becoming a nuisance there. The cabala was consulted, and it told her that for the next phase she must pour sea water into a place where two rivers joined; this must be done on 15 May. Casanova would join her at the end of the month for further sacrifices. The place was obviously Lyon, where the Rhone and Saône meet: an unfortunate choice on the part of the spirits, for Lyon was the place where Casanova had sent the poxy Passano/Querilinth/Saint-Germain.

Mme d'Urfé went. Casanova sold the precious metals and kept the jewels. Then he set out with Marcoline for Lyon. On the way they had the adventure with Henriette near Aix-en-Provence. On 28 May 1763 they arrived at the Hôtel du Parc in Lyon, and Casanova at once called on Mme d'Urfé. The Count d'Aranda was with her.

Next day the hard-worked cabala tackled Madame's difficult questions about the bastardy, her lying-in and her finances. The answers were clear and, considering Casanova's determination not marry her (or anyone) himself, well thought out. She was to have the baby in Paris; but first she must will all that she possessed to the son to be born. Paralis, who was on his way to England, would send her a husband from that island. The Count d'Aranda had told Mme d'Urfé the truth about his own background, and Casanova intended to see that the little monster was handed back to his mother in England, as she (once Teresa Imer/Pompeati, now Mme Cornelys) was clamouring for his return and threatening law suits if she didn't get him.

The air of desperation about these plans is unmistakable. The sun is setting. There is no more to be got out of Mme d'Urfé. It is a question now of escaping with what he already has, without police inquiries.

Once more, the enemies were closing in. Passano was going about Lyon swearing that Casanova had poisoned him, and was ruining Mme d'Urfé: that he was also a sorcerer, forger, and counterfeiter (all these were capital offences at the time). Passano must be silenced; but no one knew where he lived. Casanova became uneasy, and laid a criminal charge of conspiracy against the man. From hiding Passano issued fearful threats through his lawyer about the evidence he possessed of Casanova's villainies, evidence which included a letter from the Abbé Gaetano, Casanova's own brother. But, Passano concluded, he was a family man, and he would forgo vengeance for a mere £1,000. Casanova angrily refused the suggestion, and told his lawyer to press his charges against Passano, which would force Passano into court if only to plead justification.

This worked. Next day Passano wrote that for a mere *hundred* pounds he would leave Lyon and abandon his defence. Casanova loftily refused, but next day Passano went, leaving a signed retraction of his charges. Casanova's friend the silk merchant and banker Giuseppe Bono had paid the hundred louis on his own account. Passano disappears from the tale of Mme d'Urfé (but not from that of Giacomo Casanova).

Mme d'Urfé went on to Paris to make ready for her confinement, and Casanova followed. His main problem now was to get d'Aranda to ask to go to London, as Mme d'Urfé had taken such a liking to him that she would never order him to go. Casanova found the proper bait when he remembered that d'Aranda was still only seventeen. He told the youth that his mother wanted to see him at Abbeville, about halfway to Calais. He was to accompany Casanova that far on the latter's journey to London; meet his mother; and afterwards return to Paris riding post – that is, on the horses kept in stables a few miles apart along the main roads for the use of government messengers and the like, and of private citizens at a price. The glitter in the bait was that to ride post he could dress up as a courier, in topboots and a magnificent suit with the arms of France embroidered on the sleeve.

So, early in June 1763 Casanova took his leave of Mme d'Urfé. The Laforgue translations (*see* Appendix) make him write 'I took my leave of my worthy Madame d'Urfé with an emotion which I had never experienced before'. What he actually wrote was, 'After having taken leave of Madame d'Urfé . . .' He ought to have been ashamed of himself; perhaps he was – but he didn't say so. Mme d'Urfé had played out her part and, in my opinion, was probably already showing some disillusionment with him. He never saw her again.

In his *Story* he quickly tidies up the loose ends of the whole long, involved, and rascally tale. He finds priestly brother Gaetano staying with impotent brother Francesco in Paris. They pack Gaetano off to Rome, where he drops out of Casanova's ken for six years. La Corticelli is found suffering from starvation and syphilis. Casanova pays for her to be sent to a home and cured, but she dies in treatment, leaving twelve louis to 'Signora Laura'. (La Corticelli did not die at this time but during Casanova's next visit to Paris, in 1767. He frequently muddles events of the two periods.)

Casanova and Giuseppe Pompeati, alias the Count d'Aranda, set off for Calais and England. When young d'Aranda found that his mother was not in Abbeville, he made a break back toward Paris and the easy life as Mme d'Urfé's protégé. Casanova sent a real courier after him. The lad was caught before he had reached Amiens, thirty miles away, and ignominiously dragged back, and so on 11 June 1763 taken to England in Casanova's train.

Madame d'Urfé died of an overdose of a medicine called the Panacea, late in July 1763, Casanova says. He received the news on 1 August in London. She left a recently executed will, bequeathing all that she possessed to the child soon to be born to her. Casanova was to be the governor of the child. But the daughter had already seized all the land, also a pocket book containing 400,000 francs (about 40,000 dollars or £16,000).

The tale of Madame d'Urfé had ended, not only for Casanova, but for the sublime madwoman herself.

And now, as with the great escape, we had better look at this marvellous tale with a more suspicious eye. The central fact of the story is certainly true. There can have been few in Europe's floating 'faro society' who did not know that the Venetian adventurer was taking the French marquise for a very large sum. The only cause for undue remark, however, would have been admiration at the long period for which he kept his ascendancy, and at the size of the haul.

Lorenzo da Ponte told it, in much simplified form. He was a little younger than Casanova, just as crooked, a gambler and adventurer, who fell in with Mozart and wrote the librettos of *The Marriage of Figaro*, *Don Giovanni*, and *Così fan tutte*. He and Casanova were too much alike to be friends. His autobiography was published in 1823 and in it he says he will tell a story about Casanova which he swears that Casanova will not tell about himself: as we know, he was wrong. His story is this: Casanova told a rich old lady he could give her perpetual youth. To prove it, he hired a young whore, made her up to look old and bent, and then said charms and incantations over her in the presence of the old lady. After a time the girl suddenly appeared out of the smoke in her youth and beauty. The old lady, whom da Ponte never names, was taken in. She allowed Casanova to give her a drug, from which she would awaken young. While she was unconscious Casanova stole all the gold and jewels from her house, and made his escape. But his servant, in turn, stole most of his loot from him.

That is all, according to da Ponte, and I don't believe a word of it. That was not Casanova's style at all. He needed respect – from other charlatans, perhaps, but respect nevertheless – far too much to have committed a cheap bit of thuggery like that; for which Madame d'Urfé would obviously have called in the police. Besides, there is plenty of evidence for Casanova's version. Passano's letters to Mme d'Urfé, in which he tried to tell her about Casanova's villainy, are extant. So are letters from the banker Bono in Lyon.

The very end is different from what Casanova would have us believe. The Marquise d'Urfé did not die in 1763, but in 1775. Her will was unremarkable, and contained no mention of pregnancy or of Casanova. But she did order the disposal by burning of two packets of papers – which might have been her letters from Casanova. No one will ever know. It was done. Casanova's reasons for killing her off in 1763, and keeping to that myth when he wrote thirty years later, are a mystery. She was an important figure and the facts of her death would have been known to anyone who was interested. I think the clue is in Casanova's own remark, which I have quoted, about her being dead or returned to her senses, which would have meant the same thing as far as he was concerned. She did not die in July 1763; she came to her senses.

11

London: the Cock Ensnar'd

Casanova arrived in England on 11 June 1763, travelling in the style
to which he had accustomed himself. He had hired a private packet
boat to cross the Channel, but allowed the Duke of Bedford to come
as his guest. (The Duke's arrival was noted in the *Gazette*. Casanova's
was not mentioned.)

He thought the British Customs officers at Dover were curt and
rude, equally to the Duke as to himself; and adds that in this matter
the English officials cannot be compared with the French, an observation that sounds very odd to the twentieth-century traveller. But, in
general, he liked England:

The island called England is of a different colour from anything on the
continent. The sea is extraordinary, like an ocean, for it is subject to tides; the
water of the Thames tastes different from the water of any other river in the
world. Cattle, fish, all food tastes different from ours, the horses are of a
special type even to their shape, and the people have a special character,
common to the whole nation, which makes them think they are superior to
everyone else. It is a belief shared by all nations, each thinking itself the best.
And they are all right.

I noticed first the cleanliness, the solid fare, the beauty of the country and
the main roads, I admired the beauty of the carriages provided at the post
houses for those who travel without one of their own; the fair price for the
stages; the ease of paying; the speed with which they move, always at a trot,
never a gallop; and the shape of the towns we passed through between
Dover and London. Canterbury and Rochester have large populations
though their width is nothing in relation to their length.

He never explains precisely why he went to England, but it is
almost certain that he meant to interest Lord Egremont, the Secretary
of the Treasury, in a state lottery on the pattern of the one the
Calzabigi brothers had run in France. He never saw Egremont, who

died soon after he reached London, but he stayed on nearly nine months, trying to dazzle or perhaps bribe his way into a position where he would be empowered to run such a lottery. Many in high places could expect to make a lot of money out of a state lottery. Remembering the great wealth of England, he was gambling for very high stakes. He gambled all the money he had won from Mme d'Urfé; and he lost.

It is in describing the early part of his stay in England that he accidentally lets slip the evidence which shows that he may have become a French citizen. Because he was out of favour with the Venetian Government, it was the French ambassador who presented him at court (to King George III and Queen Charlotte). He relates that when the Queen asked him what his nationality was, he said he was Venetian. In the manuscript the following words have been crossed out after 'Venetian': *n'étant Français que pour m'être naturalisé* (only being French through naturalization). Before this even, when Casanova is describing his first visit to the ambassador, the following words are crossed out of the manuscript: *qui en vertu de ma naturalisation m'annonçait pour Français . . .* (who, because of my naturalization, announced me as French).

One is left wondering why he didn't admit and use his French nationality from then on. Many scholars suggest that as a keen royalist and supporter, not to say user, of the established order, he was so disgusted by the excesses of the French Revolution that he did not wish to be associated with a people capable of such behaviour. This might have been the case in 1797, but we are talking about 1763. I think, personally, that he decided to carry his secret to the grave because the secret was connected with the reason for his French naturalization itself; and that is another mystery, but probably linked to espionage.

He had a connection in London who, he expected, would put him in touch with large numbers of the sort of people who would be equally helpful to him whether in espionage or in forwarding the project of the lottery. This was Teresa Imer/Pompeati, the mother of Giuseppe. She was now Mme Cornelys, and a very well-known figure. She had rented Carlisle House in Soho Square, and held fêtes there twelve times a year. At first she had been all the rage with society, but by the time Casanova arrived her assemblies were attracting fewer of the upper and more of the entertaining class. She was heavily in debt and speckled all over with law suits. Nor did she trust Casanova, and when he arrived to hand over Giuseppe, hoping to be lodged, lionized, and introduced into society, perhaps at her expense and as her fancy man, she gave him a cold reception. He left in a huff and had little to do with her thereafter, except that he bailed her out of debtor's prison once, he says.

Partly because he was a snob, and partly because theirs was the milieu in which he had to work, Casanova soon made many aristocratic acquaintances. Among those with whom he says he gossiped, gambled, or shared an interest in saleable sex were Caroline Fitzroy, Lady Harrington – also known as the Messalina of Stable Yard – and various Ladies Stanhope, her daughters; the Duchess of Northumberland; Augustus Hervey, Lord Bristol, who was secretly married to the notorious Miss Elizabeth Chudleigh in 1744 (but the secrecy had not prevented her walking out of his life the next day); Lucy, Countess Rochford, or perhaps Elizabeth, Lady Rochefort (Casanova's reference is not clear); the 10th Earl of Pembroke; Lady Betty Germaine; a surname-less Sir Edgar (in reality, W. E. Agar), 'who enjoyed life and indulged his passions'; the Duchess of Grafton; the Duke of Cumberland, Butcher of Culloden and uncle of the King; Lady Coventry; and Miss Chudleigh herself, in front of whose house he managed to fall off his horse and put out his collarbone. Casanova chivalrously calls her 'the young lady', but she was forty-four. She had her marriage to Hervey dissolved in 1769, and at once married the Duke of Kingston.

It was an England, and a London, very much less disciplined, very much more outgoing, than we know today. After his attendance at court, for instance, Casanova took a sedan chair to go home, because a man in court dress could not walk the streets without the mob pelting him with mud. And here is his description of a night at the theatre:

We went to Drury Lane . . . the company could not perform the play that had been publicized, and the audience was in uproar. Garrick . . . came forward and tried in vain to calm them. He had to withdraw . . . the king, the queen and the rest of the fashionable audience left their boxes and rushed out of the theatre, abandoning the theatre to the fury of the incensed crowd. In less than an hour nothing remained but the walls of the theatre. After this devastation, the enraged mob went to sink themselves in beer and gin. In a fortnight the theatre was rebuilt and the play again announced, and as the curtain went up on Garrick . . . a voice from the pit yelled 'On your knees'. A hundred voices took up the cry 'On your knees', and the English Roscious was forced to kneel and ask forgiveness in this humiliating way. Then thunderous applause broke out and all was over. Such are the English – particularly Londoners.

These Drury Lane riots actually took place on 25 January and 24 February 1763, that is, six months before Casanova reached England. So either he said he was there in order to give the unlikely tale greater credence; or he really was there . . . which means that he was not in Milan with the bewitching Spanish countess.

And there is the tale of the Lady of Ranelagh. After a visit to the pleasure garden of Ranelagh (there was another, cheaper one at Vauxhall) he found that his hired coach had gone. It was about midnight. A beautiful woman gave him a lift in her private carriage. In return Casanova gave her kisses and (apparently) a quick pleasuring. He also gave her his name, and asked for hers, but she said only that they would meet again. They did, in Lady Betty Germaine's anteroom. Casanova spoke to the Lady of Ranelagh. She said politely that they had never met. The dumbfounded Casanova asked if it were possible that she did not remember him. The lady replied coolly, 'I remember you perfectly, but a piece of folly is not a title of acquaintance.' She returned to her newspaper.

It is a funny story in its own right, and it is observant of Casanova to have chosen it to tell – even if it did not happen to him – because it is deeply rooted in the facts of British social *mores*. I heard it told in 1939 of a peer's daughter. Returning to England after a visit to Viceregal relatives in India, she spent the voyage in a violent affair with a subaltern of Indian Cavalry. Shortly after the voyage and the romance had ended at Tilbury Docks, the man met the girl in Piccadilly. He went up, smiling, to greet her. She looked through him. The subsequent conversation follows Casanova's text, except that the final line was 'Since when has an affair on a P. & O. counted as an introduction?'

Before taking up the women who assuaged his leisure hours, we should look briefly at a couple of his male acquaintances, and a letter. The letter was written to the Most Serene Prince (this was the proper way to address the government of the Venetian Republic) on 18 November 1763; in it Casanova told them he had found the secret of fast-dyeing cloth, which in the past had been done in the East; and that he would give this great secret to his motherland, after demonstrating its worth to the Venetian envoy in London, at the Prince's command. The letter is extant, and seems to indicate that Casanova was giving up hope of the lottery, and trying to repeat his Paris history: going from the lottery to the silk-dyeing.

Then, as now, everyone seemed to turn up in London. All manner of shady and downright evil ghosts from his malodorous past arose now, usually with nothing but bad for him. The most notable was that same Castel-Bajac who brought in Queenie Demay to testify against him in the Paris abortion case. (In London he passed Casanova forged banknotes against a gambling debt.) Another was the Count Pocchini whom he had first seen as an exile on Cerigo in 1741, and two or three times since, hawking 'daughters' around the capitals in a version of the badger game. And a new one, Ange Goudar, who is a good example of Casanova's bipolar attitude toward his fellow rogues. Goudar was one of these – there are several – whom Casanova professes to despise, who aid his enemies, who cheat him and slander him; and who yet keep on appearing at his side in a guise indistinguishable from friendship.

Gambling, spying, or organizing a lottery, whatever it was, there had to be women. As Teresa Imer/Pompeati/Cornelys had refused to invite him into her bed he got himself a female companion by the most direct method: advertising. In a masterpiece of literary research the great Casanova scholar J. Rives Childs tracked down the advertisement in *The Gazetteer and London Daily Advertiser* for 5 July 1763.

Mrs Redaw, probably a Frenchwoman from her occupation, obviously made a preliminary screening of the applicants, sending on to Casanova only those who might fill his needs. After interviewing a great many girls, Casanova rented the floor to Pauline, a young Portuguese lady. After some time had been spent in reconnaissance and courtship, he talked her into sex by reading lascivious poetry to her. She was soon begging for practical demonstrations, and Casanova happily obliged. After sex, Pauline told the story of her life. It is thick with melodrama, contains a good dose of transvestitism, which we can now recognize as one of Casanova's obsessions, and sufficient detail is given so that Pauline ought to be readily identifiable. But she never has been and so – pretty, passionate, and perhaps partly imaginary – she passes out of Casanova's story.

He had other mistresses of Pauline's type – briefly, a little Swiss girl whom he had first initiated three years back; no less than five Hanoverian sisters introduced to him by Goudar, with their mother volunteering to make it six: but the core of his sexual experience in England was a woman very different from pretty Pauline or the placid Germans.

She was called La Charpillon and he had met her before – in Paris, in the summer of 1759. She was a trollop of thirteen then, and called herself Mlle de Boulainvilliers. Casanova had bought her some trinkets of strass.

The family history explains much about her. Her grandmother was Catherina Brunner, a child of the manse in Berne, who ran away to be mistress of one Michael Augspurgher. They never married, but she had four children by him, all girls, and adopted his name. Soon all the girls, and their mother, were expelled from Berne for immoral behaviour. They went to Paris, where about 1746 one of the girls had a child of whom the putative father was a M. Boulainvilliers, Marquis de Saint-Soire. This child, christened Marie Anne Geneviève Augspurgher, sometimes called herself Mlle de Boulainvilliers, and it was for her that Casanova bought the trinkets. At some period the Augspurgher women transported themselves to London and there continued to practice their professions. So now Marie Anne was not a Paris trollop of thirteen but a London trollop of eighteen, working in concert with her mother and at least one and sometimes two of her aunts (sisters of her mother). The other girls of her profession called her Champignon, but British inability to pronounce damn-frog-lingo had turned this into Charpillon.

Meeting her by chance, Casanova remembered that the Ambassador Morosini had given him a letter for her, in Lyon. This was explained when he learned that she had been Morosini's mistress during his stay in London. But now he also heard the girl's real name, Augspurgher, and realized that someone in the family owed him 6,000 francs, or about £250. That was the value of their bills of exchange which a third party had used to pay a debt to Casanova; but when Casanova tried to collect on the bills, the co-signers (three elder Augspurgher sisters, La Charpillon's aunts) had vanished. One of these wicked aunts was with her when they met, and her alarm may be imagined when she learned that the Chevalier de Seingalt now facing her was the same M. Casanova to whom they owed 6,000 francs; and who could send them to prison if they didn't pay up, for he still held their bills of exchange.

The family lived in Denmark Street, Soho, but it was not the address (quite respectable in those days) which led Casanova to suspect that the girl's virtue was unlikely to be impregnable. She was a tart, and her family owed him a lot of money. It was going to be easy. He was thirty-nine, she eighteen.

He opened his attack by sporadic flirting. He gave her his address and invited her to visit him. She told him she would like to make him fall in love with her, and then torment him. Casanova protested that this was a monstrous project; he would be on his guard. La Charpillon said that nothing would save him, except never to see her. She laughed as she spoke. As Hitler warned the world in *Mein Kampf* of what he intended to do and how he intended to do it, so La Charpillon warned Casanova.

He describes her: long, thick chestnut-coloured hair, blue eyes, rosy complexion, fairly tall, small-breasted, sensitive of feature and gracious of movement. She was a woman of the town, but Casanova was soon stupefied to find that the features of this little tramp were beginning to dim the aristrocratic image of Portuguese Pauline.

Casanova can be excused for thinking the affair would follow an easy course. He would invite her to his house. There would be fondling, a show of resistance, mention of money or jewels, and *holà*, she would spend a few hours on her back. Then he would tire of her, give her a diamond ring – or, more likely, bequeath her to a rich Englishman or another sex-starved ambassador . . . and on to fresh fields.

When Casanova made his first assault on what was for form's sake described as her virtue, he got her as far as a sofa. There she escaped, and made it clear that there would be no further advance until Casanova gave her aunt a hundred guineas. Well, not a gift, really, an investment: the aunt would use the money to make and sell the Balm of Life (a Fountain of Youth nostrum). The aunt would get rich, La Charpillon would get rich, Casanova would get very rich.

Casanova declined, and made up his mind to have nothing more to do with her. She was a bad girl, a gold-digger.

Three weeks later one of the aunts called. Why didn't Casanova pay them a visit? La Charpillon was in bed with a cold, but she'd be delighted to see him. Casanova, consumed by rut, rushed round to Denmark Street. The girl was in her bath. The aunt let Casanova into the room. There were shrieks, protests, inadequate holding of hands over pudenda – but nothing more. Casanova had to masturbate to relieve his over-excitement.

That did it. He didn't want the beastly girl any more. Glad to be cured, he gave the aunt her hundred guineas and left. At home he felt even better. It was all over. He'd never see La Charpillon again.

A few days later he met her in Vauxhall Gardens. And tried again. Failed. Went home. Determined, *absolutely determined* to keep away from her. Most dangerous, horrible female.

Now came the dubious Chevalier Ange Goudar, to congratulate him on giving up the girl, but . . . really, there was no way of getting over an infatuation except by satisfying it. As the old proverb has it – there are more ways of killing a cat than by drowning it in cream, but it's probably the best. Casanova felt the lust bursting his loins. Goudar was right: there was no escape except in fulfillment. Goudar advised him to go directly to the girl's mother, and offer her a hundred guineas for a night with La Charpillon. Casanova agreed. Goudar would take the offer.

Next day, at breakfast, La Charpillon presented herself at Casanova's house. She gave a magnificent performance as the wronged, insulted girl. Had she not told him in the very beginning that neither money nor violence would get him anywhere? How *dare* he offer to buy her, as though she were a . . . a . . . a . . . *common prostitute?* Especially when (tears glistened in the blue eyes) she loved him. If only he'd court her, come every day to see her, ask for nothing . . . (sobs: exit).

Casanova was devastated. He had been a brute, a monster. He began to pay the divine girl the visits she had asked for, not forgetting to take an expensive present each time.

The two weeks cost him four hundred guineas. Then he formally asked the mother whether the girl was to spend the night with him at their house, or at his.

It was to be at La Charpillon's, on a bed put up on the parlour floor. They undressed, put out the candles, got into bed. Casanova moved to take possession.

He failed – all night. She had wrapped herself in a long nightgown, with arms (and presumably legs) crossed, her head down. Casanova tried tears, argument, remonstrance, everything. She did not budge. She never said a word. He tore her nightgown to pieces, tore with his hands at her face, and finally, mad with rage, took her by the throat to strangle her. Then he staggered home, vomited, and went to bed with a high temperature.

Physically he felt dreadful for some days, but that was a trifle. What mattered was, he was cured. Never again!

Goudar came with news. La Charpillon had wanted to let Casanova enjoy her, but mother had made her promise not to, because Casanova would abandon them all as soon as he'd had her. But he, Goudar, had a plan which would get Casanova into the sanctuary. As a matter of fact, it wasn't exactly a plan, it was a chair . . . A porter brought it in, and Goudar sat in it. Springs leapt out, prisoned his arms, caught and forced his legs apart, tipped the seat. There he was, spreadeagled. Had he been a woman, say La Charpillon, the target area exposed front and centre . . . And this marvellous chair was Casanova's for just one hundred paltry guineas.

Casanova refused. He wanted nothing more to do with her, not even trapped in a trick chair.

But two weeks later La Charpillon called in person. He turned his face from her. She lifted her skirts to show him her bruises. Up to here. Here. A little higher. Casanova looked, and was lost.

Why? How could he be such an idiot, after all that she had done to him? He answers himself – 'because she was beautiful, because I loved her, and because her charms meant nothing unless they had the power to drown all reason'.

La Charpillon went into her act. Two hours later Casanova had agreed to set her up in a little house in Chelsea, with a proper stipend, as his titular mistress, just as Morosini had done. Next day, at Denmark Street, the contract was signed. The mother got a hundred guineas.

Casanova took La Charpillon to the 'country house', and eventually to bed. He found she was in her period, at least she was wearing the washable cloths which in those days served for sanitary towels. He went to sleep. In the morning he lifted her nightie, took off the cloth, and found she was not menstruating. She awoke and he said he would forgive her everything, but just let's do it *now*. She screamed that he had no right to examine her like that. He answered angrily. She screamed louder . . . It ended with La Charpillon, half dressed, yelling, swearing, stamping, and bleeding heartily, but from a blow Casanova had given her on the nose.

The landlord came up. La Charpillon returned to Mother. Casanova spent twenty-four hours in a sort of stupefaction, trying to work out what had happened to him — the world — justice — God.

Goudar came back with a message from the Augspurghers: don't try to get any of your money back, or else. Or else what? Or else La Charpillon would bring a false accusation against him. In another of those asides which seem to make time stand still, Casanova adds, 'Those who know England, especially London, don't need me to tell them what sort of lies these were which gain ground so easily among the English.' The accusation would, of course, be sodomy.

Casanova called at Denmark Street that same evening. (By now we must all share his own stupefaction at his behaviour.) No one spoke. La Charpillon sat embroidering, head down, now and then wiping away a tear. In a few days Casanova was as frantically in rut as ever. He brought her extravagant presents, wrote her an extravagant letter. She replied tenderly. Carried away with joy, Casanova rushed round to Denmark Street, bearing with him his ultimate weapon, the incriminating bills of exchange. He gave them to La Charpillon, who wept with wonder at his generosity.

They went up to her room. Casanova kissed her. She crossed her legs. Feeling an icy chill in his spine, he asked whether it would be the same all night. She said, '*Yes*'.

He went home and to bed.

The next day . . . (but this is fantastic) . . . she was round at his house. He asked her to give him back the bills of exchange. She didn't have them on her. He cursed and raved and swore and at last dissolved in helpless tears. La Charpillon said calmly that she had sworn never to let a man have her in her own house. She had come to his house to surrender herself to him. Casanova had her in his hand – at last ... perhaps. For his anger was too overwhelming now to be turned into desire. The girl spent all day with him. He made no approach to her. She went away.

Next day Casanova met Goudar in Green Park. Goudar said none of the Augspurghers would mention Casanova. He was well rid of them. But now rats of bitterness soured Casanova's stomach. The girl had got the two bills of exchange from him without any return. He had to have them back.

But she turned up again, at a party which transferred itself to Richmond, probably to the Star and Garter. La Charpillon, walking with Casanova in the gardens, said she would give him back the bills of exchange in the same place where he had given them to her, that is, in her bedroom. Casanova lost his temper at this, and raved abuse at her. Although the rest of the party had overheard the scene – at least the abuse – La Charpillon sat by Casanova's side at dinner, behaving as though they were lovers. After dinner she led him into 'the maze' (can they have been at Hampton Court, not Richmond?) where she sprawled on the grass, made him sit beside her, and began to use all possible means to excite him. Casanova forgot his furious sulks and responded to her kisses and the liberal display of her charms, including the one that interested Casanova most. He made ready for his moment of triumph ... she jerked herself away. That was enough for now, she said firmly: more later, in his house.

Casanova thinks that for a moment he lost his senses, but the truth is that for a moment he regained them. He held her down, drew his pocket knife, gave her a quick nick in the neck for earnest, and said he'd kill her if she didn't let him have her, *here, now!*

La Charpillon (one has to admire her animal guts as well as her animal cunning) lay still. He could rape her, if he liked, but afterwards she would just lie there until someone came to carry her away, and she would explain to everyone what had happened. Casanova was already over his momentary sanity. He got up and rejoined the rest of the party. A moment or two later La Charpillon came up, and put her hand on his arm, all smiles.

Back in London Casanova decided that he must give up the girl. Finally. *Definitely.* She was irresistible to him, therefore he must have nothing to do with her, except ... except that he wrote to the mother demanding the bills of exchange. If they were not returned, he would have to take steps. The mother replied curtly by letter that her daughter would give him back his bills when he learned to behave himself. Casanova, once more boiling with rage, took his pistols and stormed off to Denmark Street.

There he saw the young man who did La Charpillon's hair every week going into the house. Casanova waited in the street. He had to wait a long time but finally, about midnight, he managed to slip in unannounced. He opened the parlour door, and there was La Charpillon, on her back on the sofa, and there was the young hairdresser, mounted in the very saddle that Casanova had not yet attained (perhaps, he must have thought sometimes, the only man in London who hadn't).

The scene began. The hairdresser jumped off, La Charpillon shrieked, Casanova laid about with his cane, servants, aunts and mother rushed in, Casanova smashed the pier glass (his last extravagant gift to La Charpillon) and all the other furniture his hands or stick could reach. The harpies howled louder and louder until Casanova bellowed that he'd break their heads if they didn't shut up.

A certain quiet fell. Casanova demanded the bills of exchange. The old women didn't have them. La Charpillon, who had slipped out in the pandemonium, had them. The street watchman came to enquire into the hullabaloo. Casanova bribed him to go away and stay away. Then he began to think what he had done . . .

Poor little La Charpillon was wandering the streets of the wicked city, alone, half-dressed. Casanova trembled at the danger the frightened young girl was in. He gave money to the servants to go and find her. They went out to look for her. Casanova sat silent under a gradually strengthening barrage of abuse from the three older women. The servants came back: they couldn't find La Charpillon.

Casanova . . . but only his own words can express the sheer lunacy of his actions: 'I was stupid enough to express my repentance to the three old crooks. I pleaded with them to have a search made for her as soon as dawn broke and to let me know when she returned so that I could fall at her feet to beg her forgiveness and promise never to see her again. On top of that, I promised to pay them for everything that had been damaged and to leave with them a bill of exchange signed in my name.' Then he went home.

At eight in the morning one of the Augspurghers' female servants came to tell him the poor girl had just come home, in a bad way. She had been put to bed, with a fever, which might turn out very seriously, as she was in her monthly period. When Casanova pointed out that he had caught the hairdresser in the act, the servant said,

'Oh, that proves nothing. He's not fussy.' Casanova went to Denmark Street to ask after La Charpillon's condition. An aunt begged him to go away. The poor girl was in delirium, crying out his name in terror.

Casanova staggered home, sick with despair. He could not eat or drink or sleep. The next day he went back to Denmark Street. The aunt told him the girl was worse. Her period had been arrested. The doctor gave her twenty-four hours to live. Casanova pressed £10 into the aunt's hand, told her to see that the girl lacked nothing, and went home. On the way he met Goudar and asked him to find out La Charpillon's true condition.

An hour later Goudar told him that La Charpillon lay at death's door, stricken with fever and convulsions. Casanova could not sleep. He spent the night striding up and down his room and drinking.

Two days later he went to the Augspurghers. The mother half opened the door but would not let him in. Her daughter, she sobbed, was in her last agony. An old, thin man came out of the house murmuring sepulchral platitudes about the will of God. No, it wasn't a doctor, the mother said, it was a minister; and another was upstairs.

Casanova went slowly home, his knees buckling. He had killed the girl he loved. He decided to commit suicide.

First, he put his papers and jewels in order. Then he bought a number of lead balls, which he stuffed into his pocket along with his pistols. Then he set out for the Tower of London. He didn't feel bad any more. As a matter of fact, he felt pretty good. All was settled at last. It takes a brave man to fix his affairs with such sang-froid, an intelligent man to think of buying the balls of lead so he would sink, a determined man to walk so far with such fell intention. (I can't help wondering why it had to be the Tower of London, which is a fair step from Pall Mall. The Thames, even in 1763, flowed past Westminster, too. Perhaps Casanova's determination to be respected demanded that only the Tower, witness to so many heroic and aristocratic deaths, was noble enough to witness his.)

He tramped on, walking slowly because of the great weight of the lead balls. At Westminster Bridge he met his rich and profligate young friend, Agar. As on other occasions in his life, high comedy intruded upon the fundamental tragedy. Casanova saw Agar coming and tried to avoid him, but failed. Agar took his arm; Casanova begged to be left alone. Agar told him he looked awful. Casanova said no, he felt fine . . . and so on, until the leechlike Englishman persuaded Casanova to turn back and dine with him and a pair of whores. Casanova reluctantly agreed. He would kill himself after the dinner: but first he had to get those lead weights out of his pockets, for he was ready to faint.

After a brief rest at the Cannon coffee-house, Agar sent for the girls. They all had dinner. Blind musicians were called, the other three stripped and danced the hornpipe naked. (This is what blind musicians were for.) Casanova had not eaten or slept for three days and they let him remain dressed on his promise that if he felt an erection coming on, he too would strip. After the dancing Agar copulated with the two girls, one after the other, but not even this prime voyeurist spectacle could arouse Casanova.

He decided to kill himself the next day, but he couldn't get rid of the insatiable Agar, who insisted on taking him to Ranelagh. There some revellers were dancing a minuet. One of the women, who danced with an ethereal grace, was wearing a dress and hat just like the ones he had given to poor dead little La Charpillon. The unknown danced so gracefully that Casanova watched her, melting in grief, until she turned round. It *was* La Charpillon.

She took one look at his face, and ran. Casanova sank onto a seat. He began to shudder and shake uncontrollably. Icy sweat burst out all over him. Agar thought he had epilepsy. Casanova's heart pounded so fast that he dared not stand up. After a time his pulse began to slow down. He felt warm. The sun came out. He was cured! He took Agar home, told him all, ate ravenously . . . and decided to have the three old Augspurgher trots arrested, for he had a letter from the mother acknowledging that La Charpillon had the bills of exchange.

Next day he laid a sworn information before a magistrate. Goudar came to point out that Casanova had proved that he was cured; or, alternatively, that he was more in love than ever. He offered to act as go-between if Casanova wanted to come to terms with the Augspurghers. Casanova said the only settlement he would accept was 6,000 francs.

A fortnight passed, the three old women in prison, La Charpillon at liberty and refusing to approach Casanova. Then Agar reappeared, with money for Casanova – 250 guineas, which equalled 6,000 francs. He had become La Charpillon's lover, and to please her was thus now buying the old women's freedom by making good their bills of exchange. Casanova gave the young man a receipt and said to himself, 'Now surely all is over between myself and any and all Augspurghers.'

He should have known the girl better. A few days later he was returning late at night from a ball, when a posse of constables arrested him. The next morning he was brought before a blind magistrate.

Casanova thought it was Henry Fielding, author of *Tom Jones*, but it was his half-brother Sir John. Fielding politely, but without delaying for any nonsenses such as hearing the evidence, sentenced Casanova to imprisonment for life. (Fielding seems to have spoken in Italian, and cannot have made himself clear.) Casanova seems to have thought this procedure quite reasonable, except that he had still not been informed of the charge against him. What was it? Fielding told him he was charged with intending grievous bodily harm against this pretty girl here, La Charpillon. There were two witnesses. The girl went in fear of him. *Dunque* Casanova must spend the rest of his life in jail.

Now that Casanova knew what he had to deny, he denied it. The witnesses were liars, he said; and they probably were, for at that time one frequently saw the word *Evidence* written on signs in windows, indicating that witnesses could be hired within.

Fielding promptly freed him, provided he found two householders to go surety that he would never assault La Charpillon. Casanova spent half an hour in the terrible and terrifying atmosphere of Newgate, and then went free, delighted to see that La Charpillon was not allowed to leave the court until she had paid the costs of his arrest.

This incident is documented. The records of Clerkenwell Court show that James Casanova, Gentleman, appeared before Sir John Fielding, magistrate, on 27 November 1763. The householders who provided the recognizances for his release were John Pagus, tailor, and Lewis Chateauneu, wine merchant.

There is an interesting side-light on Fielding in *The Memoirs of William Hickey*. The following extract refers to the year 1767, three years after Casanova's stay:

We established ourselves into a roaring club, supped at eleven, after which we usually adjourned to Bow Street, Covent Garden, in which street there were then three most notorious bawdy-houses, all which we took in rotation . . . (One) was kept by Mother Cocksedge, for all the Lady Abbesses were dignified with the respectable title of Mother. In these days of wonderful propriety and general morality, it will be scarcely credited that Mother Cocksedge's house was actually next, of course under the very nose of that vigilant and upright magistrate, Sir John Fielding, who, from the riotous proceedings I have been a witness to at his worthy neighbour's, must have been deaf as well as blind, or at least well paid for affecting to be so.

That last cut allows us to guess at another possible explanation of Casanova's rapid release. And this time he really was free, even from

La Charpillon, who later became mistress of the famous John Wilkes. Wilkes undertook to do what had always stuck in Casanova's craw — provide for her mother, grandmother, aunts and great-aunts, as well as for the girl herself.

Casanova was free to hang himself by other ropes, which he soon did. One day, dining alone at the same Cannon coffee-house which provided such varied entertainment for its clients, he met a certain Latvian Baron Henau and his mistress. They joined forces. Casanova soon got the mistress, a murderous dose of venereal disease, and a forged bill of exchange for 520 guineas. By the time he found out it was forged, Henau had skipped to Lisbon. The banker who had discounted the forged bill inferred that he would give Casanova twenty-four hours to pay. If not . . . it was a capital matter.

Casanova was destitute. He had already decided to leave London and had asked Senator Bragadin to send him £200 so that he could clear his debts before going. Now, without money, with no way of getting any, racked with what was probably syphilis, he could not wait. He fled. He was so weak and delirious that he had to stop six hours in Rochester to rest and be bled. He reached Dover and the packet sailed. The white cliffs dimmed.

He never saw England again. It is a tragedy that his time there brought him so much misfortune, and ended so badly, for he always loved and admired England. There was something almost spiritual about his feeling for the country, its people and institutions, as though he had recognized in this new queen of the seas some attitudes and enchantments of his own mother, the old queen, Venice.

The language, at any rate, never frightened him, as it has done so many foreigners. He went at it head on — like some heroic Italian fox-hunter galloping at hard, high fences, sword in hand to slay the cruel fox. Here are some of his spellings: COVENGARDE, DRURI-LAINE, GRIM-PARC, PIQUE-DILLE, KINGTSINTON, S. POL, BUK-INGAN AUS, STROMBIR (as opposed to 'small beer'), BOULINGRIN, CHIRINCRAS, PALE-MALE, AUSEKEPER, WETER, ROCHEBIF, PINGBROS (these establishments are marked by a three-ball sign), VISK (as in 'Let's play a few ROBERS of VISK') . . .

To La Charpillon Casanova left, indirectly, a souvenir of their vile relationship. It was a parrot. He bought it soon after the episode in Fielding's court, hung its cage by his bed, and taught it to say a pretty French phrase. When the parrot had thoroughly learned the phrase, and endlessly repeated it with maniacal chuckles, Casanova sent it back to the parrot market to be exhibited for sale for fifty guineas. For a long time no one bought it, for the price was very steep, although hundreds came to hear it, and its apothegm became the catch-phrase of the town. Many lawyers listened, in particular, and great were the debates as to whether a parrot could be sued for slander. Finally Lord Grosvenor bought it for La Charpillon, who presumably wrung its neck, for its famous phrase was 'The Charpillon is a bigger whore than her mother'.

12

An Affair of Honour

Surely, now, to Portugal, where his mysterious project would make
his fortune? But no, he headed in the opposite direction, pausing
only long enough in Wesel for the good Doctor Wilhelm Peipers to
'cure' him of his syphilis. He travelled almost continuously for three
and half years, but gives no reasons for his movements. It has been
suggested that he was organizing the renascent Freemasons, but I
think he was certainly on the same quest as in England – trying to
run a state lottery.

His route, in broad outline only and omitting some long detours,
was: Calais, through Belgium, Hanover, Berlin, Riga, St Petersburg
(Leningrad), Moscow and back, Warsaw, Breslau, Dresden, Vienna,
Augsburg, Württemberg, Cologne, Spa, Paris. It adds up to about
4,500 miles, and this is the time to enlarge a little on just what
Casanova's odyssey implied.

In these years there was a daily stage coach which left London for
Oxford at 7 a.m. High Wycombe, 27 miles, was reached at 5 p.m.
The next day the coach reached Oxford, after another ten-hour day
for a further 27 miles. The average speed was therefore 2·7 m.p.h.
when actually on the road. A rather faster coach to Birmingham
covered the 115 miles in two and a half days, at, say, 4·6 m.p.h. Even
allowing for the occasions when Casanova rode post, or had his own
carriage, he must have spent about one thousand hours in carriages,
and one hundred nights in coaching inns.

The rates were not cheap: 21/- to Birmingham, for instance, or,
say, £1 (2.40 dollars) per 100 miles, with 14lbs free baggage and 1d
per lb excess. It was not comfortable. The coaches had room for six
passengers inside and two or three on the roof, but it was not until
about this period, 1760, that any provision was made to keep the
outside passengers on the curved roof, by giving them bars to hang
on to. Behind the body of the coach there was a huge basket in
which travelled, bundled together like the farm merchandise they

were, chickens, eggs, vegetables and wealthy peasants; poor peasants travelled by oxcart, which was cheaper, and slower. The French diligence, such as that used by Casanova on his first journey from Lyon to Paris, was very similar to the British stagecoach. It was usually drawn by five horses, and driven by a postilion on the off-wheeler, rather than the near-wheeler, as was the English custom.

In Italy roads and coaching facilities were alike terrible. Goethe said that the postchaises were just the ancient litters with two wheels added – 'You are tossed about as you would have been centuries ago'. The postilions employed at the posting houses were universally dishonest and untrained, and frequently drunk. The rates of hire varied from province to province. Vaussard, in his *Daily Life in Eighteenth Century Italy*, gives the following official rates for Milan: for a saddle horse, 3.10 lire (about 2/– or 25 cents) per stage of six miles; for a post-chaise, 10.10 lire (about 6/– or 75 cents); for a four-wheeled, three-horse carriage, 14.10 lire (8/– or about 1 dollar). The postmasters charged foreigners more if they thought they could get away with it. Lower rates were available to anyone who obtained the right authorization beforehand; but then the postmasters would go to great lengths to avoid producing a carriage at all and, if forced, would order the postilions never to move out of a walk.

Such were the conditions in which Casanova made his tremendous journeys.

After a short fruitless stay in Brunswick, where he received no encouragement from the reigning Duke (a Freemason), he went on to Berlin. Here the younger Calzabigi was already running a lottery for Frederick the Great (a Freemason), but the King had just cancelled the state's financial backing and left the lottery on its own. Casanova tried to get Calzabigi to go into partnership with him. He had no success, but he did have an interview with Frederick, a man whose spartan tastes were directly opposed to Casanova's.

They met in the gardens of Sans Souci. The King began by taking off his hat and asking Casanova 'in a terrifying voice' what he wanted. The subsequent conversation covered fountains, taxes, Calzabigi's lottery and the military power of Venice. It ended with Frederick looking Casanova up and down and saying, 'Do you know that you are a fine man?' This remark stung Casanova to the quick. Was it possible, he asked the King, that after their elevated conversation His Majesty should notice only those qualities in him which were shared by the least of His Majesty's guardsmen? The king smiled – 'kindly', Casanova says, but I doubt it: King Frederick was not a kindly man; and that was the end of their talk.

A few weeks later the King offered Casanova an appointment as tutor to a new corps of cadets. Casanova makes it sound awful. He describes how he took one look at the thirteen-year-old hobbledehoys and the barrack where they were to be lodged and left shuddering; but not before the Great King had ridden up and created a scene because he found a cadet's chamber pot was dirty.

This is all quite remote from the actuality. The cadet corps was to consist of fifteen young noblemen chosen for their intelligence; and the five tutors were to be famous savants. The place that Casanova turned down was given to an eminent Swiss, de Meirolles. The boys were not lodged in a barrack, but in upper rooms of the Royal Stables in the Breite Strasse; but only until their Academy could be built. The King's offer was in fact a good one, and flattering to Casanova's self-esteem; but there wasn't enough money in it.

In Berlin at this time he met a couple called Greve, and paid his court to Mme Doris – platonically, he says, but a much later reappearance of her name makes me wonder. And here in Berlin, where Casanova's very existence seems guaranteed only by his own veracity – and who would trust that? – suddenly independent light shines from the wings and there is Casanova, on stage marvellously lit: 'I dined at Rufin's, where Nehaus, an Italian, wanted to shine as a great philosopher, and accordingly doubted of his existence and of everything else. I thought him a blockhead.' Thus James Boswell, writing in his Journal for 1 September 1764. Nehaus or Neuhaus means, in German, New House – or Casanova; and there is documentary evidence that Casanova sometimes called himself Neuhaus in Germany.

Between Prussia and Russia lie those Baltic lands since wholly swallowed up by Russia. Casanova travelled through Courland where he came to intimate terms with the ruling family, the Birons. Duke Ernest was a big powerful man of seventy-four who had been lover of the Russian Empress Anna Ivanovna, and Regent of Russia after her death. The Duke's son, Charles, Prince of Courland, was a man of Casanova's own age and tastes, a Freemason, cabalist and spendthrift who landed up in the Bastille for petty crime.

Casanova arrived in Mitau, the capital, with an introduction from Prince Charles to his father, and no money. There is no mention of a lottery, but at dinner the conversation happened to turn on mines and minerals and Casanova, true to his genius, spoke at length and with considerable force on the subject. The next day the Duke begged him to make a two-week tour of the Duchy, and prepare a report on the mineral situation with recommendations for improving it. Turning himself with no trouble into an engineer, he visited five iron and copper mines, prepared his report, and received two hundred ducats in payment. The Duchess, he reports, took the greatest care of him, and at the end of a banquet gave him with her own hands a glass of liqueur. He took it for Tokay, at the least, and praised it accordingly: but it was only old English beer.

Still trying, he went to Russia. With considerable acumen he managed to get an interview with Catherine the Great by talking about calendar reform (Russia still used the Julian calendar, which was eleven days behind the rest of Europe; hence the 'October Revolution', which took place on 7 November Gregorian style). Casanova urged Catherine to put Russia on the Gregorian calendar, but she said there would be a rebellion, because the peasants would feel she had stolen those eleven days from their lives. Besides, several Saints' Days would vanish. In short, no!

At a second interview Casanova must have raised the subject of a lottery, and the Empress said that for all practical purposes it would not work. In short, no!

Russia fascinated him in a macabre way, but he didn't like it (except the communal naked bathing), perhaps because his piles became so bad there that he almost had to have them operated on, without anaesthetics, a prospect to jaundice anyone's view. He shared the common opinion that the only thing any Russian understood was a good beating, and tells a funny story about a horse on the journey from St Petersburg to Moscow, which went sick and refused to eat. The coachman pleaded with it, kissed it, hugged it, all to no purpose. Then, losing his temper, he tied the animal to a post and beat the hell out of it with a large stick for a quarter of an hour. The horse began to eat ravenously.

Nor, in spite of the lack of any true freedom in Venice, could he hide his scorn of the Russian tyranny:

We reached Moscow in the time the *chevochic* had predicted. It would have been impossible to have travelled any faster, as the same horses were used for the entire journey. A Russian told me that the Empress Elizabeth had done the journey in fifty-two hours.

'You mean she issued an ukase saying that she had done it,' said a Russian of the old school; 'and if she had wanted to she could have covered the distance in even less time.'

His sexual adventures are unimaginative, except two. The first was with Zaira, a fourteen-year-old girl he bought for a hundred roubles. He taught her Venetian but she remained excessively Russian. She read the cards, became madly jealous and tried to kill him with a bottle. He soon traded her in.

The other excitement was at an orgy not many *versts* outside St Petersburg, where Casanova passed up the main course (a French adventuress) but couldn't resist one of the side-dishes, a beautiful Lieutenant Lunin. Until Casanova's true text was at last published by the firm which held it, the dénouement of this episode, as of the affair with the wily Ismail in Constantinople, was suppressed from the original and therefore did not appear in translations. Here it is:

After dinner, seated in front of the fire between [Lt Lunnin] and the French lady traveller, I told him of my suspicions [that he was a woman dressed as a man] but Lunin, jealous of the superiority of his sex, displayed the proof of it on the spot and, interested to find out whether I could remain indifferent to his beauty, he took hold of me and, believing that he had found he pleased me, put himself in a position to make both of us happy. And that is just what would have happened if La Rivière, annoyed that a young man should poach on her preserves in her presence, had not grabbed him from behind and forced him to defer his exploit to some more convenient time.

This struggle made me laugh; but, not having been indifferent, I didn't think I ought to pretend I had been. I told the woman to mind her own business, which Lunin took as a declaration in his favour on my part. Lunin showed off all the treasures of his body, even his white breast, and defied the woman to do the same which she refused to do, calling us b . . .; we retorted by calling her a w . . . ; and she left us. The Young Russian and I exchanged tokens of the tenderest friendship, and swore eternal love . . .

I have not discussed Casanova's homosexual tendencies until now because he himself didn't. As I noted when remarking on the Ismail incident, Casanova seemed to be testing the temperature of the water – trying to judge by the reaction of readers, who would not be born until after he died, how they would take the revelation that he, the universal bull, was also, and perhaps by preference, a fairy. He has dropped enough clues ever since – passion for Bellino before he knew it was Teresa; his delight in transvestitism; his relations with the Duke of Maddaloni – and now for some reason he decides (looking into those not yet existent eyes) that it is going to be all right; he will not lose respect if he tells the truth; so he does.

He has not told the whole truth, though. A page of notes in his handwriting, found among his papers, contains the following notes, as though for chapter headings: *Mes amours avec Camille (en prison); Le Duc d'Elboeuf; Pédérastie avec X. à Dunquerque.* Camille is a man's name in French. The Duc d'Elboeuf was a notorious sodomite of the time; and the last phrase needs no explanation. But he never describes those incidents.

Much of his *Story* now becomes more logical. The affair in the seminary was probably an early homosexual experience, and nothing very unusual, or indicative, at that age. The meeting with Bragadin looks quite different, and more real. Casanova said that as he was leaving the wedding ball he noticed that the old senator had dropped a note. Of course he had! He wanted to pick up Casanova. Then in the gondola it was a different kind of heart attack altogether that hit Bragadin. He took the young man home to the other aunties, Dandolo and Barbaro; and soon Casanova had shown that he could keep all three of them happy. In Casanova's version, Bragadin's affection for the waif is very touching; and, unless one believes that the fact of homosexuality changes the character of acts and emotions, it still is touching. Casanova was still an unmitigated scamp and nuisance to them. They still cared for him, still tried to save him from himself, still did their best to keep him out of trouble, still rescued him when he managed to get into it. They still sent him money and still tried to obtain his return. Nor can they have had much sex out of him, because he was away from Venice so much. It was a genuine father-son relationship, and because there was no blood tie, the sexual undertones can be accepted.

More reconsiderations: I think the Inquisitors put Casanova under the Leads to break the three old men of their infatuation with him, rather than for the necromancy and cabalism, or at least that both were factors.

It will be recalled that the banker Hope of Amsterdam did not have a daughter, and that Esther was either an illegitimate daughter or a niece. There is another supposition. Hope did have a son. The reason that Casanova could not stay, marry the girl, and inherit the millions, might be that his playmate was not a girl.

One would be wise to suspect that his relations with his servants, such as Costa and Leduc, were homosexual; and I personally think that this is also true of Antonio Balletti and Le Cadet, of whom he was very fond.

The revelation, or acknowledgment, of sexual bipolarity makes Casanova a difficult, complex and constantly varying figure. As a sexual animal, he changed from situation to situation, from person to person. The affair with Lunin was homosexual lust, but the association with Bragadin began, at least, as a simple sale of his body, the way all his family and everyone else in the theatre, of both sexes, sold theirs. To some women he made love because their female bodies aroused his male desire, to others because he would get money or advantage out of it, to others because he fell in love, and to yet others because it was expected of him, because he would be sneered at if he didn't. And perhaps the sneer would have been 'Fairy!'

The fear of being sneered at is the only reason Casanova half-hid his tastes. It was a question of the climate of his time and place. Ancient Greeks did not feel ashamed of homosexual capability; nor do modern Arabs and Pathans. In many other periods and countries, homosexuality has been accepted without guilt of perversion or taint of effeminacy. Casanova lived in a betwixt-and-between time. Lieutenant Lunin went on to become a lieutenant-general, so no one can have worried much about his feminism; but Casanova, the actress's bastard, obviously worried about his. We can say that homosexuality was not, *per se*, respected, but that its status depended on the status of the homosexual. If he were the Duc d'Elboeuf he would be suffering from a faintly comical aberration; if he were a dancer, he would be basely selling his perverted body.

However he may have succeeded with the gorgeous Lieutenant Lunin, our deviate had no further prospects with the Empress, among whose several hundred lovers he was never to be numbered; so he headed back westward, the first stop being in Warsaw. Here King Stanislaus II of the Poniatowski family was almost a vassal of Russia, a cosy situation, as he was one of those who *had* been Catherine's lovers. Casanova swaggered himself into a position of some intimacy with the Polish court, and might have achieved his ambition here, only the Polish monarch 'was weak enough to allow himself to be swayed by slander'.

In other words, Casanova failed again with his lottery; but there did occur here an event comparable in importance in his life only with his escape from the Leads. This was his duel with Major General the Count Franciszek Branicki, the Royal Postoli, Knight of the White Eagle, Colonel of Uhlans and friend of King Stanislaus. The duel arose out of a feud between two actresses, La Binetti and La Catai. For various reasons Casanova found himself in La Catai's camp, as was Tomatis, a theatrical producer, while Count Branicki was in the Binetti camp. Tomatis made life as disagreeable for La Binetti as he could. She told Branicki, who ordered a soldier to give Tomatis a box on the ear.

Tomatis swallowed the insult. He had 40,000 ducats invested in the theatre production, and if he had called out Branicki or succeeded by other means in avenging himself, he would have had to leave

Poland and lose his money. At least, that was the way he saw it, but the gentry of Warsaw, including Casanova, considered that he should have done *something*.

On 4 March Casanova went to the ballet. He was in the *prima ballerina*'s dressing-room afterwards, exchanging mild gallantries, when Count Branicki walked in and said he loved the lady. Casanova, who had never seen or spoken to her before this, said in effect 'Fine, she's yours'. Branicki then called him a coward for giving way. This insult was later amended by Branicki and his accompanying bully boys to 'Venetian coward'. Casanova was a Venetian but no coward, by anyone's account, and what he did he would certainly have done even if 100,000 ducats had depended on it. He told the Count that a Venetian coward might yet kill a brave Pole outside the theatre; and waited outside for a quarter of an hour with his sword in his hand. No one came, possibly because duelling was banned inside Warsaw, and for a certain distance around, on pain of death.

Casanova played cards that night with Prince August Czartoryski, the king's uncle, of whom, eventually, he asked advice. The Prince said, 'I never give advice in these affairs, in which one must do everything or nothing.' Casanova went to bed. He awoke at 5 a.m. with the phrase *everything or nothing* dinning in his head. He decided that, for him, it must be everything. There and then he wrote out a challenge to a duel to the death, and sent his servant off with it to Count Branicki.

Everything or nothing. The phrase, in context, is clear enough: one must either risk one's life, or swallow the insult. But to Casanova it had a deeper meaning. All his life he had demanded respectful treatment from all men, especially such as were born noble or rich – that is, with the advantages he did not have. A few days earlier he had seen Tomatis swallow a deliberate insult. As far as any pretensions to gentility, to a position among aristocrats was concerned, Tomatis was finished: he had been put in his place – a fellow from the theatre. Casanova's family was of the theatre, and plenty of people knew it. If he did not want to become *nothing* again, if he wanted to maintain any pretensions, to continue to be accepted in the world where he lived and made his living, he must fight. And, if he survived, a duel with Count Branicki would bring *everything*. The gentry and aristocracy of Europe only enforced the code of the duel, and only accepted challenges based on it, among themselves. One did not duel with tradesmen, servants, or actors, any more than one did with women. If Branicki accepted Casanova's challenge, therefore, Casanova would never again have to explain, or prove, that he was a gentleman. The Count would have done it for him.

Casanova must have waited with mixed but powerful emotions for the Count's reply. The Count, by a chance useful to Casanova's purpose, was also something of an adventurer. The real Count Branicki was a Polish patriot of very old, very high family, who is said to have destroyed his coat of arms when he heard that an upstart quisling called Franciszek Korczak had assumed his name. It was this Korczak, favourite of the king and head of the pro-Russian party, who fought Casanova. A member of the real Branicki family would probably have refused to fight, but Korczak, although he was of petty nobility, must have felt the pressure of his assumed name.

So he accepted Casanova's challenge, insisting only that the duel must take place that very day or never (he gave no reason) and must be with pistols (he probably feared that Casanova was a professional fencing master). At three o'clock in the afternoon he drove up to Casanova's in splendour: a carriage and six with coachmen; two grooms leading saddle horses; two aides-de-camp; two hussars; four servants standing behind the carriage; a lieutenant-general and an armed footman inside with himself – a total of fourteen horses and fifteen men to deal with one 'Venetian coward'. But this was the way the Polish nobility lived, and it certainly helped Casanova's reputation that the duel should be conducted with such panoply.

He got into the carriage, having no servants and apparently no second, and it drove off. After half an hour, that is, when still well within the area where duelling was punishable by death, it stopped. Everyone entered a large garden. For form's sake the lieutenant-general, Czapski, tried to stop the duel, then Casanova and Branicki took up the pistols that had been prepared.

Branicki swore that the pistol Casanova took was a good one. Casanova snapped, 'I am going to try its goodness on your head.'

He was later convinced that this chance phrase won him the duel. A hit in the head, with the large lead balls used, was almost always fatal, and if not, disfiguring. But the head is a small target and in fact duellists seldom aimed at it, but rather at the centre of the body. The thought of a head wound panicked Branicki, and he spent so long raising his pistol to cover his head, aiming along the barrel, that the two men actually fired together. Both were hit, Casanova in the left hand and Branicki through the body. Branicki fell. Casanova ran to him, and the Count's noble thugs tried to kill him. Luckily for him, Branicki had enough voice left to tell them to leave him alone.

Then Czapski and Casanova helped Branicki to a nearby inn. Branicki thought he was dying, and told Casanova to flee for his life. Casanova went outside and found no one in sight. All the horses and carriages and men had galloped off to get doctors and inform Branicki's relatives. A country sleigh came down the snow-covered road, and Casanova bought a ride in it. As soon as he was under the rough covering, Lt-Col. Biszewski, one of Branicki's chief aides, galloped past waving a bared sword, eager to avenge his master; but he did not think to look in the rustic sleigh. So Casanova reached Warsaw, and took sanctuary in the Convent of the Recollects, which was actually a monastery. The porter tried to bar his entrance, but Casanova kicked him out of the way.

Casanova now had to face four enemies, all intent on killing him. First, as he had fought a duel inside the forbidden zone, the High Constable would have his head as soon as he left the religious sanctuary. Second, Biszewski and Branicki's Uhlans, hearing that their master had been killed, were raging up and down the city to wreak vengeance on the perpetrator of the deed. Third, his wound was liable to turn gangrenous. And fourth, the doctors seemed determined to finish him off if the wound didn't.

His adventurer's luck held. The High Constable, not wishing to be cheated out of Casanova's head by a mob of unruly lancers, had the monastery surrounded by dragoons. This saved Casanova until it was known that Branicki would live, when the Uhlan's fury subsided. Then the king pardoned him for duelling, which called off the High Constable. The wound did indeed turn gangrenous. The bullet had hit a metal button on Casanova's waistcoat, giving him a stomach wound, then ricocheted into his left hand, where it had lodged. Four surgeons in conference pronounced it essential to amputate his hand. He refused to let them do it, being convinced that his hand was on the way to curing itself; and so it happened.

Free and fit, he set off on a brief tour of Poland, which he found an eccentric land indeed. He was lodged in magnificent rooms totally devoid of furniture: one was supposed to travel with one's own; and he was offered a number of girls, all with their heads covered: 'Never mind about the face if the rest's all right,' the Poles said.

He returned to Warsaw in triumph; and was ordered to leave Poland within a week. His calumniators had been at work, and heavens knows there was plenty to calumniate. Casanova pretended considerable anger, but in fact he had achieved all he could hope for. He had fought a duel with a Knight of the White Eagle and been proven a gentleman.

He set off on his travels once more. In Dresden was a nest of Casanovas, headed by his brother Giovanni, like Francesco a painter and like Giacomo a scoundrel: this one got himself into trouble in

160

Rome in 1761 by selling some of his own works to the art expert Winckelmann as Old Masters. Winckelmann was considerably put out, and when Giovanni Casanova was expelled from Rome a few years later on a charge of issuing false bills of exchange it was, rather too handily, Winckelmann who gave the principal evidence against him. At all events, Giovanni kept his position as Director of the Dresden Academy of Fine Arts.

Also here were Casanova's mother, whom he had not seen for thirteen years, and his sister Maria Maddalena, married to Peter August, a court musician. But none of them could sway the royal house into giving Casanova his lottery licence . . . so on to Vienna. Here he found the elder Calzabigi, now under the protection of the powerful chancellor Kaunitz; but there was nothing for Casanova, who had the incredible stupidity to involve himself with yet another of the peripatetic Pocchini's 'little girls'. This one recited smutty Latin verses and invited Casanova for fornication or sodomy, as he preferred – an invitation which ended, instead, in a fixed card game, and a summary order from the security chief, Count Schrattenbach, to leave the country. (Casanova manages to misspell this detestable fellow's name in a marvellously obscene manner: Schrotemback.) Casanova bitterly protested at the expulsion, but as the Empress Maria Theresa herself was behind it, he had to go.

And that, as far as central and eastern Europe was concerned, was that. He had failed everywhere, partly from a general distrust by all monarchs of this form of lottery, and partly from a specific distrust by one and all of Giacomo Casanova, Chevalier de Seingalt. London had broken him – he said so himself – and the downhill pace was getting quicker. He was never rich again. He kept his pride – indeed he augmented it – but it was turning querulous and petty. He had always wanted to be famous and respected and he could see now that he had come pretty close: he was infamous and suspected.

He headed for Paris, by way of Spa, where he hoped to make some money at the gaming tables. Here he fell in once again with Antonio della Croce. Self-ennobled to the rank of Marquis, della Croce had yet another girl with him. She was sixteen or seventeen, and pregnant. Her name was Charlotte and she had run away with him six or seven months earlier. Casanova, who was forty-two, fell in love with her, while racking his brains to discover what della Croce had that such a succession of superior women should leave home for him and his rather obvious villainies. 'He was not what you would call good-looking; he lacked a sophisticated wit and polish and his manner of talking was unappealing.' So Casanova was not surprised when della Croce took him aside and told him he was flat broke and intended to fly (to Warsaw, for some unstated reason) – alone. He handed Charlotte into Casanova's care and left.

Casanova took the girl to Paris, lodged her, and arranged for her confinement. On 13 October 1767 she caught a fever. On 17 October she had a baby boy. The next day the midwife gave Casanova a certificate. It was worded as follows:

We, J. Baptiste Dorival, Councillor to the King, Commissary of the Châtelet of Paris, formerly Superintendent of Police for the Cité, do certify that there has been taken to the Foundlings' Hospital a male infant appearing to be one day old, brought from the Faubourg St-Denis by the midwife Lamarre, dressed in swaddling clothes, in which there was found a certificate to the effect that he had been baptized this same day at St-Laurent under the name of Jacques Charles, son of Antoine la Crosse, and of Charlotte X.X.X. Wherefore . . .

Casanova adds:

If any of my readers wish to know the mother's real name, I have given them the means of finding out.

That curiosity was not satisfied until 1894, when someone took the trouble to search the records. These confirmed Casanova in every detail. Charlotte's name was Lamotte.

Eight days later, at five o'clock in the morning, Charlotte died.

Before closing her lovely eyes, an hour before she died, she bade me a last farewell, telling me it was the end, and before letting go of my hand she took it to her lips, in the presence of the priest, who had confessed her at midnight. The tears which I shed now, as I write, are probably the last by which I shall honour the memory of this sweet creature, a victim of love . . .

He stayed closeted with the corpse as he stayed close to the living girl's side during her confinement and last agony. Then gradually he surfaced to the world in which he must live. His brother, the impotent battle-painter, gave him some letters that had come for him. The first he opened informed him that Senator Bragadin was dead.

I had no tears left to weep with. The man who had been my father for twenty-two years, who had gone without, and even into debt, to support me – was dead.

For three days he shut himself in his brother's house. Then he took up again the burden of living. There was still the Countess de Rumain, who was sure that the spirits had sent him back to Paris to solve all her troubles with his infallible cabala.

On 4 November he went to the theatre. The Marquis de Lisle said in a loud voice that this actress's son had stolen a million francs from his aunt, the Marquise d'Urfé. Casanova challenged the young man to meet him outside the theatre. De Lisle did not come, but two days later King Louis XV, in a *lettre de cachet*, ordered Casanova to leave Paris in twenty-four hours and France within three weeks. No reason was given except that such was the King's good pleasure.

It was time, at last, to go to Portugal . . . surely?

13

The Long Road Home

Casanova left Paris toward the end of November 1767 and, travelling via Orleans and Bordeaux, probably entered Spain through the Pass of Roncesvalles. From Pamplona he travelled on south, cresting the lip of the great Castilian steppe at Agreda. Agreda stands steep and severe on the edge of the escarpment, looking north over the hundred-mile-wide basin of the Ebro, but it was not its appearance but its name which gave Casanova the shudders, for it was here, in 1627, that Sister Maria had written that *Mystical City of God* which nearly drove him insane under the Leads.

On, over roads which were by universal agreement the worst in Europe, to Madrid, where he presented his letters of introduction and set about getting himself a girl. Her name was Ignazia, a cobbler's daughter, and there is nothing remarkable about her except her rigid Spanish religious fanaticism, and the curious way in which it aroused a complementary response in Casanova. Although most of his women were Roman Catholics, the fact that they would have to confess their sin and might be excluded from Communion had never bothered them, or him. With Ignazia the obstacles to seduction were almost purely religious.

In assessing the girl's character Casanova again bares the ingenuous side of his make-up. He needed a woman initially to take to a public ball. The picking-up was easy. He went to church, looked over the available fillies, chose one, followed her home, went into the house, and asked her father to be allowed to take her to the ball. Since every girl in Madrid wanted to go, and mother would go along as duenna, there was no problem here. The fandango itself, as then performed, seems to have been a public miming of the sexual act in dance rhythm. Ignazia was a simple virgin, but danced in so copulatory a fashion that the frenzied Casanova asked her then and there when he could expect to be 'made happy'. Ignazia said she would tell him the next day. Next day the simple virgin sent him a young man who wanted to marry her, with a proposition: Casanova would lend the young fellow a hundred doubloons; the young man would marry Ignazia: then (this part was not spelled out) Ignazia, being safely married, would make Casanova 'happy'. Casanova rejected the young man very coldly, but never seems to have appreciated that the girl had acted like a scheming, over-smart hussy.

The long-drawn affair with Ignazia did eventually make him 'happy', but he would have done better to have left her to her young man and himself taken up the veiled invitations extended to him by the Marquesa de Villadarias. This lady was a notorious nymphomaniac who could not wait one moment for satisfaction when the amorous fury seized her, an affliction which led to some astonishing scenes on dance floors and drawing-room carpets.

The rest of the Spanish story is a sad catalogue of arrests, imprisonments, quarrels, misunderstandings and sickness.

Early on, he spent two nights in prison on a trumped-up charge. One suspects again the determination of Authority to get rid of him before he Created Trouble: but he had a most powerful ally in the Count de Aranda (the real one). Aranda was the King's chief minister, and a Freemason, and he soon got Casanova out of jail. But when arrested Casanova had been staying with the painter Rafael Mengs – the same Mengs at whose house in Rome he had been dining when Papal envoys brought him the Golden Spur. Mengs was now court painter to Charles III, the worthy and fantastically ugly Bourbon trying to rule Spain, and the arrest at his house caused a quarrel between the two men, because Mengs objected to the scandal.

Next, Casanova fell ill on his way to Aranjuez, where the Venetian ambassador would have introduced him to the King. Not only did this sickness lose him entrée to the Court, but it caused him to be excommunicated for failing to attend mass on Easter Sunday.

Nevertheless, he had hope. There *was* an opening in Spain suitable for a man of his talents. The post was Lieutenant Governor (or perhaps First Deputy would have to suffice, as he was a foreigner) of a colony of Swiss-German immigrants in the Sierra Morena. The colony had been proposed by a Bavarian adventurer, Lt-Col. Kaspar Thürriegel. With the advice of his chief ministers, Campomanes and Aranda, the King had authorized Thürriegel to import 6,000 colonists of Catholic German stock. He signed the magical formula YO EL REY to the contract on 2 April 1767, and appointed as first Governor an extremely capable native of Peru, Don Pablo Olavides – also a Freemason.

The difficulties of establishing northern Europeans in the Sierra

Morena, the burning range of hills which faces south across the Guadalquivir, promised to be considerable. Apart from problems of economics, agriculture, industry, culture, custom and law, the King and Campomanes privately proposed to use the colony as a lever to lift Spain into the modern world. The constitution of it forbade the setting up of any abbey, monastery, or religious foundation: and it made strict rules curbing the privileges of the Mesa, a stockowners' society all-powerful in the rest of Spain. How our Venetian imagined that he was going to master this mass of complexities, one does not know; but he probably would have succeeded, for he understood human nature, even if he did not often follow his own advice, and he was certainly capable of conducting the necessary intrigues, and of using force and threats when necessary. Nor was his counsel to be faulted. As he wrote, in part, to Campomanes, on 27 May 1768: 'It is proper . . . to forbid the installation of any person whose vices could provoke laziness, love of luxury, debauchery, disease, or libertinism . . .'

With Aranda's support, and perhaps Olavides' also, all that was lacking for Casanova to get employment in this great project was the favour of his ambassador, for when dealing with foreigners the advice of their ambassador was always sought. The Venetian ambassador to Madrid was Alvise V Mocenigo, a particularly good subject from Casanova's point of view because he was an active homosexual, in the female, or catamitic role. His lover was a handsome embassy secretary, Count Manucci, and Count Manucci had become a firm friend of Casanova, whose wickedness in escaping from the Leads was gradually being forgotten.

Suddenly all doors were slammed in his face. For some time the shocked Casanova could not even find out what had happened. No, he had not broadcast the fact that Ambassador Mocenigo was his secretary's queen. Everyone knew that already. It was much worse: he had let slip the fact that Count Manucci was no Count, but the son of a miserable Venetian merchant who would stoop to anything to make a few sequins – even to spying on Giacomo Casanova, leading to the latter's imprisonment.

Manucci's anger was implacable; Mocenigo would do anything to please his lover, and everyone else took their cue from him. Aranda advised his fellow-Freemason to leave Spain, since he now had no hope of employment under the Spanish Court or Crown.

So Casanova went . . . on, at last, to Portugal, surely?

Alas, no. His narrative has a couple of ominous references to that country and finally 'I had no longer hopes of doing anything in

Portugal' ... The penultimate mirage had faded. Flat broke, he decided to sell a gold watch and snuffbox, and with the proceeds make his way to the last distant Eldorado – Constantinople: there he would try his fortune 'without turning renegade' (for that would lose him all that he had gained by the famous duel). But he never did go to Constantinople, and from now on he really had only one object in life. He would gamble and cheat and make love again. He would borrow and give and take. The journey, far from being direct, would look like the wanderings of a drunken snake. But the goal was sure, and unalterable, his motherland and mother, the more cruel the more loved: Venice.

Casanova left Madrid early in September 1768, travelling via Zaragoza and Sagunto to Valencia, where he fell in with Nina Bergonzi, an Italian dancer who was mistress of Count Ricla, Captain General of Catalonia. Nina was the product of sexual relations between her father and his daughter, who was therefore Nina's mother and sister. If the father had not died, Nina would have been next in line for the same treatment. She first engaged Ricla's attention by showing her drawers when doing a simple hop-skip routine on stage. In Spain a dancer who showed her drawers was automatically fined. Nina cursed mightily, but paid the fine, and took care not to show her drawers again: she danced without them, causing, as the narrator drily put it 'an eruption of sparkling high spirits in the theatre such as had never been known in Barcelona'. The Captain General fizzed with the rest, and quickly installed the girl as his mistress.

By way of introduction Nina had herself pleasured in front of Casanova by Ricla's resident spy. With her background she was, not unnaturally, a monster of viciousness. She liked to torment Ricla by committing outrageous infidelities and ensuring that he received full reports of them. She forced her body on Casanova, too, but it was for this sadistic purpose, not for her own or his direct pleasure. As bait she allowed Casanova to win some money from her at cards.

When she insisted that he follow her to Barcelona he ought to have realized the danger he was in; but he went, and it is an indication of his decline that he permitted her to install him in an inn and provide him with a servant and carriage, at her (or Ricla's) expense. It was not long since the mere hint of such a thing would have pulled his sword from its sheath, for gigolism was *the* mark of the theatre, and hence *the* imputation he must never lay himself open to.

Since Nina also insisted that Casanova visit her every night after the Captain General had left, Ricla could hardly help knowing what was going on. Indeed, the whole city knew. But Casanova had, once again, temporarily lost his senses, for, as he ruefully remarks, 'There might have been some excuse for me if I had been in love with her, but having no feelings for her . . .'

Casanova was only a pawn in her war against mankind; so in another way was Ricla.

The Count duly played his part. On 15 November at midnight, as Casanova was leaving Nina's house, two men tried to assassinate him. Casanova ran his sword through one, and fled for his life down the dark alley, followed by a pistol shot from the other man. The shot holed his greatcoat, under the armpit.

In the morning Casanova was arrested, taken to the citadel, and imprisoned in the Torre de Santa Clara there. Nothing was said of the attempted assassination, or of the fact that Casanova had probably killed a man. Officially he was arrested only because an ill-wisher had whispered that his passports were false. This ill-wisher was none other than the porno-taster Passano, failed Querilinth, who did indeed owe Casanova a monumental grudge, and, for our hero's ill fortune, happened to be passing through Barcelona.

Casanova spent six weeks in jail while his passports were sent to Madrid for verification. Since the round trip journey could have been made inside a week with ease, Ricla was also clearly showing his displeasure. Casanova used his enforced leisure to further his one desire. In 1676 Amelot de la Houssaye had published a markedly derogatory *History of the Government of Venice*. The Venetian Establishment had waited a long time for someone to refute de la Houssaye's calumnies and Casanova now set about doing it. He says he started and finished the work inside the six weeks of his imprisonment, with no references but his memory: but there is proof in one of his own letters, dated July 1768, that is, some months earlier, that he had written or drafted most of it by then.

Another acquaintance he had last seen in Lyon now helped get him out of the trouble Passano had got him into. This was the banker Bono, who arranged for an important friend to speak to Ricla on his way through Barcelona on 26 December 1768. Two days later Casanova was released from the Tower, given back his passports, told that he was absolutely innocent, and ordered to leave Barcelona in three days and Catalonia in seven. Time was when such an order would have led to scenes of Homeric fury, threats of vengeance, non-stop rides to Madrid . . . but Casanova left quietly and, dodging another attempted assassination in the sullen crags of the Pyrenees (this one engineered by the still raging Manucci), entered France near Perpignan.

The long, halting journey back to Venice continued. At Aix-en-Provence he went for a drive in an open carriage, it was cold and he had no cloak. Although half frozen when he returned, he did not go to bed but spent a couple of hours in the popular eighteenth-century sport of Break the Maidenhead. It was played like this: a young woman, still possessed of a hymen or a reasonable facsimile, announced that she will allow any gentleman, for a small charge, to try to rid her of the nuisance: when the gentleman sets to work she bends her spine in such a way that the pubic arch closes the entrance to the vagina. Casanova saw the trick at once, but could not force the door. All he got for his two hours was a severe pleurisy. He came close to death, but was devotedly nursed back to health by a mysterious old woman whom he presumed his doctor had provided. When he felt better, he went out to call on Henriette, at the nearby house where she had passed a night with Marcoline. Henriette wasn't there, but his devoted nurse was. She told him the story. Henriette had heard of his illness, and sent the woman, an old servant, to look after him. Casanova wrote to Henriette, who replied affectionately, but told him not to visit her. She had grown fat, and although he had actually seen her in Aix before his illness, he had not recognized her. So they never met again, but began a correspondence which lasted many years. She wrote him forty letters, and what happened to those letters has been one of the chief concerns of casanovists ever since.

It was in Aix, too, that Casanova met the third of his century's classic charlatans (Saint-Germain and Casanova himself being the other two) – the man later notorious as Count Cagliostro, but at this time still calling himself Giuseppe Balsamo. Casanova has one of his sharp descriptions: 'He seemed to be about twenty-four or twenty-five years old. He was short and quite well-built, showing on his pleasant face all the signs of boldness, impudence, and roguishness.' Balsamo, here posing as a pilgrim on his way back from Santiago de Compostela, showed Casanova that he was a skilful forger and copyist. He was also a cabalist, crook and near-genius, who was to invent his own brand of Freemasonry, dominate the world of quackery, and persuade considerable numbers of people that he could make gold, prolong sexual potency, and extend human life to 5,557 years.

Casanova went on his tortuous way – to Lugano now, where he had his *Refutation* of Amelot de la Houssaye printed, taking care that the Inquisitors at Venice should know how and by whom the Republic's sacred institutions were being defended. In Lugano he was dumbfounded to find the Baroness de Roll von Emmenholtz, the

Ludovika whose leg had made him forget Einsiedeln, and for whose love he had mistakenly served the loathsome Lame Lady. The Baron, her husband, was High Bailiff of Lugano on behalf of the Swiss Confederation, and although Ludovika did not renew their sexual acquaintance, the friendship enabled Casanova to move in respectable circles, a fact duly noted and reported back to the Inquisitors by the Venetian consul.

The *Refutation* printed, Casanova moved on to Turin; Parma (here he borrowed more money); Bologna; Pisa (here he sold the jewelled cross of his Golden Spur); the baths of S. Giuliano (here he met Bonnie Prince Charlie, but it was a long way from Culloden Moor, Flora Macdonald and the bonnie boat to Skye: Charles Stuart was fat and fifty-one, and next year the wits of Rome were calling his new wife the Virgin Queen because her husband's enthusiasm was reserved for the bottle).

. . . on to Leghorn (the Russian admiral Alexei Orlov offered him a trip to Constantinople, and he nearly went, but remembered in time that Venice was his destination).

. . . to Pisa again; Siena, and an adventure with an English girl called Miss Betty, only remarkable for one delightful and very Casanovan touch. They were travelling together and at Buonconvento, half a day's journey out of Siena on the way to Rome, Casanova says that Betty 'was agreeably surprised to see the steaks and plum pudding I had ordered for her'. The imagination boggles at the picture of Casanova instructing the cook of a small Italian posting inn in the preparation of these British national dishes, early in the extremely hot summer of 1770.

From Rome Casanova passed quickly to Naples, where he found that the Duke of Maddaloni, on whom he had clearly hoped to sponge for a time, was dead. But he found instead the kind of drifting, vicious society which perfectly suited his talents. Apart from strangers and new operatives in the field his chief cronies were Tommaso Medini and Ange Goudar. Medini was the adventurer with whom he had first crossed swords, literally, in Padua in 1746; Goudar was the equivocal 'friend' from London; and the three of them, crooks one and all, were also good writers. Medini made an excellent translation of Voltaire's *Henriade* into Italian *ottava rima*. Goudar wrote *L'Espion Chinois* and the *Histoire des Grecs* (a very highly regarded book on card sharpers, who were called 'Greeks'; well, if Goudar didn't know about 'Greeks', who did?).

Goudar was installed with a gambling den and a pretty wife as bait. The wife Casanova had known in London when she was Sarah, an Irish barmaid. She was moving up in the world, for now she was mistress of the young Fernando IV, King of Naples; was, that is, until the Queen intercepted a note in which Sarah told the King she was awaiting him with the eagerness of a cow awaiting the bull.

Casanova swam out into these foetid, slowly circulating waters of Neapolitan society. He gambled, winning and losing large amounts – but losing more than he won. He quarrelled and fought a duel with Medini once more. He acted as guide, cicerone, and shill to the rich and titled who visited Naples, never omitting to introduce them to Goudar's gaming tables. Notable among these were the scapegrace young Francesco Morosini, and his tutor the Count Simon Stratico; Francesco was the nephew of the powerful Procurator, who could do a great deal to help, or hinder, Casanova's return to Venice. Casanova had time for an affair with a much younger girl, which may have caused him to write the following lines about his close friend the British consul: 'He was a brilliant man and yet he had married a mere girl . . .' The consul's name was Sir William Hamilton and the 'mere girl' he married in 1791 was Emma Lyon Harte, who thus became Lady Hamilton.

Always restless now, Casanova left Naples and headed back towards Rome. On the way he visited the widowed Donna Lucrezia who was now living at Salerno with her (and his) daughter Leonilda. Leonilda had married a seventy-year-old marquis and Freemason. The marquis badly wanted a son to inherit the fortune which he did not wish to pass on to the vulture-like relatives surrounding him. Casanova did his best for his brother Mason in this small matter. Then, ignoring Lucrezia's final plea that he stay with them the rest of his life, he went on to Rome and a position, in a certain circle of society, which he describes as like a 'marker at billiards'.

The centre of the circle, for Casanova, was his old friend Cardinal de Bernis, ambassador of France and, from the splendour of his way of life, known as the King of Rome. The Cardinal lived in the palace which is now the Banca di Roma. Among those in orbit around him were the Princess Giuliana of Santa Croce, his titular mistress; the Duchess of Fiano; and the latter's *cavalier-servente*, the Prince of Santa Croce. No wonder they needed a marker to keep the score . . . Casanova became their shadow and sycophant, the retailer of gossip and sitter-beside of beds, the indispensable outsider and ashtray-emptier.

For his personal needs he took a room in 290 (now 32) Piazza di Spagna, and seduced his landlady's one-eyed daughter, Margharita Poletti, to the great chagrin of another lodger, the Abbé Cerutti, who wanted the girl for himself. But even with Margharita's ministrations it was a boring time as he waited for the efforts of his friends to bear fruit in Venice. He embellished it by improving the lot of some wretched girls shut up in a convent (probably the S. Caterina). The constitution of the convent, which was for poor girls and foundlings, had been foolishly written, in that the girls could only be released by someone asking for their hand in marriage; but they were not allowed out, so no man could see them to decide he wanted to marry them; nor could visitors see them in the convent, because interviews were conducted through a thick double grating which admitted almost no light. Upon this dark den of misery Casanova descended like a ray of sunshine. Through Cardinal de Bernis he had the rules relaxed, one by one. In no time he was taking a couple of inmates to the theatre, for, as he rightly pointed out, the girls had to learn how to behave in decent society before they were really fit to be let out into it. So, after the theatre there were little supper parties at an obliging inn, where clothes were exchanged, punch slurped down by the gallon, oysters sucked from lip to lip or allowed to slide down between dewy, budding breasts. The romping continued round the table or on the couch till long past midnight. The three girls who took this master's degree in society living were called Emilie, Armelline, and Scholastica.

In the middle of these instructional debauches he had a letter from his daughter Leonilda. She was six months pregnant. Casanova could not repress a shudder, he says.

He became at this time a member of two famous Academies. One was the Arcadians, or *L'Accademia degli Arcadi*. It arose out of the literary salon which Queen Christina of Sweden had founded after her abdication and retirement to Rome. On her death in 1689 several friends, wishing to carry on the purpose of the salon – to encourage the study of writing and poetry – founded the Arcadians. Each member of it took the name of 'a shepherd of Arcady'. Casanova chose *Eupolemo Pantaxeno*. The standing of the Academy, and, by inference of Casanova, as a man of letters, may be judged by the fact that Goethe became a fellow-Arcadian sixteen years later.

The other society was the less famous *Accademia degli Infecondi di Roma*, for which Casanova had to compose an ode on Christ's Passion. He went to the peace and quiet of the country to do this, being much aided by girls called Guillelmine, who was his brother Giovanni's illegitimate daughter, and Jacomine. He did not carnally possess Jacomine, but he did everything else – and with her established a new record in his sexual career; she was nine, and his own daughter by a previous affair.

But suddenly he is on his way to Florence, and suddenly Barbaro, another of his three old protectors in Venice, is dead: and suddenly, for the first time, the smell of fear pervades his *Story*. It is not the heroic fear, but real fear . . . fear of old age, of loneliness, of destitution, of empty years and an unregarded death. For a moment these grim, colourless shadows obliterate the Armellines and Scholasticas, the Leonildas and Jacomines . . . He faced the truth and decided he would change his mode of life. No more gambling, drinking, whoring, feasting, duelling! No, he would practise a studious manner, and devote himself to writing something Important. Translating the *Iliad* into modern Tuscan-Italian, for instance.

So, when he had settled into an unfashionable inn, he put on a black suit to denote that he was poor and did not intend to live the high life, went to the Pitti Palace, and asked the young Grand Duke to grant him asylum. Leopold, later Holy Roman Emperor, rather ominously replied that as long as his conduct was good, the laws guaranteed his freedom. Casanova knew better than anyone how much that pious nonsense was worth, but he could only bow, mouth his gratitude, return to his inn, and start to write.

'As long as his conduct was good . . .' Unhappily, Casanova was incapable of good conduct, and even when he did manage to keep the sheet clean for a few weeks, disreputable friends or rumours came and trampled their dirty feet over it. Like many a reformed drunkard his past forced him back into channels he would like to leave. Here in Florence Count Stratico turned up with his charge, young Morosini. Stratico had broken his leg and begged Casanova to keep Morosini company in his stead. If Casanova wanted the Morosini family to help him return to Venice, he could not refuse. So, in the line of duty, back he went to the brothels and drinking dens.

Next Medini appeared, as though linked to Casanova by an invisible string; and where Medini was, there was crooked gambling. Medini and his accomplices, a pair of clever young scoundrels called Alvise Zen and Premisla Zanovich, soon found the perfect lamb – an Englishman, naturally – in the young Earl of Lincoln, nineteen-year-old heir to the dukedom of Newcastle-under-Lyme. They sheared him of 12,000 guineas.

Within the week Zen, Zanovich, and Medini were ordered out of Tuscany; and so was Casanova, who had no hand in the business, he says, and he may be telling the truth. It was no longer necessary to have even the pretence of a reason to kick Casanova out of town.

He went to Bologna, and made his presence known to the Cardinal-Legate who governed the city – Branciforte, a noted Freemason and pederast. Under these friendly auspices he once more settled down to write. The *Iliad* progressed slowly and Casanova's discouragement must have been increased by the knowledge that there were other and better translators in the field. (Goudar declared that Casanova, in wishing to put Homer into a new pair of trousers, had only made the poet bare his fundament.) Casanova found diversion in a little pamphlet entitled *Lana Caprina*, a patchily brilliant satire on the condition of women; but one of the reviewers of this book was the Abbé Cerutti, who was very scathing; which only goes to show that authors should never touch critics' girls.

In Bologna, too, Casanova made the acquaintance of a very famous singer, Carlo Broschi, whose career casts as clear a light as any on how such as Casanova and Cagliostro could lead such brilliant lives in this eighteenth century. Broschi was a *castrato* whose stage name was Il Farinelli. He became a favourite of King Philip V of Spain and was the only person who could charm his successor, Ferdinand VI, out of his catatonic melancholia. Over ten years Ferdinand made him sing the same four favourite lyrics 3,600 times. In return the eunuch Farinelli became a Knight of Calatrava, a Grandee of Spain, and the most influential man in the kingdom.

Of much greater importance to Casanova was a chance which enabled him to open a correspondence with Pietro Zaguri. Zaguri was a young Venetian nobleman who seems to have admired Casanova, the city's *enfant terrible*, from afar, and now undertook to win his forgiveness from the Inquisitors. As a first step, he advised Casanova to live close to the borders of Venice, so that the state spies could report more easily on his mode of life. Casanova therefore decided to go to Trieste, across the head of the gulf from Venice.

To reach Trieste without passing through Venetian territory he planned to go by sea, via Ancona. At Sinigaglia he gave a ride to a Jew, Mardoque. When they reached Ancona Mardoque offered him lodging in his own house. Casanova accepted the offer, accompanied his host to the synagogue, and afterwards walked alone thinking:

It was in Ancona that I had started to enjoy life to the full; and when I thought about it, it was quite a shock to realize that this was thirty years ago, for thirty years is a long time in a man's life. And yet I still felt young.

What a difference I found when I compared my present physical and mental state with the way I was then. I scarcely recognized myself as the same man. The vision of a brilliant future no longer faced me and I realized that I had wasted my time and therefore wasted my life.

He shrugged off the morbid fit. Things were not that bad yet, for

174

Mardoque had a beautiful young daughter, Leah, and no ship was going to Trieste for some days. He set siege to Leah's virtue, using this time another of his favourite weapons, his little collection of erotic pictures. Leah resisted him with a sort of offhand disinterest that piqued him, and he had given up hope when, seeing a light late at night, he looked through a keyhole and saw Leah and a young man practising all Aretino's most athletic posturings, but there was no actual penetration: they pleasured each other only by hand or mouth. The scene infuriated Casanova beyond endurance: to think that the wretched girl should use *his* Aretino for the benefit of this young oaf!

He sailed with a sigh of relief at having rid himself of his infatuation, but a storm came up, the vessel returned to Ancona, and without waiting for orders the sailors took his baggage back to Mardoque's. His trial began again.

This time Leah set out to conquer him. He managed to remain cold through long hours while she pleaded her love, justification, and regrets in his darkened bedroom; but he did not trust himself, and searched frantically through Ancona to find a whore who would reduce his head of steam. He didn't find one he could rise for, and had only his bad temper to defend him when Leah came to his room again, wearing nothing but a short slip and chemise. This time she did not plead, but dropped the slip, took off the chemise, threw back the covers, and slid into bed with him. In a moment he was enwrapped by her arms and legs, and her mouth was seeking his. He gave up the struggle, reflecting that at eighteen she knew a lot more about human nature than he did at forty-seven. She was a passionate lover and, to his amazement, a virgin.

He put off his departure another month, but Leah was no substitute for Venice, and so at last on 14 November 1772 he set sail on a Neapolitan man-of-war just cleared from quarantine, and on 15 November landed at Trieste.

Trieste was then a part of the Holy Roman Empire. The officials with whom he was most concerned were the Intendant (Governor) and the Chief of Police. From early 1773 the Intendant was Count Adolf Wagensperg, with whom Casanova succeeded in establishing a close relationship – a fact which, by now, will make us fairly sure that Wagensperg was a Freemason. The Chief of Police and security was Anton Pietro Pittoni, lecher, gambler, cabalist and Freemason, who seems to have been appointed on the set-a-thief principle.

Casanova took a room in the big municipally-owned inn, La Locanda Grande, and settled into his part: the ascetic scholar, immersed in his tomes, who yet prays daily that the Puissant Prince will forgive his youthful peccadillo and permit him to return to the bosom of the only mother he has ever known. He was much encouraged by an early visit from Pietro Zaguri, and it is probable that the two men now made the plan for Casanova to perform small diplomatic and secret investigations for Venice. To that end Zaguri introduced him to the Venetian consul, Marco de Monti.

While he waited for something to turn up Casanova returned to his *Iliad*, and now also began work on a *History of the Troubles in Poland*. He also wrote a comedy which was performed at Trieste and Gorice, and allowed the ladies to talk him into staging another for their benefit.

Still waiting . . . there were brief flurries with a little Slav servant-girl who didn't like her lover-employer and ran for succour to Casanova. And an affair with a Negro woman, more out of curiosity than lust. And suddenly Wagensperg found a way to help Casanova. He gave him advance information of the Imperial Government's intention to send their goods into Italy by a route which would bypass Venice altogether, unless Venice lowered its exorbitant 4 per cent *octroi*. Casanova could make capital by sending the information at once to the Inquisitors so that they could enhance their much-prized reputation for knowing everything before anyone else. This he did: the report, which went to the Savi della Mercanzia, or Board of Trade, was dated 17 June 1773. The Venetian authorities ordered that Casanova be given a small money payment, and issued a guarded commendation of his zeal. Casanova rubbed his hands and looked around for further opportunities.

In October 1773 three new Inquisitors took office: Francesco Grimani, Francesco Sagredo and Girolamo Zulian. Casanova's friends wrote that if his pardon could not be obtained from this board, they would be inclined to throw in the towel: for Grimani (not of the same branch as Casanova's guardian) was a good friend of Casanova's 'uncle' Dandolo; Sagredo was an intimate and follower of the Procurator Morosini; and Zaguri swore that he could answer for the vote of Zulian.

Another opportunity presented itself: the weekly diligence from Trieste to Mestre, for Venice, went by the direct route, more or less round the curve of the coast, via Monfalcone and Latisana. At the cost of a few hours more, it could go via Udine, farther inland. Udine was the capital of Venetian Friuli. If the diligence went through it, its trade would be increased, and their Grim Excellencies across the bay would be pleased. Casanova went to Wagensperg, who agreed to help. Casanova prepared a thorough report and recommendation, setting out all the reasons why the diligence should go through Udine, which Wagensperg then presented to his council as his own, daring them to reject it. The change was made and on 10 March 1774 the Inquisitors instructed Consul de Monti to give Casanova £35 and an expression of their thanks.

Here intervenes the last affaire described or mentioned by Casanova in his *Story*. It concerns an actress, Irene Rinaldi, whom he had known (in every sense) for many years. The last time he had seen her it was in a voluptuous three-sided homo-hetero orgy with Marcoline, at Avignon in 1763. (Eleven years, but how short it had suddenly become.) Irene was acting in Trieste, and she had a daughter of about ten. She ran a crooked little gambling salon to augment her income, and was foolish enough to cheat Casanova, who crossly advised her to be careful. Then he writes:

She left with the company at the beginning of Lent. I saw her three years later in Padua, where I made a much more intimate acquaintance with her daughter.

Those are the last words that have ever been found of any version of *The Story of my Life*. From here on, all that we know of the life of Giacomo Casanova comes from other sources, not from his own incomparably biased and brilliant observation.

A little earlier than this there had begun the affair of the Armenian monks, a business of stunning complexity which Casanova soon saw was insoluble, since no solution could please both the Venetian Inquisitors and the Intendant of Trieste. His interest therefore was to make his part seem as important as possible, but be sure to bow out altogether before the inevitable disaster could be laid at his door. He was thus playing a game of bluff with the august and omniscient Inquisitors; and it was the penniless adventurer who turned out to have the sharper wits.

The dispute centred on a community of Armenian monks in communion with Rome, whose monastery was on the Isle of S. Lazzaro at Venice. After the founder died his successor behaved in such a high-handed manner that the monks mutinied. The Patriarch of Venice stepped in and expelled four of them. They went to Trieste, bought a house, lived on alms from the wealthy Armenian community, and started plans to set up an Armenian printing press to rival the one at S. Lazzaro.

The Most Serene Prince was nothing if not vindictive. It could not bear to see the banished fugitives defy it at such close range. The Inquisitors determined to ensure that the monks failed in their endeavours, and were forced either to return to Venice begging forgiveness or to move on to another more distant province of the Empire. They therefore told de Monti to do all he could to achieve their ends. He replied, proposing to employ Casanova. On 29 January 1774 the Inquisitors agreed, but warned de Monti to be careful.

Now begins a bulky correspondence between the Inquisitors, de Monti, and Casanova. De Monti says he has contacted Casanova. Casanova himself, on 8 February, swears eternal zeal, and reports where the monks live. Next, the Inquisitors want to know about the printing press. Is the type being cast by the monks, or bought? If the latter, where? (They are thinking that if it is being bought in Venice, they can prevent it.) . . . 18 March . . . 6 May . . . 20 May . . . 10 June . . . all through spring and early summer the letters wing across the head of the Adriatic.

But the monks are obviously getting on well, for in that letter of 10 June Casanova comes up with a Machiavellian plan. He is going to suggest to the Intendant that the court of Vienna forbid the monks to publish anything in Armenian until it has been passed by a censor. This would raise impossible difficulties. Who speaks Armenian, at the court, to be censor? Who is going to pay him – except, clearly, the monks themselves, by means of a crippling impost? To have this plan approved and forwarded to Vienna a bribe would be necessary to the Austrian officials.

The Inquisitors sent sixteen sequins, about £15. Casanova pointed out, in effect, that he was not trying to bribe the town dog-catcher, but a senior official of the Imperial Government. After elaborating on methods by which their Venetian Excellencies could be sure that none of the bribe money had stuck to his own fingers, he suggested two hundred sequins as a more appropriate figure.

But at this point Casanova sensed that the moment had come to get out. The affair was never going to be solved to the satisfaction of the Inquisitors, and his sole aim now should be to find himself at a safe distance when they started throwing the mud. Accordingly on 26 August he wrote a brilliant and touching letter. He can do no more for his beloved Republic, he says. His health is failing. He must leave Trieste if he is to survive the coming winter. With the utmost regret he has set his departure for the middle of September. Farewell, most honoured and respected patrons! If it is written that Casanova must die abroad, unforgiven, then he will face the prospect as a son of Venice should (*stifled sobs; music up and over; tears, carefully wiped off, stain the paper*) . . .

It worked. On 3 September 1774 the Inquisitors ordered him a safe conduct, in the following words: 'We, Inquisitors of State, for reasons known to us, give Giacomo Casanova a free safe-conduct good for the whole of the current month, empowering him to come, go, stop, and return, hold communication wheresoever he pleases without let or hindrance. Such is our will.'

That same day they sent the safe conduct to de Monti, with instructions to give it to Casanova and to order him, on arrival in Venice, to present himself to Marcantonio Businello, Secretary to the Inquisitors and the Council of Ten.

On 10 September the Consul wrote to the Inquisitors, telling them how Casanova had received the safe conduct: 'He read it, and re-read it, then he kissed it again and again. Finally, after a short interval of silent self-concentration, he burst into a flood of tears.'

That day Casanova left for Venice, travelling by land. At some time the next day, 11 September 1774, after an exile of eighteen years, he stepped again onto the soil of Venice. He was home, in the arms of his mother. Everything would be all right, after all.

14

Autumn in Venice –
the Scholarly Spy

The Prince de Ligne, a friend, describes him:

He would be a good-looking man if he were not ugly; he is tall and built like Hercules, but of an African tint; eyes full of life and fire, but touchy, wary, rancorous – and this gives him a ferocious air. It is easier to put him in a rage than to make him gay. He laughs little, but makes others laugh . . . He has a manner of saying things which reminds one of Harlequin or Figaro, and which makes them sound witty.

The Prince has not mentioned the smallpox scars that Bettina Gozzi bequeathed him nearly forty years earlier, nor the great beak nose and strong chin which, as the famous engraving by Berka makes clear, dominated his face and expression. But it will serve to give dimension of physical reality to the wanderer who passed the flat plains by the sea and came at last to Mestre and there, as he must have, took a gondola toward the domes and towers painted in opalescent colours above the lagoon.

He settled in with Dandolo and had to live very quietly, as (he said) he wished to. His fixed income was about £11 (27 dollars) a month, half left to him in Barbaro's will and half allowed to him by Dandolo. This very year of his return, 1774, the Council closed the Ridotto, the gambling hall where Casanova had certainly expected to pass some time and make some money. That left only his pen to augment his income. He was still working, slowly, on the *Iliad*, and the *Troubles in Poland* (the first volume had already come out in Trieste; there were supposed to be six more). In Trieste, too, they were producing a cantata that he had written and Francesco Petrucci set to music; but there was no money in that for him.

Still, he was back . . . Giacomo Casanova; the famous Casanova who had escaped from the Leads under the dogeship of Alvise IV Mocenigo; Casanova the scholar, confidant of the Inquisitors and duellist with the Polish general; Memmo's friend. It was going to be all right.

Up to a point, it was. Or it could have been if he had not been Casanova. Memmo and Zaguri, important patricians, did invite him to their houses. It was at Zaguri's that he met a man of similar tastes and background to his own, Lorenzo da Ponte, a sort of priest, as Casanova had once been, and so calling himself Abbé; but not yet writing librettos for Mozart. There were other less noble friends, especially sardonic old Signora Manzoni, who had never had any illusions about him and loved him for what he was, not what he might have been. There was an immense correspondence to decorate the drab present with memories of a glittering past; besides, it saved him from the hard and uncongenial discipline of writing professionally, for gain. There was Dandolo . . . only, in truth, what did they have to talk about now, except how wonderful it had been when Bragadin and Barbaro were alive? And many doors which had been hospitably opened to him when he first came back now began, without fuss, to close. Everyone who wanted to hear his famous story of his escape had heard it. The invitations dwindled to a thin trickle.

If there were lovers, they have left no record. Women there must have been – whores, occasionally an actress or a dancer, but not the young stars now, only the older, *passée* women. Of the sensuous rich and high-born – none. The widowed Countess Orsini-Rosenberg liked to think of herself as an author now, and had a little literary salon, but she never gave a hint that she would like him to treat her again as Miss X.C.V. She was probably still in love with Memmo, in the senseless, marvellous way women have – after twenty years! Besides, she was as penniless as himself.

Yearly on Ascension Day the Doge took to sea in the mighty *Bucintoro* to marry the Adriatic. Yearly carnival swept upon the ancient city with masque and licence. The events had not changed, but the times had. Louis XV was dead in France – where two reigns had covered 131 years – and heaven knew what would happen, for young Louis XVI was said to be too kind, to *think* too much, to govern that great ungovernable. There were rumours of revolution in the wild Americas, and the reports of death were beginning to mean more to him than the reports of marriages and births. Sir John Murray was dead in Venice, who had once been English Ambassador here, who had liked Casanova to watch him make love to that pox-ridden old hag Ancilla. And Jeanne Camus de Pontcarré, Marquise d'Urfé, was really dead; the evil gossip would spring up again at the news, and then perhaps die away for ever.

Back to work: the *Iliad, Canto XVI* . . . but there was word from Businello, Secretary to the Inquisitors. A Genoese diplomat, the Marquis of Roccaforte, needed a secretary. That name stirred a memory. The family name of the Roccafortes was Spinola. This man must be the Carlo Spinola who had broken the bank at a Milan gambling house in Casanova's presence back in '63. He was a marquis and a count, but a dubious character . . . had been Genoese ambassador to London; to Vienna (expelled for bad behaviour); married to a Countess von Stahremberg, but separated since he found her in bed with his secretary. Now he wanted another secretary.

It must have been clear enough to Casanova what the Inquisitors wanted: any little scrap of information he could pick up. It should not be difficult to learn things, rummaging through Spinola's back correspondence, listening, eavesdropping a little. What value there might be in such stale gossip and long-cold intrigues was something else again, but of that Their Excellencies were the best judges.

He became Spinola's part-time secretary in 1775, and worked with him, perhaps an hour a day, perhaps a morning a week, from 1775 until a fearful explosion rent that, and all his other Venetian relationships.

1776 . . . the Americans declared their Independence, and the Inquisitors hired Casanova as a confidential agent, or spy, on a piece-work basis. He was given the spy name of Antonio Pratolini, and ordered to report on matters adversely affecting religion, morals, public security, commerce and manufacture. He submitted many reports to the Inquisitors: forty-eight are still extant. They cover a wide range. One of the earliest, dated 8 September 1776, concerns a rumour that the Emperor Joseph II was planning to invade Dalmatia (which belonged to Venice) as soon as his mother and co-ruler, the Empress Maria Theresa, was dead. On 12 December of the same year Pratolini reported on a project of the Imperial Government to make Fiume a free port, thus opening up communications between the Adriatic and Hungary. Also in December he warned that the ballet *Coriolanus* was highly seditious stuff . . .

But the end of the next volume of the *Iliad* seemed as far off as ever . . . and, ah, here was news that would have stabbed deep. There was announced the death, in Paris, of Madame Maria Maddalena Blondel, daughter of the famous Silvia Balletti. This was Manon, who had loved him, and he had sworn to marry her, and broken his promise. She had married Blondel, lived unhappily, and now she was dead, thirty-six years old. No one could call it his fault. Except Manon, and himself.

Back to the *Iliad*, and the cold room, and the thin food and the thin clothes . . . The next letter came from Dresden: Mother died on 29 November. Did he remember her once, as a child barely able to walk? Was it *her* golden hair (she must have dyed it) of the first dreams? Did she, when he tried to tug at her skirt, slap his hand because she was talking to a man? She must have always been talking to men, getting something out of them, the natural lords of creation (as Casanova, equally disadvantaged by birth, had done from titled lords). Strong-minded, strong-willed, had she ever seen anyone but herself in that mirror she called her life? Goldoni thought she was a good actress, in her time. Others, himself included, thought she was atrocious. How many lovers? How many intrigues? Had she died happy? Who knew? Who cared?

1777: at last the second volume of his *Iliad* saw the light. He heard that Onofrio Paganini's troupe was playing Padua, only twenty miles away. He could go that far to see Irene Rinaldi, and to make 'a much more intimate acquaintance with her daughter'. He could not expect to hold the girl long. She was barely thirteen, and had a great future before her as a courtesan.

Back to Venice . . . and a letter from Valgiorgio. Bettina Gozzi was dying. He went to her and she died in his arms. She had been the first woman to bring him to the magical spurting of his seed.

And John Wilkes's mistress was dead. They used to call her La Charpillon.

1778: the third volume of the *History of the Troubles in Poland* published; but there were no more subscribers and the scoundrelly printer refused to print any more without payment, so that was the end of that. The third volume of the *Iliad* appeared to the same dirge – no more subscriptions, no more money, no more printing.

Here was some good news, for a change! Voltaire was dead, the atheistical scoundrel who had scorned Casanova's admiration eighteen years ago. All the world grovelled at his feet and a French publisher was putting out a book of the encomiums written about him; just the occasion for a slashing attack on the man, the myth, and his sycophants. It might not sell, but that did not matter to a gentleman, which Voltaire certainly was not, with his acquired *de* . . .

Rousseau, dead; Mengs, friend and enemy for twenty years, dead; Marco Dandolo, the last person in the world to know Casanova as a father might, and better, dead.

The anti-Voltaire book came out. Described as 'a monument of enraged dialectic', it proved only that Casanova was a true Venetian: he never forgot or forgave a slight.

This year, 1779, Casanova did at last find a girl. Her name was Francesca Buschini, and that is about all we know of her, except that she was kind and uneducated, a seamstress when she could get any work, and she loved Casanova. He moved out of Dandolo's and lived with her in a small house at the Barbaria delle Tole, near the church of S. Giustina. She was his bedfellow, companion, and house-keeper – mistress is too exotic a word for such a simple soul – from now until he left Venice, and she continued to pine for him long afterwards, thereby losing whatever chance she may have had of marrying. In return he took her inside worlds she had seen only from the outside, as unattainable, the worlds of theatre and tavern, and that half-world where aristocracy liked to trail its satin skirts in the slime. Whenever he was away from Venice they corresponded. Thirty-two of her letters have survived.

In May the Inquisitors sent him to Ancona to investigate the commerce between the Papal States and Venice, most of which would pass through Ancona. He spent two months in the region, and renewed his affair with Leah. On 7 October of the following year, 1780, the Inquisitors changed his status from piece-work to civil service. He was taken on the payroll at a salary of 120 lire, or about £5 10s. a month. At the same time he launched two new ventures. With another man he brought a company of French actors to Venice from Florence, where they had been playing without success. The company performed at the S. Angelo theatre in Venice from October 1780 to February 1781. To advertise it, and to inform the general public, which did not understand French, about French comedy in general and the plays of this company in particular, Casa-nova published a weekly magazine called *Le Messager de Thalie*. Every issue of the magazine was written from cover to cover by Casanova . . . in French. One must admire his magnificent con- sis-tency here; but the outcome was equally consistent. It was a disaster, not to be averted by Casanova's despairing gesture in calling the last issue of his magazine *Talia* and writing it in Italian. Nor can the spy Pratolini have helped when he reported to the Inquisitors, in Dec-ember, on the unparalleled licence that reigned in all theatres when the lights were put out.

At the same time Casanova had been canvassing subscriptions for a little private magazine of his own, called *Opuscoli Miscellanei*. Seven numbers of *Opuscoli* appeared, and then it died from the same malady as all his other writing ventures – lack of funds. The subscribers, who had paid for a year's issues, were offered instead a copy of Casanova's next book: *Venetian Anecdotes of the Fourteenth Century.*

The *Messager de Thalie* was dead, *Opuscoli Miscellanei* was dead, the theatre troupe had left, and the Inquisitors did not think much of Casanova's reports, which were in truth not at all exciting, because he could no longer move in circles where he would meet important people or hear of important intrigues. The funeral bells tolled more insistently: Sir John Fielding, the magistrate who had heard La Charpillon's case against him in London; the Empress Maria Theresa, who had ordered him out of Vienna the last time he was there; Alvise V Mocenigo, the sodomitic ambassador who had ruined his Spanish projects; Count Ricla and Nina Bergonzi; Bono, the good banker of Lyon . . .

In May 1781 Pratolini reported that one member of the Grimani family, patricians, seemed to consider himself exempt from the Venetian rule, enforced on pain of death, that patricians must not have any dealings with foreign envoys or their suites. The puffed-up person committing this crime was the Abbé Grimani, who happened, not coincidentally, to have been Casanova's guardian when young. The Inquisitors made their secretary 'gently remind' the Abbé, their fellow patrician, of the rules. The Abbé, I'll be bound, in turn reminded the Inquisitors that his family had had this impossible and now spiteful Casanova hanging round their necks for fifty years, ever since his brother had been idiot enough to bed Zanetta Farussi.

In November, licking his lips, Pratolini reported that there was an art class where they had nude models. In December he sent in a list of the chief works of pornography and blasphemy to be found in private collections in the city.

Rather mysteriously (unless we remember the Abbé Grimani), the Inquisitors responded to Pratolini's reports by dismissing him from their salaried employment. Casanova/Pratolini almost strangled himself in his contorted grovelling: 'Recognizing myself absolutely unworthy of addressing my vile letter . . . invoke, on my knees, the mercy of the Prince . . . respectful supplication . . . wisdom of your Excellencies.' It is enough to make a man throw up, and Casanova probably did; but if he wanted to survive in Venice, he had no choice.

It made no difference. The Inquisitors dismissed him just the same, though they did pay him once more for a small item he sent in the following year.

The *Aneddoti Veneziani* was published . . . and the long downward ramp of Casanova's life suddenly tilted, jerked, and threw him off. He was not to die in Venice, withering where he had flowered.

It came about through the Genoese diplomat, Carlo Spinola, for whom Casanova was still part-time secretary. Spinola was so sure that he could arrange a marriage for himself with the daughter of Prince Esterhazy that he bet a certain Signor Carletti 250 sequins, or nearly £225, on it. Spinola lost, for the lady married someone else; he also conveniently forgot his bet with Carletti. Carletti contacted Casanova and asked him to remind Spinola of the debt of honour, and secure payment from him; or, at the least, get a written acknowledgement. Casanova asked Carletti what was in it for him. Carletti said a substantial reward. Casanova agreed to take up the matter on these terms. The third person present at the undertaking was to be the witness. This third person was Zuan Carlo Grimani, and the meeting had taken place in his palace.

Casanova spoke to Spinola, and obtained from him a signed acknowledgement of the debt. He took this to Carletti, who gave him not money but a document promising some money against Spinola's payment. Casanova lost his temper, and a fearful scene ensued. Carlo Grimani took Carletti's part and the air grew thick with abuse, insults, and blows offered and parried. Casanova appears to have been struck, but did not draw his sword. He was in the house of a Grimani, and he depended for his very existence on the goodwill of the patrician body. Besides, whatever Polish counts might do, patricians of Venice did not duel with commoners. And Casanova was now fifty-seven.

The next day, nevertheless, rumours of the quarrel began to fly and Casanova heard that he was being called a coward. The few doors still open to him closed. He had, as we know, a notably low boiling-point. If people were calling him an actress's cowardly bastard, he'd give them a few more names to bandy about. He wrote and published a furious pamphlet called *Nè Amori, Nè Donne, ovvero la stalla ripulita* (Neither loves nor women; or, the stable cleaned out). It was a scandalous attack on the patrician society of Venice. In it Casanova revealed that he himself was the fruit of illegal relations between his mother and this Zuan Carlo Grimani's father, Michele; and, that, on the other hand, Zuan Carlo was not the true son of his father, but the result of an affair *his* mother had had with Sebastian Giustinian. In an obscurely relevant gesture Casanova dedicated the work to the nobleman who had countersigned his claim to gentility: Count Branicki.

The Giustinians claimed descent from the Roman Emperor Justinian, but no one welcomed Casanova's revelations. Casanova had ruined his life – again – but he must have felt an enormous relief at having shouted out loud what he had heard whispered all his life, at having finally excised the cancers which had been eating his heart since childhood: the grasping whorishness of his mother and the patronizing scorn of the Grimanis.

Shortly after the publication of *Nè Amori, Nè Donne* the doyen of the patrician body, the Procurator Morosini, sent for him and told him to leave Venice and, this time, not to come back. Casanova had no choice but to obey. No part of Venetian life was not controlled by the patricians. The three Inquisitors of State, in particular, could do anything, with, without, or against the written law, provided only that they were unanimous in their secret decisions. If he refused the banishment he faced the Leads, the Wells, or a garrotting.

His mother city had turned on him, as his fleshly mother had neglected him. He was not sorry to go. He left Venice on 13 January 1783, for Trieste; returned briefly on the 17th to pick up some of his belongings and say goodbye to Francesca Buschini. Then he set out for Vienna, over the snow-covered Brenner Pass.

15

Winter in Bohemia –
the Old Librarian

As so often in his life, his departure was far from final. In this case he got only as far as Vienna. There, still boiling with undistilled spite against the society that had rejected him, he somehow managed to get at the Venetian ambassador's diplomatic bag. When the bag reached Venice it contained, along with routine diplomatic reports, a warning that Venice would be destroyed by an earthquake on 25 May of that year, 1783. Someone in the Council didn't know how to keep his mouth shut, and the rumour spread. The destruction of Lisbon nearly thirty years earlier was still a terror in people's minds, and that, combined with the superstition of the age and perhaps a general sense that decadent humanity was about due for another Flood, caused Casanova's message to be widely believed. Patricians deserted the city in droves, land values fell, business declined. Confidence did not return until the fatal date passed without incident.

Casanova now found that he had to pay a last visit to Venice after all. He was well advised not to leave his barge when he passed through on 16 June, embraced Francesca Buschini, and returned to Mestre. From there he crossed the Alps by the route via Bolzano, the Brenner Pass, and Innsbruck to Augsburg; then on to Frankfurt and Aachen.

He soon received a lady visitor. It was Catina Pocchini, wife of the pimping Count with the relays of 'daughters'. Now he was dying in want, and his wife begged Casanova for help. Casanova had usually been generous to fellow scoundrels in distress, even when he had been a target of their villainies. But the tightening grip of the years, and the final rejection by Venice, had changed him. He was a bitter man, becoming paranoiac. He laughed in Catina Pocchini's face, wished her a beautiful death, and went on his way.

The next stop was Spa, where an Englishwoman hired him to

accompany her to Amsterdam. We do not know in what capacity he was hired, but we may guess, since the woman was not young or beautiful. Whatever he had to do, he did it well enough so that when they reached Amsterdam she made him a proposal, or proposition, so blood-curdling that he left her on the spot. She gave him twenty-five guineas as a *douceur*, and he never saw her again, and never revealed what the terrible proposal was. In view of the catholic sexual arrangements in which he had been happy to take part, one is baffled to think of anything that could have shocked him in that line. There is one obscure clue. Casanova wrote to a friend that although he could never reveal the proposal 'a great event might, in time, enable you to find out'. This seems to point to a political plot of some kind.

On to Brussels, where he got drunk 'because his reputation demanded it'. This letter astonished Francesca Buschini, for she had never seen him even slightly the worse for drink; and it is a fact that although he had got drunk in his time, he was amazingly abstemious for a period when a gentleman thought nothing of lowering four bottles of claret and port at a meal. The drinking bout in Brussels also, rather mysteriously, put his teeth in better condition, but they were to give him trouble for the rest of his life, from all the mercury the doctors had used on him.

All the time he was trying to raise money, in particular from the Procurator Morosini. At the end of August Francesca had to tell him the fate of his last appeal to the old man. When she gave the Procurator his letter, he groaned before he opened it, complaining that Casanova was always in trouble. After reading only a page, he put it down and told Francesca that he wished Casanova well, but he would never write to him again. With this final bowing-out of his most influential acquaintance – Morosini had never been exactly a friend – he reached Paris in the middle of September.

In Paris he joined his brother Francesco, the impotent battle-painter, now remarried and devoting his talents to keeping out of debtors' prison. Casanova had hoped to get employment with or through an old friend, Jean d'Alembert, the eminent scientist and Immortal; but d'Alembert died a few weeks after his arrival, and so another door closed. He met the great American Benjamin Franklin, who invited him to a meeting of the Academy of Science on 23 November. Franklin talked about the problems of steering balloons, and Casanova was not impressed. For a moment the word *Madagascar* glows eerily in the gloom: he will go to Madagascar . . . but why, or how, he never says, and as he does not go the exotic glimmer fades.

Having found no employment, and no welcome, the roll of dead patrons and lovers still thudding in his ears, he left Paris late in the year, with his brother Francesco. They headed east, looking for positions. Dresden – nothing; Vienna – here Francesco came to rest, in a position suited to his peculiar talents, as painter and 'master of pleasures' for the powerful Kaunitz, Chancellor of the Empire. But there was nothing for Giacomo, who kept on travelling through the terrible winter of Central Europe, on the appalling roads, and he was now fifty-nine: Dresden again, Berlin, back to Prague . . . nothing. Down the length of Bohemia and Slovenia: to Vienna once more in the middle of February 1784, less than a hundred days after leaving Paris.

Here, at last, he found work. His friends in Venice, though they could not help him there, must still have had influence, for after what he had done it is astonishing to learn that the man who now employed him was the Venetian ambassador to the Empire, Sebastian Foscarini. Foscarini needed extra help because Vienna was the scene of negotiations to end a state of war between Venice and Holland. Casanova knew the men who were the cause of that war: the brothers Zanovich, one of whom had been in the plot to rook young Lincoln in Florence. By confidence tricks they had now defrauded certain Amsterdam merchants of large sums, mainly because their *bona fides* had been vouched for by the Venetian envoy to Holland, Cavalli. When the frauds came to light, the Dutch Government demanded compensation from the Venetian Government, as its official representative was responsible. Venice refused to pay, and on 9 January 1784 Holland declared war. Actual hostilities were suspended when the Emperor Joseph II offered to mediate. On this, the Dutch and Venetian ambassadors to Vienna began to work out a settlement.

Casanova happily prepared Foscarini's papers for the negotiations, and probably spied in the brothels and coffee-houses to find out what the Dutch really meant to press for and how much they were prepared to sacrifice. From this came his *Lettre historico-critique sur un fait connu, dépendant d'une cause peu connue*, a well-written resumé and presentation of the Venetian case in the dispute.

From Venice, churchmouse Francesca wrote that she and her mother had no money and didn't know where to get any. She noted, apparently without irony, that Casanova was attending dinners and balls, dancing minuets and quadrilles, and in general living the life to which he had accustomed himself. It was only in such circles, however, that Casanova could meet people who might be useful to him, people with whom he had most in common, and people who enjoyed his startling, frenetic company as much as he relished theirs.

One day, dining at the ambassador's table, he was introduced to the Prince de Ligne and his nephew, Count Waldstein. De Ligne was an Austrian diplomat, field-marshal, and *littérateur*, about ten years younger than Casanova. Count Joseph Charles Emmanuel Waldstein, lord of Dux and Oberleutensdorf in Bohemia, was not quite thirty years of age; an unstable, strange young man, who talked of the mysteries of the cabala. Casanova's ears pricked. If the Count wanted to know about the occult sciences, there was an adept in the room: Giacomo Casanova. The Count responded enthusiastically. Later they exchanged handshakes, and by the secret grip Casanova learned that the Count was a Freemason. Casanova made such an impression that the Count invited him to come to Dux whenever he wished, and stay as long as he liked.

Casanova could only give one of his low sweeping bows (they were becoming more old-fashioned every day now, but he did not notice, or could not change). Things were looking up. He was doing well with the ambassador. He had found and fallen in love with a young woman called Caton, and was actually thinking of marrying her, although his bleeding piles, falling teeth, unpunctual erection, and forty-year age superiority must surely have limited romance. But he pulled back from that abyss in time, and vented his adventurous spirit in planning a balloon journey. If the winds were right he would cross the Alps to Trieste, thence to Venice and Francesca. He was still very poor, and could not help Francesca financially: perhaps also he felt how barren the outcome of the affair would be for her, so he wrote renouncing her. In return the wretched girl had to confess that in her need she had sold some books he had left with her for safe-keeping. He did not write to her again for a year and a half, either in pique or because he really did want to cut the tie.

Now the shady Abbé da Ponte turned up, and was with Casanova when the latter recognized a familiar face in the crowd – a rattish, mean, rascally face. He pounced, and seized the man by the nape of the neck. It was Costa, the servant who had decamped with Mme d'Urfé's gifts twenty-four years earlier. Casanova threatened to have Costa punished for the old crime, but Costa escaped to a coffee-house, and after a few minutes sent out a rhymed message, in which he pointed out that although he had indeed robbed Casanova, Casanova at the time had been robbing someone else: they were equally to blame and should let bygones be bygones. Casanova scowled, then laughed, and murmured, 'The rogue is right'. Thus da Ponte, in his *Memoirs*; and although he was as unreliable as Casanova and a good deal more spiteful, the story rings true.

All in all, life was going well when, on 23 April, Ambassador Foscarini died. Casanova was out of work again.

He tried to become secretary to an old friend, Count Fabris, but this fell through. He turned for the third time to thoughts of the religious life, and toyed with the idea of becoming a monk; but his still-violent energies could not be dissipated in the cloister.

He was back where he had started, penniless, alone, and becoming more lonely every moment on the world's cold stage. Balbi the renegade monk was dead – a scoundrel of scoundrels, but his companion on the sloping leads of the Doge's Palace. His youngest brother Gaetano, the renegade priest who had abducted Marcoline, was dead. Father Gozzi had followed Bettina into eternity. General Kettler, Mimi von Groote's *cicisbeo*; the Comte de Saint-Germain; Pocchini; Lady Harrington – all dead.

He wandered through Moravia and Bohemia; to Brno, Carlsbad (a desperate journey to meet the Princess Lubomirska, who had been one of his protectors in Poland twenty years back: but clearly she had nothing to offer him now). He headed for Berlin. At Teplitz the Prince de Ligne had his castle, and here he gave up, or was persuaded to abandon the journey to Berlin, and take up instead the invitation extended to him at Foscarini's table by the Prince's nephew. Dux (now called Duchcov) is five miles south-west of Teplitz (Teplice) on the main road to Most and Plzn.

It is a gently rolling landscape, now pockmarked with mines but then purely rustic. Dux is a village with a lake and running water and trees, and the huge château of the Counts Waldstein opening directly upon the market-place. Depending on the point of view, Dux and its castle would seem like a marvel of feudal calm, a scholar's dream, or a bleak northern prison, only to be endured because it, and it alone in the whole world, offered food and shelter. Casanova, Venetian cosmopolite, saw it as the bleak northern prison. So, when Count Waldstein offered him the post of librarian at a salary of 1,000 florins, or 80 guineas a year, plus his keep, he accepted – but not with great joy.

The principal personalities at Dux were, first, Count Waldstein himself, an equivocal and not very attractive figure. He loved horses to distraction, and had as resident mistress a superior female servant-girl called Caroline, but he never married, and died a bachelor in 1814. He may have been a homosexual, suppressed or active, as well as a Freemason, practical joker, feckless *flâneur* and world traveller.

The major-domo of Dux, who arrived just after Casanova, was Feldkirchner, a warrant officer who had been given lieutenant's rank on retirement, Casanova soon came to detest him, and never managed any closer approximation to his name than Faulkircher. This sounds much nastier, so we too will call him that. Faulkircher's assistant was Wiederholt, which Casanova writes 'Viderol'.

Casanova soon learned, to his chagrin, that the Count was absent from Dux more than he was present, thus leaving him to the unspeakable Faulkircher and Viderol. However, the Count's younger brother Ferdinand lived a few miles off at Oberleutensdorf, and Casanova could seek occasional refuge there, or with de Ligne at Teplitz.

Now Casanova possessed all that he had so often claimed he needed in order to write great books: an assured income, room and board, a place to write, peace. The first fruit was published the following year, *Soliloque d'un Penseur*. A diatribe against such as Saint-Germain and Cagliostro, it was written specifically to gain the attention and favour of the Emperor Joseph II. Casanova hoped that the Emperor would rescue him from his exile at Dux. Joseph may have remembered that Casanova was the fellow who had snubbed him in his own palace a few years earlier. On that occasion the Emperor had expressed his scorn of those who bought honours. Casanova suavely agreed, adding 'And what, then, are we to think of those who sell them?' Da Ponte's version of this famous interview is that Casanova tried to interest the Emperor in organizing Chinese fêtes for the people of Vienna, and was turned down – nothing more. Whichever version is true (probably da Ponte's: Casanova was never a man to snub royalty, except in his imagination. He admitted in a letter about this time that in the Emperor's presence he found himself trembling violently, and unable to speak) – the Emperor did not take the bait: Casanova stayed at Dux.

Francesca was in Venice, Caton in Vienna, but the female sex sets its gins everywhere, and however obvious the net, Casanova was the man to step eagerly in. In his first letter to Francesca Buschini after the long sulk he told her about a sweet, desirable and altogether worthy young person. Her family adored him, she adored him, she looked after him in every respect, she merited his love and regard, and on her he spent what few sous he could save from his stipend: thus he regretted he could send nothing to Francesca. Francesca, who should have been born an early Christian martyr, wrote back politely, but restraining her enthusiasm for the young person.

Così fan tutte: the sweet young person became pregnant and had the ingratitude and lack of taste to accuse Casanova, now sixty-one, of being the prospective father. Casanova may well have been among those present, but the actual husbandman was adjudged to be a house painter who married the girl – Anna Kleer, daughter of the castle porter – early next year. Casanova wrote to Francesca complaining of the inconstancy of women.

She was sinking deeper into penury. Writing did not come easy to her, but without her mis-spelled, ungrammatical playbacks to Casanova (*I see that you have been in bed with your usual ailment . . . that you have travelled five posts to see the Emperor*), we would not know what he was doing. She was a woman of the earth as this extract about her dogs shows: 'Here's some news which will make you laugh, though not me, when it happened I was very angry. Partagna took Aida's virginity and she bled a lot. I held my bitch and tried to staunch the blood while letting that damned Partagna finish the job, but afterwards I gave him a good beating.' And, pushed by misery, she could be poetic: 'Where are all the pleasures you used to get for me? Where are the theatres, the comedies, we once saw together?' Now she sinks from our sight, leaving no further mark, except upon our hearts.

In 1787 Casanova became associated with a work which some have called the perfect opera, *Don Giovanni*. The principal evidence linking him with it rests on the memoirs of a Prague professor, A. Meissner, whose notes were published by his grandson. Meissner tells a romantic tale: *Don Giovanni* is due to open in a couple of days and the cast have not yet received the overture. Mozart says there is plenty of time for that. He refuses to work on it, insists instead that everyone go for a picnic in the country. One of the guests at the picnic is a tall, imposing man of about sixty. After some horseplay the cast get together and decide they will lock Mozart into an upstairs room of the country inn until he has written the overture. The trick is played and Mozart locked in. He leans out of the window, protesting, and then the saturnine old man speaks up. He says that the cast have done wrong, but the great composer will understand their anxiety: let them release Mozart, and he is sure that Mozart will allay their fears by giving them the overture before morning. All agree, for he speaks with magnetic force and power. He goes upstairs and frees Mozart, who duly writes the overture.

There is no other evidence for this scene as described; but one can wonder why Meissner would have gone to the trouble to invent it at a time when Casanova was regarded as either unspeakably base, a total liar, or both. On the other hand, da Ponte, the librettist of *Don Giovanni*, does not mention it, and if the picnic took place he would certainly have been there: but he did not like Casanova.

Casanova was certainly in Prague at the time, and it is reasonable to assume that he had gone to attend the opening of the opera, which took place at the National Theatre on 29 October 1787. It is interesting that there were found in the castle of Dux manuscript notes in Casanova's hand, re-writing parts of Act II of the opera. It may be too much to describe him as a collaborator on the libretto, but I am sure that he was associated with it in some way.

He returned to Dux, to a lowering atmosphere of mutual dislike. The Dowager Countess, who can have had no idea of her son's real problems, wanted the servant Caroline sent away so that the Count would marry a girl of his own class, and father a little Count. The Count himself was trying to marry Caroline off to Viderol, but she refused, for reasons which will become apparent, and which throw an equivocal light on both the Count and Viderol. Caroline glowered at Casanova because he had passed a censorious remark about her status. The quarrels with Faulkircher and Viderol rumbled permanently under the rest. (And Frederick the Great was dead; and the Baron de Roll; and his sister's husband, Peter August; and the Abbé Bourbon, bastard son of Louis XV by that Mlle Roman-Coupier whom he had advised to go to Paris and become the king's mistress in 1760; and, ah, here was another bad one, the woman who knew him as none other had or ever would – Signora Manzoni, aged eighty-one.)

He returned grimly to writing. In the next year he published the *Story of my Escape from the Leads*; visited Leipzig and Dresden; hired and fired a personal cook who gave three men-servants venereal disease in short order, although she was 'old, ugly and ill smelling' – which throws a light on what life at Dux must have been like; and published his *Icosameron*, a philosophical-scientific-prophetic novel in five volumes.

It was a disaster. A literary journal in Jena published a criticism of it; no one else read it, and the expenses of publication wiped out all that Casanova had saved, borrowed or otherwise amassed at Dux. (The real Count de Aranda was dead; and the notorious Miss Chudleigh, once Duchess of Kingston; and Bonnie Prince Charlie; and Doctor Algardi of Augsburg, who had cured him of the horrendous venereal chancre in 1761; and his erstwhile best friend, Manon's brother, Antonio Balletti.)

In his beloved Paris, the people seemed to have gone mad. They sacked the Bastille, and Europe sussurated with whispers of worse to come, with the King and Marie Antoinette barely more than prisoners. Hard on the news came a story involving Casanova himself. Some years back the Prince of Courland had found himself in the Bastille over a little matter of forging bills of exchange. At the time the police had taken his papers, and kept them. Now the mob was gleefully publishing all the papers the régime had guarded so carefully, so long. Among them was a letter from Casanova to the Prince, describing how to set about making the Philosopher's Stone, that magic device whose touch would convert all base metals to gold. So now Europe was laughing at him! Even these Bohemian cattle among whom he had to live were sneering at him!

Casanova considered suicide. Bohemia was an outer province of cultured Europe, and Dux was in a secluded corner of Bohemia. Casanova's rooms, symbolically, were situated in a remote wing of the château and gave only on the outer courtyard. The rooms were littered with papers – copies of the *Icosameron* which no one could ever buy; notes on *Don Giovanni*, for which da Ponte had got the credit; threatening demands from creditors; Francesca's last letter, unanswered; drafts of a begging note, unwritten; copies of his essay on usury which should have won him the Emperor's 500-ducat prize, only the Emperor had suddenly died before he could award it.

The Revolution in France was destroying the value of what he had devoted his whole life to become. He lived among peasants and servants and the world was going to the dogs. He was afraid of death but not of dying. Once before, in London, he had decided to kill himself – but that would have been a heroic and romantic act, to be compared with Cesare Borgia's riding out to certain doom among the lances of Navarre.

Life is a burden to me. What is the metaphysical being who prevents me from slaying myself? It is Nature. What is the other being who enjoins me to lighten the burdens of that life which brings me only feeble pleasures and heavy pains? It is Reason ... Reason tells me imperiously that I have the right to slay myself, with the divine oracle of Cen: *Qui non potest vivere bene non vivat male*. These eight words have such power that it is impossible that a man to whom life is a burden could do other than slay himself on first hearing them.

But Casanova held his hand. Why? I believe that he did not kill himself because he knew that he had not fulfilled himself. A final work remained. The *Icosameron* was a pouring-out of the contents of his mind; and his mind was brilliant, turgid, contradictory, by turns sharp and obtuse, incisive and careless. His life, on the other hand, as life, was superb throughout, and he knew it. No one had lived as he had, and he knew it. Facing the fact of obliteration, I believe that he saw the glimmer of eternity in the recording of that life. He had not lived in one place, or with one person, so there was no other witness to all he had done and been. He had not carved his genius in marble, or spread it in paint, but lived it in a series of plastic events. Like a dancer, he had written on water and drawn in sand, and the tides of time and death would soon wipe out all trace of him. Like a great tune, his life must be written down to survive as it was lived, part unbelievable truth, part credible fantasy, all throbbing, burning, pulsing with life. Only he could do it. He put away his pistol then, and took paper, and primed the candles, and began to write . . .

It would be quite wrong to think that the writing of his *Story* used up all his time or energy. He soon found a means to convert the bucolic calm of Dux into a seething stew of animosities. The long-standing feud with Faulkircher and Viderol boiled over when Faulkircher told Stelzel, the Count's inspector at Dux, that Casanova would not be in financial straits if he had not wasted his money on having his *Icosameron* printed. Such a remark would gall any author: to the paranoiac Casanova it was an intolerable insult. He began writing letters:

In the ordinary course of events, M. Faulkircher, there would be nothing in common between you and me at the Castle of Dux, where I am employed as librarian and you as major-domo; but the extraordinary is so much the fashion of our times that we can almost count on it . . . Courage then, M. Faulkircher; reply to these letters; but be good enough to let me have your answers in French, or Latin, or even Spanish . . . I pay a translator; you do the same and let us not be ashamed of publishing our ignorance – mine of German and yours of all the other languages of the universe . . .

He reached the end, re-read it with satisfaction, sharpened a phrase here and there; then put it away in a drawer and turned to the growing pile of manuscript headed *Histoire de ma Vie*. There are twenty letters to Faulkircher, all written in pure bile, and none of them ever delivered.

When the atmosphere at Dux threatened to stifle him, he could drive to Teplitz or Oberleutensdorf. He continued a vast correspondence, among it a series of letters to an earnest little inspector of finances called Opiz. Casanova had a mathematical theory of how to square the cube, and began to bombard Opiz with papers on the subject, but the fellow turned out to be much too stupid to see the obvious rightness of Casanova's mathematics. Indeed, he refused to buy the rights to Casanova's treatise on astral mechanics and the properties of light, though it was offered to him for the laughable sum of fifty florins. How could a man like that expect to understand the squaring of the cube?

There were further journeyings, too, most notably to Vienna, where he saw Charlemagne's crown placed on Leopold's head. At the festivities the Count Rosenberg told him 'with an equivocal smile' that his stepmother had died of cancer in Padua, aged fifty-four. That was the woman who had been Miss X.C.V., and who later wrote a few instructional works and a large novel, *Les Morlacques*.

At the coronation, too, Casanova took particular interest in a certain young Italian marquis; naturally, because he was the marquis's father; and unnaturally, because the marquis's mother was also Casanova's own daughter. This was Leonilda's son, outcome of Casanova's selfless efforts to help his fellow Freemason, Leonilda's ancient husband, get an heir.

These meetings must have softened him, for when he returned to Dux he wrote to Carlo Grimani in Venice, humbly apologizing for all the dreadful things he had said in *Nè Amori, Nè Donne*. A little later Leonilda wrote from her estate near Salerno, inviting him to spend the rest of his days there; but something, for good or evil, made him refuse. He must reach the final curtain here in Dux, alone in the theatre with fools and barbarians.

In the faithful pursuit of your military duties [M. Faulkircher] you displayed your talents to such good effect that you reached the very respectable rank of Warrant Officer; and this in less than fifty years! . . . Ever since you came to Dux and saw me, and learned what my employment was you have been vainly furrowing your brow to understand why Count Waldstein should throw away 1,000 florins a year on a librarian. In your zeal for his interests you advised him to get rid of me . . . Permit, M. Faulkircher, that I submit for your consideration the general opinion on your friendship with the little scoundrel Viderol . . .

Count Waldstein, who was certainly associated with Bohemian royalist groups working for the restoration of the French monarchy, now set out on an extended journey of noble intent. He hoped to become a real-life Scarlet Pimpernel, and went to France and England to engineer the escape of aristocratic prisoners from the Terror, especially Louis XVI, Marie Antoinette and the Princess Lamballe. His absence, and Casanova's increasing frustration, carried the castle feud to its highest, and lowest, point.

My patience has foiled your plan and forced you to think of some insult I could not possibly tolerate. You ... have ordered the commital of an act which you would have considered dishonouring as a warrant officer, and which you would certainly have refused to carry out if one of your own officers had ordered you to ... You told your vile hanger-on to make an effigy of me in a substance that one does not name in polite society ... Your scoundrelly Viderol, a true hangman's servant, having torn a portrait of me from one of my works and daubed my name on it with the epithet you taught him, then stuck it on the door of the privy, plastered with his ordure or yours — for the foul connection between you makes the mixing of the two easy ...

One can almost see the foam flecking his lips as he furiously scribbles ... And more notes on squaring the cube; and a system for winning the Rome lottery; and metaphysical problems: 'whether it is possible to compose a Latin distich of the greatest beauty without knowing either the Latin language or prosody'; and wagers: 'I wager that it is not true that a man who weighs a hundred pounds will weigh more if you kill him'; and a last kick at dead Voltaire — 'Voltaire, the hardy Voltaire ... who ridiculed our dogmas, doubts, and ... is not ashamed, being reduced to the extremity of life, to ask for the sacraments, and to cover his body with more relics than St Louis had at Amboise'.

And real letters, that were mailed, flew off to the Count's mother; and de Ligne; and Zaguri in Venice, who counselled that the matter of the plastered portrait was very delicate and Casanova should try to await the return of Waldstein for justice. But Faulkircher and Viderol meant to drive him away before the Count got back, for Casanova was highly regarded by all the gentry, who were inexplicably ready to seek his company, and forgive his faults, for some extraordinary quality they saw in him. To the likes of Faulkircher and Viderol he was nothing but an arrogant, vicious, bad-tempered old man, as base-born as they, or worse, giving himself impossible airs.

... when his Highness the Prince Antoine of Saxe came to visit the castle with the Archduchess his wife, you ordered your pansy-boy to mount a horse, with another stable lad, to do the honours to their Highnesses ... That was another of your ignorant stupidities there, Mr Retired Warrant Officer, for to do the greatest possible honour to the heir-presumptive to a throne you yourself should have got into the saddle, and in uniform ...

The insults and threats continued, and Casanova went to a justice of the peace in Dux to lay an information. The justice merely said

199

that the castle and everyone in it came under the jurisdiction of the Count; and Viderol actually beat Casanova up in the street. There was no redress.

Since you were forewarned, that the two princesses were coming, it seems to me that you as major-domo of the splendid cellar of Dux should have had a Tokay served instead of a wretched local wine ... If you knew anything about human nature, Mr 2nd Lieutenant, if you could conjure up any sort of a picture of the mentality of a man of honour, you would never have considered doubting, twenty months ago, that it was *ten* florins I put on the Count's dressing-table while your loathsome nancy was doing his hair ...

But the Count was in London, keeping bad company, as usual. The correspondence with the idiot Opiz broke up in recriminations and accusations. The lengthening shadows covered another woman who had woven a voluptuous thread through his life – La Calori, who had called herself Bellino the first time he met her fifty years ago. He could only turn to the great bright tale taking shape under his hand, and write thirteen hours a day, and talk to the one being who really appreciated him, Melampyge. She was a well-bred fox terrier, born in 1791 of a sire belonging to Caroline. Casanova loved her and she travelled on a cushion beside him on his journeys.

The Count returned at last and dismissed Faulkircher and Viderol. Casanova had triumphed, but surely he must have secretly missed those two gorgeous targets for his arrows, perfect lightning-conductors for his frustration? He had also mended his relations with the rest of the castle staff – or, seeing his victory, they had mended their ways toward him. He became friendly with Caroline, and must have written quite suggestively about her, for Zaguri enthusiastically proposed that Casanova bring the 'beautiful and amiable Caroline to Venice' and arrange a party; but that never came off.

He was getting restive. Where could he go? Who would rescue him from this bleak tundra? He remembered the bride of Berlin, Doris (née, rather distressingly, Droopen) Greve. He began a letter to her: 'After a silence of twenty-nine years ...' But what followed? What did he suggest? He does not tell us, except that Doris did not answer.

From Dresden Teresa Casanova, the daughter of his brother Giovanni, wrote that she had met a charming man who had begged her to send her uncle Giacomo the warmest expressions of his regard. His name was Antonio della Croce ...

Della Croce! With his niece! It wasn't possible! The man must be seventy if he was a day. Casanova seized paper and pen ...

There is a wonderful description of him at this period by the Prince de Ligne:

Let no one imagine, however, that in this port of tranquillity which Count Waldstein's good nature had opened for him against the storms, he did not seek them. It was an inherent need of his nature. No day passed when there wasn't a quarrel in the house, on account of his coffee, his milk, or a plate of macaroni that he'd asked for. The cook had forgotten his polenta; the head groom had given him a bad coachman to come and see me; dogs had barked in the night; the Count had invited so many guests that *he* had to eat at a little side table. A hunting horn had shattered his ears with piercing discords. A priest had bored him in trying to convert him. The Count had not greeted him first, before the rest. The soup had been served him too hot, maliciously. A servant had made him wait for a drink. He had not been presented to an important gentleman . . . The Count had lent a book without telling him. A groom had not raised his hat in passing. He had spoken German and no one had understood him.

He is angry – they laugh. He shows some of his own Italian poetry – they laugh. He gesticulates in declaiming Italian – they laugh. On entering a room he bows as Marcel the famous dancing master taught him sixty years back – they laugh. At every ball he most gravely dances the minuet – they laugh. He puts on his white plumed hat, his suit of embroidered silk, his black velvet waistcoat, his garters with the strass buckles, his silk stockings – they laugh. 'Cospetto!' he cries, 'Scum that you are! You are all Jacobins, failing in respect to the Count, and the Count fails me in not punishing you.'

'Monsieur,' he said once, speaking to the Count, 'I pierced the stomach of the great Polish general. I was not born a gentleman, I made myself one.' The Count laughed.

Perhaps it was on this occasion that Casanova stalked, insulted, to his room. The Count took two pistols and followed him. There, trying to hide his laughter, he gravely offered Casanova a choice of the pistols, as though for a duel. Casanova stared at the weapons, then at the Count, then burst into tears, crying, 'How could I think of hurting my benefactor?'

The clouds gathered once more. Casanova managed to embroil the Count in a quarrel with a small local monastery. Inspector Stelzel passed a sharp remark about Melampyge misbehaving and Casanova snapped back about 'Inspectors of Dog-shit'. He took temporary refuge at Oberleutensdorf, where, alas, Melampyge fell ill and died. He said that she died because he had kept her shut up during the three heats of her life (there was no dog of the breed in Oberleutensdorf), and wrote a long threnody in Latin for her. He also tried to draft a poem in French begging the poor female's pardon for having foiled her natural instinct.

Ennui succeeded where the foul Faulkircher and the vile Viderol had failed: Casanova fled.

He asked the Prince de Ligne for letters of commendation to the Duke of Weimar, a well-known patron of the arts; and duly went to Weimar, the Duke's Thüringian capital; but the Duke had a writer in residence called Goethe, and everyone hung on Goethe's words, and treated him as a genius, even though he wrote in German. Casanova bethought himself (again, and still with no reason given) of Doris Greve, who lived in Hamburg. He almost went there now, in 1795; only his daemon prevented him, and sent him instead to Berlin, where he tried to obtain a post as librarian, academician, resident savant, anything – as long as it was away from the tomb-like isolation of Dux.

He had not changed. The man who had written the *Messager de Thalie* in French for the instruction of a non-French-speaking people now canvassed the courts and palaces of German Europe, begging a literary post by casting scorn and disgust on the German languages and German literature, which, according to him, did not exist. In Berlin also he drew several bills of exchange on Count Waldstein, without the latter's permission, and at last, after an absence of six weeks, returned to Dux. Count Waldstein had many faults, but vindictiveness was not one of them. He laughed when Casanova disappeared, saying only 'He will be back'. He laughed when the bills of exchange were presented, and paid; and now when the big, tired, white-haired old man came to the castle's great door he laughed again, embraced him, and welcomed him home. Casanova repaid him by keeping the circle amused for months with tales of his adventures on this final, futile hegira.

He returned to his rooms. Louis XVI and Marie Antoinette, his lovely, foolish queen, had both knelt to the guillotine. Dubarry, once a whore, then the extravagant mistress of a long-dead king – the mob had to have her head, too, at the age of fifty. And Philippe, Duc d'Orleans, who had called himself Philippe Égalité and voted in the Chamber for the execution of his relative the king – how the ghosts must have laughed when his head, too, stared out of the basket! And Cardinal de Bernis, who had shared women with him; and Andrea Memmo, his boyhood companion in mischief, but a statesman such that the Emperor had exclaimed, 'With four such men as Memmo, one could govern the world!' – all dead. And his own brother Giovanni, painter, scoundrel, pseudo-respectable head of the Dresden Academy, womanizer without taste, implacable enemy; and sad, saddest, a woman he called Henriette, because that was not her name; of all his loves there had never been anyone again like her.

He turned again to his manuscript. He had finished the first draft about the time of the dismissal of Faulkircher and the quarrel with Opiz. There are experts who believe that it was a much stronger draft than the one we now possess, and that Casanova decided to tone down his reminiscences from fear of the political implications of what he was writing, particularly upon the Bohemian royalists. At all events, he did work over his draft very carefully, making considerable corrections, rewriting, and doing his best to hide the identity of women he had loved and who, in defiance of marriage vows and religious oaths, had loved him. He had another dog beside him now, another fox terrier bitch whom he had called Finette. He probably loved her even more than Melampyge, because she had been given to him by a Princess (Lobkowitz).

He turned aside briefly from the central work to write an article on the changes wrought in the French language by the Revolution. This work, *A letter to Leonard Snetlage*, was the last to be published in his lifetime.

He met his last lady friend, but alas only on paper. She was the daughter of a good-for-nothing Baron Roggendorff with whom Casanova had 'done' Vienna in 1753. The baron died penniless in 1790, leaving, among other children, an heir – Baron Ernest – and Cecilia, born in 1775. Young Ernest was a friend of Waldstein's, and when his sister's fiancé was killed in action in 1796 he urged her to write to Casanova, as in need of a protector and adviser. This advice is as odd as anything in Casanova's whole story – he had neither the money nor the reputation for such a post – but Cecilia started writing to him in February 1797 from Cassovie (Kosice, in eastern Czechoslovakia); and the correspondence, all preserved, presents a fascinating picture of another Casanova, who helped, and advised the young girl, only once made her blush, and got her a position as Dame of Honour to the Duke of Courland. Her last letter was written in the spring of 1798, and by then she was worrying because her old confidant was not well.

In February 1798 Casanova fell ill. Prince de Ligne wrote him once, 'One is never old with your heart, your genius, and your stomach': but at the last the big, fantastically resilient body had begun its final collapse. He was seventy-three. He had had smallpox, epistaxis, perhaps adenoids, pleurisy, pneumonia, probably malaria two or three times, and gout. He had suffered at least eleven venereal attacks, of which three are now thought to have been gonorrhoea, one gonorrhoea with orchites, five soft chancre, one prepucial herpes, and one syphilis. The weakening of his genito-urinary tract caused by these attacks and still more by the mercury used in their treatment left the way open for minor infections to aggravate themselves. He had developed symptoms of prostatitis in 1794, and now septic infection caused by the prostatitis began to spread, his urinary passages being unable to resist.

And in the year before, the oldest republic in the world, though neutral in the war, was invaded by the French. Venice, Casanova's Venice, ceased to exist, and, in return for concessions in the Low Countries, was handed over by the conquerors to the Empire. Casanova had, I believe, no spirit to survive his beloved and Most Serene Prince.

Friends tried to get crawfish to send him, for crawfish soup was a favourite all his life (because his mother had a craving for them just before his birth, he said); but the rivers were running too high. Zaguri wrote sorrowfully from Venice, asked his own doctor about Casanova's case, and sent medicines.

The light was failing. Two of his very earliest friends now went close ahead of him, as though with torches in their hands to light his way — Teresa Imer, dead in a debtors' prison in London at the age of seventy-four; once he and she had shown each other the difference between boys and girls in a golden morning at Venice; and Father Giorgi, that secretive figure who had tried to teach him the machiavellian paths of Rome half a century before, and had failed because a girl's distress had blown away his cautionings: both dead.

If there was to be light now, in the darkening cold, it must come from the work. He picked up the manuscript, and began to read. The light grew, and changed. This was not a candle but a spreading glow from the sun, a young sun in a young morning. The barred darkness beyond the window dissolved, and the window itself, and the bars. It was 2 April 1725 and the waters of Venice sparkled in the spring morning, as a young actress lay in travail of her first-born.

Epilogue

He died on 4 June 1798. I suppose the priest was there. De Ligne may
have been. Carlo Angioloni, the man who had married his sister's
daughter, certainly was. Casanova's last words were 'Almighty God,
and you witnesses of my death, I have lived as a philosopher and die
as a Christian' – a declaration as misleading, one might think, as his
genealogy.

They buried him in the graveyard of the church of St Barbara, just
outside Dux. The church has fallen into disuse, and there is no sign of
the headstones which once surrounded it. But there is talk of restoring
the church, and it is a pleasant place, beside a lake, and Casanova rests
somewhere under the grass, where a footpath crosses from the lake
toward the village. Legend has it there was once a cast-iron crucifix
over his grave, but in time it fell down and lay hidden in the grass,
where its spiky rusted arms caught at the skirts of young girls as they
passed.

And now that, somehow unbelievably, he is dead, let us try to
sum him up. First, what exactly was he? That is easy to answer. He
was a librarian, poet, author, playwright, director, producer, gambler, lottery organizer, spy, military officer, priest, lawyer, mining
consultant, merchant banker, mathematician (in 1793 Count Waldstein hired him and Opiz to make a review of the calendar), cabalist,
con-man, police agent, student, magician, abortionist, cook, violinist,
philosopher, dancer, silk manufacturer, pimp, rescuer of damsels in
distress, love-maker, revenge-taker, practical joker, prisoner (and es-
caper from prisons), administrator of nunneries, duellist, name-drop-
per, raconteur, instructor in manners (by self-appointment) to kings,
emperors, and popes; patient – he must have spent hundreds of hours
in the hands of doctors; good Samaritan? I think so, especially toward
his brother Francesco, whom he didn't really like much but two or
three times helped out of trouble. And, of course, above all, he was a
Venetian.

Where did he go? Everywhere, three times around – except Madagascar and Lisbon. This extensive journeying points to another accomplishment. Any traveller of the period needed an encyclopaedic memory for coinages and rates of exchange. Casanova, who travelled all the time, must have been a walking computer. Currencies were not so stylized, nor so confined, as they are now. A man, especially a gambler, might be asked in, say, Genoa, to accept French louis against Dutch guilders. What were they each worth, in Genoa? England has long been famous for its untidy currency, but Casanova's Venice had Venetian ducats, current ducats, silver ducats, gazettes (a small piece of copper money; news sheets cost this amount), lire, gold scudi, soldi and sequins. And every other duchy, principality, kingdom, state and electorate as many.

Food aroused the same sort of lust in him as women; but the ladies have only two kinds of 'charm', and Casanova soon exhausted all the possible ways of describing them, whereas with food the variety is infinite; but alas, I have had no space to describe his successful assaults on larks, anchovies, mushrooms, bécasses, coquillages, crostata, eels' livers, smoked tongues, mortadella, olla podrida, and several score more – together with the arrack and beer and coffee and Hermitage and Malaga and Montepulciano and Orvieto and Pontac and Refosco and Scopolo and Tokay with which the seductions were consummated.

Like a demon he ate, and like Pan he danced . . . the allemande and the cabriole and the contredanse, the fandango and the furlana and the gargouillade, the hornpipe, the ländler, and the minuet, the pas-de-deux, the passacaille, and the polonaise and the seguidilla.

He was a man of the theatre. He saw French comedy at Berlin, Italian comedy at Paris, and opera bouffe at St Petersburg. He knew by sight every major figure of the stage, and he probably made love to half of them, of both sexes. He had attended nearly every piece of drama and opera then playing in Europe, and had a hand in writing two or three of them. He published over twenty books in his lifetime and, posthumously, the great *Story*. He spoke three languages and could at least defend himself in others.

Now, Casanova as *Casanova*, Don Juan; first, how many women? Various devoted actuaries of sex have drawn Casanova's recorded copulatory output onto graph paper; but he must have had women he does not enumerate, and we suspect that some of the affairs he does describe are imaginary. He himself says he 'turned the heads of some hundreds of women', which is a nice round figure, and good enough for me.

But women do not like to be stacked and counted like so many fleeces garnered, and in quality his women were not, over all, very high. Most were either cheap or somehow two-dimensional, and much like one another. That points to their being at least in part imagined, creations of a recurring obsessive imagination, or palimpsests of this obsession (probably his mother) painted over the dull reality.

There is no list of the male lovers, but I would bet on the Balletti brothers and of course the three dear old patricians. That 'pédérastie avec X. à Dunquerque' is a teaser. Who was X.? Was the *pédérastie* connected with Casanova's espionage in Dunkirk?

A deeper look at Casanova as a sexual actor leads to some interesting conclusions. The curtain rises; the great lover advances to centre stage; the women go down like ninepins before him. But after a while we begin to notice that all the women lack something. It seems that if a woman falls for Casanova there is something wrong with her – not always morally, but in a more general sense; she is less well endowed, less happy, less secure, less normal, than most women. Henriette, Marcoline, Crosin, Irene and others were lesbians. Teresa/Bellino was a transvestite; Margharita had a glass eye. Others were uneducated peasants, or very young, or both; and most of the rest were actresses or prostitutes. Even the nuns were handicapped. They might be superior to other women spiritually, but not in their functions as females. Then there were the cases of incest, and a girl knowingly committing incest is, again, socially handicapped.

His appeal to such women was not only to the seat of Venus, but to the spirit. He had the power to make them feel better, to lift them up, convince them they were wanted, that they were not abnormal, that they were equal to, even better than, other women. Casanova very seldom tried to seduce really well-endowed women – beautiful, normal, young, rich, or aristocratic. His target area, women's insecurity, was here shielded from him, so these women could judge him with their heads. They did not necessarily then despise or reject him. Far from it. They may even have invited a little sex, but they then established a relationship which we, now that we know the truth about his sexual bipolarity, can easily recognize. To such women – Lady Harrington, Mme de Rumain, the Princesses Lobkowitz and Lubomirska – Casanova was the tame cat, the homosexual intellectual confidant whom every sophisticated woman of the western world has known, and welcomed, as a respite from the pressures of 'normal' society. In brief, Casanova was a demon lover to the insecure, and a safe escort and correspondent to the others.

An essay on Don Juan by the Spanish scholar Gregorio Marañon takes on an extraordinary relevance, knowing what we now know about Casanova; which, to sharpen the point still further, Marañon did not know when he wrote in 1930. The character Don Juan Tenorio was created by Tirso de Molina in *El Burlador de Sevilla* early in the seventeenth century. Marañon proves that the character was based, first on folklore, and secondly, on an actual Don Juan de Tassis, Count of Villamediana. Villamediana was handsome, gallant, brave, reckless fighter of bulls and an insatiable lover of women. Every Spaniard knows that he rode into the Madrid plaza for the bullfight wearing on his hat the device *Son mis amores reales* (my loves are royal); and most believe that he was flaunting before the King the fact that Queen Isabel was his mistress (though she was not). That year, 1622, he was assassinated, and numerous popular jingles proclaimed that the King had ordered the deed.

Three hundred years later, in 1920, a researcher digging into the right royal confusion of the state archives at Simancas discovered that in 1622 the Madrid police had unearthed a secret society of homosexuals in the capital. The chief of the society was Villamediana. Homosexual activity was a capital offence and Philip IV had indeed probably ordered Villamediana's execution; but in the file there is a note in the royal hand ordering that since the Count had died, nothing should be published of his shame. Nor was it.

Marañon's brilliant essays also cover *Donjuanismo* as a symptom, and show the general characteristics of the type to be: a certain epicene beauty of form; bisexuality; need of multiple experience, that is, need of women, not a woman; usually compulsive travellers, because until modern times society was too small, in even the biggest city, to provide the required secrecy and variety; and an inner necessity to cock a public snook at established authority. We can see, therefore, that those who called Casanova a Don Juan spoke truer than they knew.

His life as a whole was shaped by two contrasting pressures: one, that of the picaresque, the other that of the secret society. Adventures, loves, events, travels, careers . . . none are planned, engineered, even done: they happen. It is a universe without principle of causation, or logic of effect: that is, existentialist. Events go the way the winds blow. Casanova is on top of the world when he senses the wind sooner than others, underneath it when he does not.

Security and mutual support against the general anarchy are to be found inside the walls of closed societies: Freemasons, spies, Jesuits, Arcadians; the theatre, the church, the underworld, the army –

interlocking and overlapping cells of privilege, each with its own passwords, signs, and code language. It was not the purpose of these societies to subvert Society, with a capital S, but to support it, and a man whose only assets were courage or intelligence or an educated mind found his future in or through one of them. We have seen Casanova try the law, the church, and the army, before he settled down with one foot in the Freemasons, one in the theatre, and at least a hand in the underworld.

Without money or high birth, soon aware that he was not the son of his mother's husband, starved of love, the brilliantly perceptive boy early recognized that he could steer one of three courses through life. He could take society apart and put it together again better; he could go into retreat; or he could play the same game as the others, and by superior wit come out on top.

He may, when very young, have thought to take the first course. His idea of becoming a preacher *might*, at least, have led to a reformer's pulpit.

We know that three times he thought of withdrawing altogether, and then realized that while he still had his enormous reserves of energy to burn he could not exist away from the battle; and so, as soon as he had drawn a few deep breaths, he ran back into the thick of events.

His third course was to beat the world on its own terms, and this is what he spent his life trying to do. His tools were a quick intelligence, steel nerves, thousand-kilowatt energy, and the constitution of a rhinoceros. His targets were the weaknesses of society, its greed, lust, and perpetual need of new sensations. It was the random juxtaposition of these, his tools and his targets, that made him from time to time what he was – gambler, dramatist, salesman, etc. . . . because he had the inborn talent to become whatever was needed. He lacked control over his own strong will and sharp wits, and when he ceased to respond to the wind (which told him to get out while the going was good), he had no plan, no attainable goal – only the haphazardly offered and unwillingly accepted living immurement of Dux.

Such are my conclusions on Casanova. Others, of course, have reached different opinions. Edmund Wilson issued a long-winded pronouncement to the effect that Casanova was different from Rousseau, which some had already suspected. Havelock Ellis noted that 'he sought his pleasure in the pleasure, and not in the compliance, of the women he loved . . .', and summed him up as 'the supreme type of the human animal in the completest development of his rankness and cunning, in the very plenitude of his most excellent wits'.

The best views of him are contemporary, because those who knew him alive recognized that his genius was in living. Here speaks the Prince de Ligne, who has already been quoted in part:

The only things about which he knows nothing are those on which he believes himself to be expert: the rules of the dance, the French language, good taste, the way of the world, *savoir vivre*. It is only his comedies which are not funny, only his philosophical works which lack philosophy – all the rest are filled with it; there is always something weighty, new, piquant, profound. He is a well of knowledge, but he quotes Homer and Horace *ad nauseam*.

His wit and his sallies are like Attic salt. He is sensitive and generous, but displease him in the slightest and he is unpleasant, vindictive, and detestable. You couldn't buy back a little joke against him for a million . . . He believes in nothing except what is most incredible, being superstitious about everything. Happily, he is honourable and sensitive, and always uses the phrase *I owe it to God*, or *God wills it*, but in fact there was nothing in the world he was not capable of doing. He loves and lusts after everything, and having had all he sees that he has lost all. Above everything, women and girls fill his head; but they can no longer arouse him elsewhere. That annoys him, that infuriates him – against the fair sex, against himself, against heaven, against nature, and above all against the year 1725. He revenges himself on whatever is eatable or drinkable; no longer capable of being a satyr in the garden, a Pan in the forest, he is a wolf at table, beginning swiftly and ending sadly, miserable that he can not begin again.

If he has sometimes used his superior intelligence to make money out of certain stupid men and women, it was for the benefit of his intimates. Throughout the disorders of a wild youth and a most adventurous and sometimes equivocal career, he has always shown tact, honour, and courage. He is proud because he is nothing. As a rentier or financier or great lord he might perhaps have found it easy to live; for no one must contradict him, above all no one must laugh at him . . . the chip is always on his shoulder. Never tell him you have heard the story he is going to tell you; pretend that you are hearing it for the first time. Never omit to greet him in passing, for the merest trifle will make him your enemy. His prodigious imagination, his Venetian vivacity, his travels, all his skills and avocations, his fortitude now that he has lost all that he once gloried in, make him a rare human being, of value to know, and worthy of true respect and friendship on the part of that very small number of people who find favour in his eyes.

That was written by the man generally acknowledged to be the most 'civilized' in Europe, a superb aristocrat, soldier, statesman, and author. Plenty of dukes would have given half their duchies for de Ligne to write about them thus.

In 1772 Lt-Col. the Baron Bavois, dying in Venice, responded thus to a letter from Casanova: 'I am a little upset that you wrote to me so formally. Remember that you are still *mio caro Giacometto*.'

Mio caro Giacometto ... tender words from a soldier he had not seen or written to, as far as we know, for eighteen years. 'A rare human being, worthy of true respect,' the great prince murmurs, bowing his heavy head before the memory of his friend. We, a hundred and seventy years later, stand pensive in front of the plaque on the wall of the church in Duchcov: JAKOB CASANOVA, VENE-DIG 1725 – DUX 1798. After all the seduction and the sodomy, all the stealing and the lying, can it be that the proud boast with which he closed his life, the declaration we found so unlikely, was true: that we are about to say farewell not only to a scapegrace scoundrel but to a Christian philosopher?

I think so, and I think that this feeling for the man has turned just about everyone who has ever started to study his life into an ardent casanovist. That was certainly the case with Arthur Symons, the symbolist poet and literary critic, who visited Dux in 1899, looking for relics and papers.

He came from Oberleutensdorf, by carriage, just as Casanova must have done many times, galloping through open country 'between broad fields, and always in a haze of lovely hills'. The huge château rose like a stage backdrop behind the crowded marketplace. Inside, shields, portraits, armour, relics of far travels, lined the corridors which had once echoed to the old man's vituperations against the awful Faulkircher. The old order still flourished in Bohemia then. Dux was still lived in. Nothing had changed since Casanova's time.

The big library, his library, had whitewashed walls covered with bookshelves under a low-vaulted ceiling. The Count Waldstein of the day gave Symons six great cardboard boxes full to pick through. Here was all that Casanova had left, almost untouched. Here were notes for unwritten treaties, uncompleted poems, unsolved equations – Symons noted how his writing had grown more shaky with age; again, the human cry – here were bills, receipts, envelopes, letters, many scribbled over with mathematical formulae. Here were comments, epigrams, lists of words, ideas for ideas. Here were letters from Manon Balletti, the Procurator Morosini, Francesca Buschini and scores of others, once as alive as Casanova, long dead, but living again because he had breathed his life upon and into them.

Symons wrote 'I seemed to come upon Casanova at home, it was as if I came upon an old friend, already perfectly known to me before I made my pilgrimage to Dux'. He was particularly struck by several drafts of the following poem, scrawled on various bits of paper:

> Sans mystère point de plaisirs.
> Sans silence point de mystère.
> Charme divine de mes loisirs,
> Solitude! que tu m'es chère!

And there, I think, is the real, secret Casanova. He has the solitude and the mystery, at last. The sun still shines in Venice. In all the world, the girls smile. Farewell, *mio caro Giacometto*.

J.M.

Appendix

The publishing history of Casanova's memoirs makes a fittingly bizarre pendant to his life. Before he died he willed all his other papers to Count Waldstein, probably in repayment of loans, but the manuscript of the *Story* disappeared, although Casanova had said he was going to leave it to Cecilia de Roggendorf.

In 1820 an emissary of Carlo Angioloni, son of that Carlo Angioloni who had witnessed Casanova's death, brought a bulky manuscript to the office of Herr F. A. Brockhaus, publisher, of Leipzig. After some negotiation Brockhaus bought all rights in the manuscript for 200 thalers (about 38 dollars or £15).

The manuscript was in twelve bundles, each one a volume. The whole was headed *Histoire de ma Vie, jusqu'à l'an 1797*, though the story ended at 1774. It was written in French. Casanova had told de Ligne and others that his native Italian was a stronger and more graceful language, but not as widely understood as French.

Brockhaus hired a certain Wilhelm von Schütz to translate the manuscript into German, and published the result between 1822 and 1828. Pirated editions soon began to appear in French, being translations of Schütz's translation of Casanova's manuscript. Seeing that he was losing his French-language market to the pirates, one might think that Brockhaus would now publish the original manuscript; but no, he hired a French professor at Leipzig, Jean Laforgue, to work over Casanova's French, and published the result.

No one could really judge Laforgue's work until Casanova's original manuscript was released. This has now been done, and we are in a position to do Laforgue justice. He was in fact one of the crassest prigs in the annals of literature. He committed all the crimes open to an adapter or translator, and some that go beyond those limitations. He altered Casanova's sharp, direct style to a florid discursiveness. He omitted some passages because he judged them obscene, and others because he chose to for reasons best known to himself. When he thought that Casanova had failed to tell us something, he did not hesitate to tell us himself, in Casanova's voice. Being himself republican and anti-clerical he amended Casanova's attitude when he could, and frequently editorialized on his own account – but again, as though from Casanova.

It would need a separate book to list Laforgue's sins, but some examples will give his method. Casanova writes that a doctor brought him 'a syringe': Laforgue changes this to 'a very necessary instrument'. In Spain Casanova is made to cry 'Spaniards, when will a strong, generous impulse take you to wake you from your lethargy and inject the spark that your flagging energy seeks? What do you need today? You miserable and piteous race, as useless to the world as you are to yourselves.' This scoutmasterly harangue is, of course, pure Laforgue: Casanova was getting on with his story.

In talking about ladies' theatricals in Trieste Casanova suddenly interrupts himself to cry 'It is a generally known fact that if a revolution is needed in Italy it is in the field of education, particularly female' – plus two hundred words more on the evils of convents: all straight Laforgue.

Here is how he inflates Casanova's sparse directness to an orotund abstraction. It is during the great escape from the Leads. Casanova is astride the roof of the little dormer, alone. He leans over and finds that a grating bars access to the window. Here is what he actually wrote next:

Perplexed, downhearted, and confused, I could not think what to do, when a natural event affected my stupefied brain like a real miracle. I believe that my sincere confession will not lower me in the eyes of the sensible reader, if he reflects that a man in a state of misery and unease is only half of what he would be in a better frame of mind. It was the clock of S. Marco, striking midnight, which . . .

Here is how Laforgue translated that:

I was confused and began to lose courage, when the simplest and most natural thing happened and restored me.

Any intelligent reader who could place himself in my shoes, who could gauge how unfortunate my lot had been during those fifteen months, who could appreciate the dangers I faced on the rooftops where one false move might cost me my life; if, indeed, you could reflect on all the difficulties which were piling up and which I had to surmount in a few hours – with doubled pressure put upon me by the law if I were to fail – then, understanding all this you will surely not let my confession lower your opinion of me. And do not forget that it is only natural, when faced with anxiety and trouble, to be half the man one is normally.

It was the clock of S. Marco, striking midnight, which . . .

That flatulence is continuous, and I stress it because its effects went far beyond mere textual exegesis. He who reads Laforgue, or any translation based upon him, must rate Casanova as a wordy boaster.

A man who expressed himself so fruitily (one thinks), a man who regarded himself with such pompous self-satisfaction, *could* not have done what he says he did. His women must have been imaginary, if only because we know that even the most patient lady will wait in bed just so long for a man's attitudinizing to come to an end. And how can this old windbag be the steel-and-whipcord hero of all-night gamblings, duels, stabbings, fights in dark alleys, drunken orgies, leaps down city walls? Laforgue is responsible for some of the delay in recognizing Casanova's *Story* for the work of flawed genius that it is.

The massacre of Casanova's text did not achieve the acceptance at which it had presumably been aimed. The first volumes were published in Leipzig in 1826 and 1827. Then there may have been objections from the authorities, for the next four volumes were printed (for Brockhaus) in Paris; and the last four in Brussels. The whole Laforgue was out by 1838.

The years rolled by. Pirated editions sprouted like weeds. Unscrupulous publishers out for a quick killing made writers put in new and imaginary incidents, to their taste. Brockhaus, sitting on the real manuscript, did nothing. Some scholars said that Casanova had never existed and the whole book was a hoax; others that he was Stendhal wearing a palpably false beard. Brockhaus, who had only to look at the original, did nothing. Casanova's picture of the eighteenth century grew more brilliant, more illuminating, even through Laforgue's ornate drapes, as the century itself retreated into history. The body of scholars needing his text for their studies steadily grew. The Brockhaus firm permitted them to beat their brains out on Laforgue's adaptations. As late as the nineteen-twenties – a century after they had bought the manuscript – they would not release the text to the group of scholars then preparing the monumental La Sirène edition, with its exhaustive notes. They would not publish, or let anyone see, Casanova's essay on usury, of which they had – and still have – the only manuscript.

In World War II Casanova's *Story* survived heavy bombing raids on Leipzig in a cellar under the Brockhaus offices. When the Red Army approached, the then heads of the firm decided to emigrate to West Germany. The U.S. Army provided a truck to enable them to carry away their most important manuscripts, including the Casanova. Soon afterwards they began to think that perhaps the world was ready for Casanova. Moving with due caution they arranged with the Paris house of Librairie Plon to publish the true text, with ample footnotes and comments. This edition was published simultaneously in 1960 in Wiesbaden and Paris.

All previous editions in English had, of necessity, been translated from Laforgue, Schütz, or a pirate (and that usually based on Laforgue). This is true of the well-known Arthur Machen translation, which inevitably suffers from Laforgue's faults. The first true English edition — that is, a translation direct from the manuscript — has been published by Harcourt, Brace, and World in the U.S.A. and Canada, and by Longmans, Green in London. The translation, by Willard Trask, is faithful to Casanova's text as well as to his peculiar Latin-Italian style.

With the true text available, casanovists turned their main effort from guessing what he had really written, to interpretation and annotation . . . and learned that Laforgue had been wasting their time even here. Scholars had vainly searched for years to trace a man named Zeroli; vainly, because the name is a Laforgue invention, where Casanova had written Z——. In the birth certificate of Charlotte's baby (page 162) Laforgue gave the father's name as della Croce; persevering scholars wasted much time looking for this in the Paris records, until someone thought it might have been Frenchified into Delacroix, or La Crosse. Under the latter name it was found — not surprisingly, since that is just what Casanova wrote; Laforgue had translated it back to della Croce.

In spite of the Brockhaus firm's odd conduct in the past, I must urge anyone who is moved by this book of mine to want to know more of Giacomo, to go first to the Brockhaus edition, in his own language, of the true text. This is the compulsory starting point. From there, scintillating avenues of further inquiry lead in all directions: Venice, music, costume, Freemasonry, cabalism, pornography, gambling, travel, theatrical history . . . let each wander at his own will.

A final footnote: the present government and town committee of Duchcov are making a considerable effort to create a Casanova museum in the château. The rooms in which he lived contain relics of his life, portraits, and maps showing his travels. The great rooms and endless corridors are stocked with furniture and paintings of the period. More needs to be done, and the manuscripts now at another ex-Waldstein castle (Dosky) and in Prague need to be brought to Duchlov, with a professional curator to work with the local authorities. Then Duchlov will become again Dux, a major re-creation of eighteenth-century high life, and a thoroughly worthwhile attraction for many different kinds of tourist and traveller — but especially for the growing band of casanovists.

Bibliography

Bazzoni, A, 'Casanova confidente degli Inquisitori di Stato' in *Nuovo Archivio Veneto*, 1894.

Bleakley, Horace, *Casanova in England*, London, 1923.

des Bordes, A. Compigny, *Casanova et la Marquise d'Urfé*, Paris, 1928.

Brunelli, Bruno, *Casanova loved her*, London, 1929.

Mémoires de Jacques Casanova de Seingalt, écrits par lui-même, twelve vols, F. A. Brockhaus, Leipzig, Ponthieu et Comp, Paris, 1826–38. Adaptation by Jean Laforgue. Reprinted in eight vols by Garnier, Paris, 1880.

Mémoires de Jacques Casanova de Seingalt, écrits par lui-même, with introductory essays by Raoul Vezé and others, twelve vols, La Sirène, Paris, 1924.

The Memoirs of Jacques Casanova de Seingalt, translated by Arthur Machen, six vols, London and New York, 1958–60.

Histoire de ma vie, six vols, F. A. Brockhaus, Wiesbaden, Librarie Plon, Paris, 1960–61.

History of my Life, translated by Willard R. Trask, six vols, London and New York, 1967, 1968, 1969.

Childs, J. Rives, *Casanoviana*: An Annotated Bibliography of Jacques Casanova de Seingalt and of works concerning him, Virginia, 1956; *Casanova de Seingalt*, Hamburg, 1960; *Casanova*, London, 1961.

Damerini, Gino, *Casanova a Venezia dopo il primo esilio*, Turin, 1957.

Dewar, James, *The Unlocked Secret: Freemasonry Examined*, London, 1966.

Dobrée, Bonamy, *Giacomo Casanova*, London, 1938.

Ellis, Havelock, *Affirmations*, London, 1898.

Endore, S, Guy, *Casanova, his known and unknown life*, London, 1930.

Graeffer, F., 'Graf Waldstein und Casanova' in *Archiv für Geographie, Historie, Staats und Kreigskunst*, Vol XIII No 123–124, Vienna, 1822.

Hazlitt, W. C., *Coinage of the European Continent*, London, 1893.

Hoyle's *Games, improved*, new ed. rev. by C. Jones, London, 1796.

de Ligne, Prince Charles, *Mélanges militaire, littéraires et sentimentaires*, Vol XXIX, Dresden, 1807.

Malmani, Vittorio, *Il settecento a Venezia*, Venice, 1891.

Marr, B., 'La Kabbale de Jacques Casanova', introductory essay in *Mémoires de Jacques Casanova de Seingalt*, Vol III, La Sirène, Paris, 1924.

Maynial, Edouardo, *Casanova and his time*, translated by E. C. Mayne, London, 1911.

Molmenti, P., *Venice*, London, 1908.

Monnier, P., *Venise au XVIIIème siècle*, Paris, 1920.

Nettl, Paul, *Casanova und seine zeit*, Esslingen, 1949; *The other Casanova*, New York, 1950.

Polišenský, Josef, editor, *Giacomo Casanova, historie mého života*, Prague, 1968.

da Ponte, Lorenzo, *Mémoires*, four vols, New York, 1898.

Rava, Aldo, editor, *Lettere di donne a Giacomo Casanova*, Milan, 1912.

Rolleston, Dr J. D., 'The medical interest of Casanova's Memoires', in *Janus*, Leyden, 1912.

Samaran, Charles, *Jacques Casanova, vénitien*, Paris, 1914.

Vaussard, Maurice, *Daily Life in Eighteenth Century Italy*, translated by M. Heron, London, 1962.

Wilson, Edmund, *The wound and the bow*, Cambridge, Mass., 1941; London, 1942.

de Wyzuva, T., 'Un épisode de la viellesse de Casanova' in *Revue des deux Mondes*, Paris, March, 1914.

Zweig, Stefan, *Adepts in self-portraiture, Casanova, Stendhal, Tolstoy*, translated by E. and C. Paul, London, 1929.

Index

CARDINAL

THE PRE-RAPHAELITE TRAGEDY
THE AESTHETIC ADVENTURE
VICTORIAN OLYMPUS
William Gaunt

First published in the 40s and 50s, these curious and humorous biographical studies have become minor classics. Gaunt's style is without an imitator. The books read like novels, full of incident and vividly recreated scenes of the daily lives of three different groups of Victorian artists, each group looking to and living up to a different ideal.

The Pre-Raphaelites – Rossetti, Holman Hunt, Millais, William Morris, Edward Burne-Jones, the best-known of them – took their inspiration from the age of chivalry, before the birth of the painter Raphael. The aesthetes of THE AESTHETIC ADVENTURE – notably Wilde, Whistler and Swinburne – saw the artist as supreme over nature, art as the only worthy condition of life. In VICTORIAN OLYMPUS Lord Leighton and his followers – Albert Moore, Alma Tadema, G. F. Watts and E. J. Poynter – took their inspiration from the Elgin marbles and the heroic ideals of the Ancient World.

The volumes which make up the trilogy may be read in any order.

THE PRE-RAPHAELITE TRAGEDY   0 7474 0152 7   £3.99
THE AESTHETIC ADVENTURE   0 7474 0154 3   £3.99
VICTORIAN OLYMPUS   0 7474 0153 5   £3.99

CARDINAL

THE CAESARS
Allan Massie

Allan Massie's self-confessed 'enjoyment of the period and characters' certainly shows in this witty account of the lives of the Caesars. As a novelist he is well set to make the imaginative leaps and connections necessary – because of the limited historical documentation surviving from the ancient world – to get to the heart of these remarkable men.

0 7474 0179 9   NON-FICTION   £3.99

THE LIFE AND DEATH OF MOZART
Michael Levey

'Essential reading for all Mozartians' *The Times*

Mozart's reputation as a composer continues in the ascendant, yet, curiously, our understanding of the man has been clouded: his personality has been seen as irreconcilable with the musical genius. This picture is unsatisfactory and unsatisfying. Michael Levey sees behind that darkened varnish the clear image of a man of immense liveliness and great humanity not at all at odds with the genius we acknowledge in the music. Simply, Michael Levey reveals the real Mozart.

0 7474 0150 0   NON-FICTION   £3.99

THE LAST MEDICI
Harold Acton

'Doomed ornamental beings, mere occupants of a remarkable museum; exotic fish hidden behind seaweed, stirring languidly in a subaqueous current of history . . .'

Strange fish, indeed, revealed here in all their decaying glory. Cosimo III, pious and profligate, ever devising new draconian taxes and punishments for the dwindling Florentine population, whilst indulging in conspicuous gluttony, grotesque paintings of double-headed calves, monstrous plants and hideous martyrdoms, and freak shows of human deformity. Cosimo's son and successor, Gian Gastone, permanently drunk, encouraging his servants to steal and sell back to him his own curios, living in his nightshirt for the last thirteen years of his reign . . .

With his enthusiastic appetite for the baroque, Harold Acton chronicles every decadent detail of the late 17th century decline of the great Medici dynasty in this classic account

0 7474 0236 1   NON-FICTION   £4.99

FOUR DUBLINERS
Richard Ellmann

Ellmann's four Dubliners are Wilde, Yeats, Joyce and Beckett, and his slim, rich book comes up with new material on each . . . His gift for uniting critical insight with biography is as freshening, as undogmatic and as humane as ever' John Carey, *Sunday Times*

'In Ellmann's best manner' Frank Kermode, *Guardian*

'A skilful and distinguished book' P N Furbank, *Sunday Telegraph*

'This brief, witty book . . . is a model of literary perception' William Trevor, *Observer*

0 7474 0276 0   NON-FICTION   £3.99

CARDINAL

THE AGE OF REVOLUTION
1789–1848
E J Hobsbawm

'A brilliant account of Europe in its revolutionary age . . . No one could ask for more' AJP Taylor

'A harsh, brilliant, powerful, fascinating book.' Peter Laslett, *Guardian*

0 7474 0290 6   NON-FICTION   £5.99

THE AGE OF CAPITAL
1848–1875
E J Hobsbawm

'This brilliant book sparkles on every page . . . With a power of decision that commands a terrified admiration, he selects basic themes, illustrates them with a wealth of reference. European and global . . . What a book! For heaven's sake, and your own, read it.' *Guardian*

'Will undoubtedly be read and valued as widely as the earlier AGE OF REVOLUTION, and that is high praise indeed' *Times Higher Educational Supplement*

'His two great syntheses on the origins of the society we inhabit – THE AGE OF REVOLUTION (1962) and THE AGE OF CAPITAL (1975) – have become part of the mental furniture of educated Englishmen.' *Observer*

0 7474 0291 4   NON-FICTION   £5.99

THE MYSTERY OF WILLIAM SHAKESPEARE
Charlton Ogburn

Could Shakespeare have been the man of Stratford who died in 1616, years after writing his last play, leaving no books, and exciting no tributes from his fellow writers? A man who could barely write his own name, but had twice the vocabulary of Milton; a man who was never referred to as a writer; a mediocre actor, forever in trouble and in debt, whose greatest role was the ghost in his own HAMLET: could this man be Ben Jonson's 'soul of the age'?

Why do we know so little about Shakespeare? Is it because we are looking in the wrong place?

Sigmund Freud wrote, 'The man of Stratford seems to have nothing at all to justify his claims, whereas Oxford has almost everything'.

'Oxford' is Edward de Vere, the seventeenth Earl of Oxford, courtier, patron of the arts, classical scholar, poet, dramatist, sportsman, Italophile and favourite of Elizabeth I. In this brilliant detective story Charlton Ogburn presents the strongest case ever against 'Stratford' and for 'Oxford'. His life time's quest has resulted in a work of enthralling historical reconstruction and imagination.

0 7474 0255 8   NON-FICTION   £7.99

COUNTRY LIFE
Howard Newby

'Howard Newby has achieved what has long been needed, a single and authoritative telling of village England's economic tale over the past two centuries'
Ronald Blythe, *Guardian*

Every age has mythologised the countryside. Our jealously guarded 'heritage' is almost entirely mythical.

With humanity and clarity Howard Newby tells the real story of country life: from the enclosure of the old strip farms to create fields and the first capitalist industry in the world, the effects of the ensuing competition and changes in the law, machinery and farming techniques, to the Napoleonic Wars and the Corn Law, the First World War and Lloyd George's budget, the Second World War and the EEC. It spans the various attempts at unionization and rioting, changing aesthetic perceptions of country living in architecture, literature and painting, and changing patterns of population and movement of labour. All are worked into an extremely readable and moving account of the real heritage of our countryside.

0 7474 0286 8   SOCIAL HISTORY   £4.99

MY LIFE
Isadora Duncan

Born in 1878, Isadora Duncan was one of the most famous dancers of modern times. Variously described as 'eccentric', 'mad', and 'a genius', she was one of the most original artistic personalities of this century. Defying convention from the moment she was born – when, as she frequently remarked, 'Venus was in the ascendant' – she was always a reckless, courageous and dedicated exponent of freedom and love. Her dancing was freestyle, improvised and unique. Dressed in a simple white tunic, she danced her way across America and Europe, found fame and (fickle) fortune, and courted love, disaster, and ultimately tragedy.

Her writing, like her life and her 'Art', is an extraordinary mixture of grace, inspiration and exquisite exaggeration. If she is to be believed – and sometimes it is difficult – she had a 'religious and awe-inspiring' effect on men, she 'discovered the dance', and her life was 'more interesting than any novel and more adventurous than any cinema'.

Her death was as flamboyant as her life. In 1927, shortly after completing this book, she was strangled by her flowing scarf, which had become caught in the wheels of the car in which she was travelling. *Isadora: My Life* first appeared the following year, and was promptly banned.

0 7474 0377 5   NON-FICTION   £3.99

GUSTAV MAHLER
Alma Mahler

'I lived his life. I had none of my own. He never noticed this surrender of my existence. He was utterly self-centred by nature, and yet he never thought of himself. His work was all in all.'

Both Alma's devotion to Mahler and her own forceful character shine through her recollections of the ten intense years they shared from 1901 to 1911. Her lively account of these last days of the Hapsburg Empire mixes domestic detail with anecdotes of such figures as Richard Strauss, Debussy, Freud and Schoenberg, personal moments with musical analysis – Alma was herself a gifted musician and helped Mahler considerably with his work when he forbade her own. Combined with a large collection of Gustav's letters and sixteen pages of photographs, her memories contribute much to our understanding of one of the most popular composers of recent years.

Edited by the eminent music scholar Donald Mitchell, who also provides the biographical listing, appendix and chronology.

0 7474 0317 1   NON-FICTION   £6.99